IN A WILTSHIRE VILLAGE

Scenes from Rural Victorian Life

IN A WILTSHIRE VILLAGE

Scenes from Rural Victorian Life

Alfred Williams

Selected from the writings of Alfred Williams
by Michael Justin Davis

ALAN SUTTON

Alan Sutton Publishing Limited
Phoenix Mill, Far Thrupp, Stroud, Gloucestershire

Alan Sutton Publishing Inc.,
Wolfeboro Falls, NH 03896–0848, U.S.A.

First published 1981
Reprinted 1992

British Library Cataloguing in Publication Data

Williams, Alfred
In a Wiltshire Village.
1. South Marston (Wiltshire) – Social life and customs
I. Title II. Davis, Michael, *1925–1991*
942.3'13 DA590.S

ISBN 0–904387–62–3

Typesetting and origination by
Alan Sutton Publishing Limited.
Photoset Janson 10/12.
Printed in Great Britain by
The Bath Press,
Bath, Avon.

CONTENTS

Dedication

For Marjorie and Joan

FOREWORD

by Jack Maisey, J.P.

Alfred Williams was born in Cambria Cottage, South Marston – a house built by his father. Twenty-nine years later it so happened that I war born there, too, in the very same room. My father was a native of South Marston and knew the Williams family intimately. He was four years older than Alfred and was at school with him.

I lived in South Marston until I was about six years old and have always maintained contact with the village. As a youngster I cycled weekly to visit my aunts – one of whom was living in Cambria Cottage. Another, Aunt Jennie, as we called her, lived opposite 'Ranikhet', the house built by Alfred and Mary Williams. She often slipped across to help Mary and to talk over the happenings of the village. She, it was, who found Alfred when he died. She had not seen him about, so she climbed a ladder and peered through the bedroom window and saw him collapsed by his bed. He had died of a heart attack.

I remember Alfred as a quiet, scholarly man – of gentle voice – and who was always ready to talk to children. To read his books now is a constant delight and an unfailing source of interest and nostalgic pleasure.

His books have fascinated Michael Davis, too, and in recent years he has made a thorough research into hitherto unknown sources of the Williams family. In his introduction he has shown Alfred Williams to be a most remarkable man – a person with a first class brain – fighting against apparently insuperable odds and winning through.

The selections from *A Wiltshire Village* and *Villages of the White Horse* are carefully chosen. Contemporaries of Williams in the district come alive again; the countryside becomes real; and one is anxious to leave the fleeting attractions of urban life for the more abiding delights of the fields.

The River Cole, the surrounding meadows (frequently flooded in winter 'like an inland sea') and many of the old houses are still there. Descendants of many of the characters in his books are living there still, also.

Visits to South Marston and the surrounding villages are always most rewarding and this book will add to one's enjoyment.

ACKNOWLEDGEMENTS

In compiling this book I have received great encouragement and help from many people, and to all of them I wish to express my gratitude. The Alfred Williams Society, through Marjorie Leigh and Joan Jefferies, has been a source of informed enthusiasm; and I am also much indebted to Leonard Clark for *Alfred Williams, His Life and Work*, a book on which I have relied. I have received invaluable help from the Swindon Reference Library, the Marlborough Branch of the Wiltshire County Library, and the Devizes Museum Library. I am particularly grateful to the librarians there, and to the following who have given me most generous personal help: Pamela Coleman, Winifred Evans, the Revd Dr F.W.T. Fuller, Jim Glover, Malcolm Jones, Colin McGregor, E.G.H. Kempson, Jack Maisey JP, Roger Pope. To them all, I offer my profound thanks, and above all to my wife, who has constantly helped and encouraged me with her unfailing devotion, wise comments and practical skills.

For permission to reproduce material for illustrations, acknowledgement is gratefully made as follows:

Wiltshire Library and Museums Service for the drawings on page 149; to Jack Maisey JP for the photographs on pages 12, 70 and 104; to David Carson for the photograph on page 61; to Roger and Shirley Pope of Pewsey for the old Wiltshire photographs which they have gathered into their collection, here reproduced on pages 25, 28 (the original photograph was found in a postcard album of Mrs Etta Reeves of The Swan, Pewsey), 34, 39, 44, 52, 57 (this photograph, in the possession of Doug Martin of Milton Lilbourne, was copied from a lantern slide of his grandfather's farm; the slide was originally taken by a visitor from London, Mr Joe Wallen), 108, 119, 128 (the original photograph is in the possession of Mrs Kit Thompson of Pewsey), 147 (the original photograph is in the possession of Mrs Weeks of Littleworth, Milton Lilbourne), 165, 166, 169, 179 and 182 (the original photograph is in the possession of Eddie Mercer of Pewsey); and to J. Kenneth Major for the photograph on page 115.

The tailpieces, from old pictures, have been drawn by Martin Roberts, to whom I am especially grateful.

INTRODUCTION

Alfred Williams was twenty-four when Queen Victoria died in 1901, and he had twenty-nine more years to live. His early years gave him what he valued most: experience of the Wiltshire country and its people. Born and bred in the village of South Marston, about four miles from the rapidly developing railway town of Swindon, he knew at first hand the age-old, traditional ways of village life. These he loved, and their passing appalled him. He deplored industrial progress: its noise, speed, superficiality and lack of concern for individuals were destroying all that he held dear. His writings are a nostalgic protest, an attempt to save what he knew was doomed. He celebrates, in his books about village life, the vigour, rich individuality, independence and sanity of village characters who had lived their lives in the Victorian age. Many of these people were very old when he came to know them. Often he records their own words about themselves and their experiences. His detailed descriptions of characters and traditions, all firmly rooted in particular parts of South Marston and nearby villages, bring to life again a world that has now vanished.

Alfred Williams had rare talent and energy, but his background was no more eminent than that of many of the villagers he wrote about. His mother, Elizabeth, was the younger daughter of Joshua Hughes, a tanner and smallholder who owned about an acre of free-hold land in the centre of South Marston, and lived at Rose Cottage. Elias Williams, a carpenter and joiner from North Wales, came to lodge there: and he married Elizabeth in March, 1870.

On part of Joshua Hughes's meadow, which is called The Hook, Elias and Elizabeth Williams built Cambria Cottage and a carpenter's shop. In addition, Elias rented a timber yard in Swindon, the expanding town where there was plenty of work for a building contractor. Elizabeth bore him many children. According to their eldest daughter, Bess, the first son was born at Rose Cottage, and then six more sons and four daughters at Cambria Cottage. Owen Alfred was born on 6 February 1877: of the boys 'Our Alfred was the youngest; but I believe he lived and died without knowing he was the seventh son.' Four boys and four girls survived infancy.

According to Bess, their father was a very good carpenter, joiner, bricklayer and architect who could work from his own plans, and he 'might have had hundreds of pounds where he had not a penny, because he developed the drinking habit.' Their mother 'was a clean and smart housewife' who bore a child annually for eleven years. Every year there was less money to feed and clothe the children, so their mother 'took in needlework and plied the trade through the midnight hours, while waiting for our father' to return, drunk. He 'would go to bed without a word, and carry a knife and put it under his pillow.'

Bess recalls one 'Sunday noon. A hot meal had been cooked and covered close till our father returned from the inn. When he arrived he was in such a strange and awful state that he said not a word; but, taking the covered dishes of food he bashed them against the wall, breaking food and dishes, and which caused us younger ones to burst into tears of fright. He then went back to the open door and stood facing us, throwing what money he had left into the room. Mother said nothing. She was nursing the youngest. . . . When father had gone, mother dished up one of her large "spotted dogs" . . . a roly-poly currant suet pudding. And we had one course only, that dinner time.'

The marriage lasted ten years. It finally broke when Elizabeth discovered a paper falling from Elias's 'trousers pocket, proving to be a notice of occupation by a bailiff, of Cambria Cottage, at which he turned coward and fled.' Bess goes on to say that her mother 'met our father's creditors — whose deficits were for timber — bricks — ironmongery . . . not a penny owing on her side for food, physic, coal or clothing . . . . She would have paid all father's debts if she could: she felt the shame of it . . . . Father went first to Nottingham . . . . He did not send regular payment for our upkeep, nor enough.'

Elizabeth and her eight children, evicted from Cambria Cottage, were given a home in Rose Cottage by Grandmother Hughes. Alfred Williams, aged three when the marriage broke, continued to live there until he married. He was, according to bess, 'a very passionate personality . . . . His self-control was wonderful.' And so were the diligence and resourcefulness of their mother. She took on the job of newsagent, and after putting the children to bed, 'circuited the village' with her eldest son 'for company (in winter) to distribute *The Swindon Advertiser* . . . . After a time the *North Wilts Herald* appeared, and mother became agent as well, for those' at fourpence a dozen. She also 'started a confectionery business, and made ten shillings to £1 weekly profit. Bess 'used to be taken when old enough to help carry the sweets' from the wholesale manufacturer in Swindon. Food 'was cheap then; and mother pocketed any pride she had and went yearly gleaning at corn harvest: and we always had a sack of flour.' But cash was essential too.

'School money had to be found; for seven years a pile of ten pence went every Monday morning. Not till baby Ada's last year or two at school did free education come.'

Alfred went to the village school with his brothers and sisters full-time until he was eight. Miss Deacon, the school mistress, singled out the Williams children for their diligence and politeness. The education they received was very simple and limited. In later life, Alfred criticized more complex types of schooling. But he must have learned extremely valuable lessons from his mother, a woman who 'often composed poetry while working in her garden, but did not stop to write any,' as Bess records. 'To take a walk with her was an education. She always pointed out some fresh beauty of nature. We did not walk by road if we could travel through the fields.' Alfred Williams's love of nature shines out in all his writings: it was fostered by his mother, and so was his delight in poetry.

Soon after his eighth birthday he became a half-timer, spending only part of the day at school and the rest of it working on the local farm of Launcelot Whitfield. Bess had started working there half-time when she was nine. 'We were so fond of the fields,' she writes, 'that to work in them was a beatitude to us! And every little helped in the house-keeping . . . . The public must have wondered why Alfred began as a farmer's boy at such an age. Our mother remarked sadly once to me, when she had read a paper report of his achievement: "No-one knows he ever had a mother". Yet, it was her genius, her great endurance, her wonderful will-power that equipped him to achieve.'

Alfred later wrote that he was very happy as a half-timer working in a gang, 'pulling weeds and thistles from the wheat. At other times we scared birds, tended pigs, and worked in the hayfield, or at corn harvest.' At eleven, like other children of his age and circumstances, he left school and became a full-time farm worker. His love of flowers, animals and birds was intense, and he learned a lot about them. Although he made few young friends of his own age he enjoyed going for walks with his sisters. The family was happy and united, and Alfred had plenty of interests. He was fascinated by all sorts of machinery: trains enthralled him. Several engine drivers gave him short rides on the nearby Great Western Railway line to London. For a dare, he had, at the age of ten, lain down between the metals of the track and stayed there while a long train rumbled over him.

In adolescence, he joined in more readily with boys of his own age, and shared their sports and pastimes. He also met Mary Peck, when he was fourteen, and he became fond of her. She had come to South Marston to help her married sister. Bess described Mary as 'a winsome and witty girl'. Alfred was increasingly restless, however. Several times he tried, although under age, to join the Navy. Pay for farm-hands was meagre. His elder brothers,

Alfred Williams, aged about 30

Edgar and Henry, were earning much more at the G.W.R. Works in Swindon. When he was fifteen he decided to join them, and the three would walk the four miles to Swindon and back daily.

Alfred began his factory work as a rivet hotter in 1892. Soon after, he became a furnace boy in the stamping shop, where metal articles were stamped out between dies under steam hammers. He enjoyed the arduous physical challenge of heavy factory work with its violent processes, and he was completely dependable. In 1893 he became a drop stamper. Although he accepted the responsibility of being chargeman of his gang, twice he refused further promotion. He would not become foreman, because he did not wish to give orders to others or sacrifice any of his individuality.

Harry Byett, who knew Alfred Williams well, described his appearance as a young man: 'He was well over medium height, spare of flesh, had squarish, angular features, powerful lower jaw; dry, wrinkled and almost colourless lips generally parted in a pleasing smile, revealing pale gums and a perfect set of well-tended, gleaming white teeth. Blue-grey, far-seeing eyes which looked straight into yours, proclaiming sincerity, and forbidding aught else in his *vis-à-vis*. Light brown hair, short cropped from time to time, as necessitated by his hot, sweating work as hammerman. Fair complexion, perfectly upright figure, head erect whether walking, standing or sitting, imparting a military bearing and a sense of invincibility when confronted with obstacles.'

In his spare time, Williams continued to roam the countryside, and he gained a local reputation for knowledge of nearby sites and customs. He took up painting: some of his pictures he sold in the neighbourhood. He also showed an interest in politics, at first as a Liberal, later as a Tory. His thirst for knowledge and for self-expression was remarkable. In 1897 he began reading English literature in earnest during his spare time, and would not waste a minute of his dinner hour.

Despite the exhausting demands of full-time factory work and his long daily walk, Williams began a four year course in English Literature with Ruskin Hall, Oxford, in 1900. Baffled by the numerous Latin quotations in the books he had to study, he determined to learn that language. 'Beginning with the books of Caesar,' he declared, 'I afterwards became bolder, and dipped with delight into the wonders of Cicero, Ovid, Sallust, Horace and Virgil.'

When he was twenty-four he became engaged to Mary Peck, although he was regarded by her family as a poor match. They were married in Hungerford in October, 1903, and after a honeymoon at Torquay they made their home in Dryden Cottage, very close to Cambria Cottage.

Every room was soon in use as a library, because Williams was reading for

London Matriculation in his spare time and now learning not only Latin, but Greek and French as well. 'I used to print a troublesome Greek word on the toe of my boot in the morning,' he later recalled, 'and allow it to remain till the evening. Never mind what your workmates think or say. They may deem you eccentric, but you know what you are doing, while they do not.' He learned astonishingly fast and crammed his days with study, rising at four a.m. and eventually going to bed at midnight, besides cycling to and from Swindon and doing a full day's work as a hammerman at the railway factory. His eyes began to suffer, and he accepted his doctor's advice to stop studying at night, but continued to study by day at every possible moment.

His wife Mary supported him in all his labours. 'She is,' he wrote, 'indispensable to my pursuits. While she knits I commune with my gods. We lead a simple and quiet life.' Harry Byett once asked her:

'Do you ever help Alf in his work?'

'Yes,' she said, 'by keeping quiet.'

At the factory, Williams was scrupulously careful not to allow his studies to encroach on his work as a hammerman. 'When learning Greek,' Byett writes, 'he made a practice of chalking a few Greek characters or words at the rear of his steam drophammer.' He would catch sight of them in passing and so they would become automatically impressed on his mind. Rather, however, than chalk up these few characters during the time of his employers, he reached his work early, and did so before starting time at six o'clock in the morning.'

Life in the factory had by now become soul-destroying for Williams. The coarser men persecuted him. An official who regarded the chalk marks as pretentious ordered their effacement. However, Williams continued to draw his Greek characters and, when the official had thick grease daubed on the drophammer, Williams wiped the grease off and inscribed his Greek in white paint. 'Men and boys in the shop,' Byett writes, 'were encouraged by the official to do any mean thing to annoy, even to the extent of throwing water over him.'

Away from the factory, Mary guarded her husband jealously against all disturbance. As Leonard Clark, Williams's biographer, writes: 'She was no scholar herself, but sympathetic to all he undertook: her nature was so finely drawn that she understood the urge of all his strivings. Hers was not an enviable existence, yet she looked upon her task as a privilege . . . . The brief companionship of their evening meal, when he poured forth all the happenings of the day, and dwelt upon his aims and desires, was her greatest joy. He would have liked to have given more time to her, but it was she who unselfishly pressed him on to his goal.'

Every Sunday they went for a country walk together. He continued to study nature with an intense delight which, despite his solitary character, he was able to share with the village children. They regarded him as someone special; and in response to their friendly greeting – 'Hullo, Mister Willums!' — he would talk to them quietly about animals or birds, or teach them poetry. Alfred and Mary Williams never had any children of their own.

Besides studying, he had begun to write. In 1904 he completed a lyrical play, *Sardanapalus*, and in 1907 two of his poems were published in an anthology. One of them was highly praised by an eminent author, Sidney Colvin. Three prose articles by Williams about his own methods of study were also published, in the *Young Men's Magazine*. In 1909 two more of his poems were anthologized, and the *Daily Telegraph* critic acclaimed him as 'one of the most remarkable men in Wiltshire, if not in England' – fulsome praise which amused Alfred Williams. This year, however, he aroused the interest of Lord Edmond Fitzmaurice, an important figure in Wiltshire life and a member of the Government, who became his patron and helped foster the publication of the first book of Williams's poems, *Songs in Wiltshire*. Meanwhile, Williams discovered the works of Richard Jefferies, the Wiltshire writer remarkable for his power of observing nature and writing about it in a poetic and philosophical way. Williams, intensely excited, felt that he had found a kindred spirit in Jefferies who had lovingly described the landscape of north Wiltshire, and had died ten years before Williams was born.

Thanks partly to Williams's friends who bought copies of *Songs in Wiltshire*, and especially to the Swindon enthusiast, Reuben George, who tried to sell copies wherever he went, the expenses of publication were covered, but only because Williams worked very hard as his own travelling salesman and spent £30 out of his savings, mostly on railway fares. The book, a collection of love songs and nature poems, was well received. Life, however, was far from easy for Williams: and his health was suffering. He wrote to William Dowsing, a poet working in the Vickers factory at Sheffield: 'What with being assailed with internal fatigue, with fag in the worst form, with poor health generally, with the worry of keeping myself together at all cost, with increasing duties at the forge, the utter lack of sympathy, and enmity of one and another, I very often feel most unhappy. My strength seems very often to be exhausted. But it is useless to feel faint. You must march forward or fall to the rear. There is no room to turn back.'

In April 1910 he was invited to a gathering of 300 poets and their descendants at the Holborn Restaurant, in London. He met the *Daily Mail* reporter there. Williams was invited to read his own poetry aloud, but he could not stay to do so: he had to catch the late train back to Swindon, to be at his steamhammer next morning on time.

Williams worked extremely hard to get his second volume of poetry published. It appeared in November, 1911, with the title *Poems in Wiltshire*. There were some translations from Greek and Latin, and one from French, and some tributes to friends, but most of the works were original nature poems. The book was praised in *The Times* and other papers, and as well received as *Songs in Wiltshire*. Williams, however, had contracted to sell half the edition of 500 copies himself, and he stood to lose money.

Realising that ill-health might force him to give up factory work and turn to writing for a living, he decided to write a book in prose. By October, 1911, he had completed *Life in a Railway Factory*, an account of his own experiences and observations. This important and provocative book remained unpublished until Williams's digestive and cardiac trouble made his doctor insist, in 1914, on Williams leaving the G.W.R. works. If the book had been published earlier, Williams would have lost his job.

Meanwhile, in the spring of 1912, he began a book about village life, 'making use,' he said 'of my own early experience on the farm, and portraying local character.' The first draft, completed in only ten weeks of his spare time, he entitled *A Wiltshire Village* and sent to Fitzmaurice. 'No composition', Leonard Clark writes, had ever given Williams 'greater release or pleasure than this honest and unadorned story of the life that went on daily in South Marston.' Fitzmaurice praised the manuscript and, in July, Duckworth accepted it for publication. 'The motif of the work', as Williams told Fitzmaurice, 'is to give a picture of rural life – an unvarnished one – as I have lived it,' and also 'to sketch the locality – an unknown corner of north Wilts. – and call attention to the farm labourer's lot.' To William Bavin, a schoolmaster friend and admirer, Williams wrote: 'Whatever I have written I have seen, though what I have described is chiefly the immediate past.'

While waiting for the publication of *A Wiltshire Village*, Williams prepared his third volume of poetry, *Nature and other poems*, a collection that includes some large-scale works, notably 'The Testament', his longest poem, which he considered 'to be the best for thought and nature feeling.' Very few of his fellow workmen bought his books of poetry, however, and this was a bitter disappointment to him. He had put all his life savings into the three volumes, and he was now so poor that he considered emigrating.

Nature and other poems was published in October, 1912, and was even more highly praised than its two predecessors. John Bailey, in *The Times*, hailed 'another collection from the Wiltshire poet' and praised its combination of 'fine taste and culture with rugged simplicity.' The *Athenaeum* compared Williams with Cowper, a poet renowned for simple, natural verse. No longer was Williams patronisingly praised as 'The Hammerman Poet' or 'The Harmonious Blacksmith': his achievement as a nature poet was taken seriously and acclaimed.

A Wiltshire Village was published a few weeks later. The reviewer in *The Times* 'found it a gentle and continuous delight' and praised the 'wonderful little descriptions. Here is a vivid portrait that will seem to many like that of an old friend – Jemmy Boulton, the carter . . . . We knew and loved him ever so many years ago.' Harry Byett pointed out later in *The Swindon Advertiser* that Williams's 'dialogue, wonderful pen pictures of his characters' and his anecdotes all reflect, 'incidentally, some of the history of the period.' Much of the book's value, Byett claimed, 'lies in the fact that every word is absolutely true, and is therefore history. This feature will be the more appreciated as time goes on.'

In South Marston itself, the 'old-fashioned, agricultural village' that Williams had described, the book – which uses no fictitious names – was not generally resented. Some villagers even complained to Williams that they and their relatives had been omitted. The vicar, however, perhaps objecting to Williams's statement that the 'sermons are long and the minister severe', publicly burnt two copies of the book because it was 'too disgusting to read', and preached against the author (who was present in the church) on a number of Sundays. Williams, though deeply hurt, managed to ignore the affair.

The book sold well, and in a few months he was writing a successor, based on weekend visits in the late summer of 1912 to neighbouring villages 'from Wroughton to the Blowing Stone all along the downside' as far as Kingstone Lisle in Berkshire. This attempt 'to depict the life and characteristics of the agricultural classes in that region', he told Fitzmaurice, would 'not be stylish literature but I hope to preserve a lot of interesting matter.'

He was also working on a fourth book of poems, *Cor Cordium*, the contents of which he described to his youngest sister, Ada. 'Half the work shows my evolution from a *doubting* to a *trusting* state in religious belief, and the other half are love poems.' *Cor Cordium* was published in October, 1913. The book, his highest achievement in poetry, was much admired and it sold well. As always, Williams was very grateful to his friends: 'I despair of getting any local support except among those who know me personally.'

Villages of the White Horse, published a month later, describes a score of villages set in twenty miles of downland. The villages were accessible by bike from South Marston, and Williams had done his research with vigour and enthusiasm. 'As to the persons and "characters" that figure in the pages, I have made a point of introducing them exactly as I found them, rough and plain, frank and hearty, honest and homely,' he wrote in his preface. 'I am proud of every single one of them. Some of the dialect and narrative may appear a little barbarous to those of refined tastes, but I can assure them it is all accurate and characteristic.' The book was highly praised by critics as a record of 'real rural life'. One reviewer commended its 'simple strength of style, its sweetness, its fine balance, its sanity of outlook, its flashes of rollicking humour, its informativeness.'

The present book, *In a Wiltshire Village*, is compiled from *A Wiltshire Village*, which provides most of the material, and from *Villages of the White Horse*, which provides the last few chapters. Williams's fine descriptions of landscape, flowers, birds and animals, and his references to Berkshire villages, have been much reduced in order to highlight his presentation of rural Victorian life in Wiltshire. He was highly conscious of the antiquity of the villages, where habits, customs and speech had evolved in centuries gone by. Victorian village life had grown from remote ages that he loved to contemplate in his imagination. He emphasised this antiquity, in his descriptions of the villages and of their inhabitants, by quoting from Greek and Roman literature in translation. His classical allusions spoil the immediacy of his writing, and they have been omitted from this book.

Williams's love of the Wiltshire landscape and its villages was a passion that he wished to share throughout his life, as the Revd. Dr. F.W.T. Fuller, who now lives at Stratton St. Margaret, still remembers. From the age of eight to thirteen he knew Williams, who was forty-eight when they first met in 1925.

Between the publication of *Villages of the White Horse* and that date, Williams had experienced much. In 1914 he left the G.W.R. Works and tried market gardening, without success. *Life in a Railway Factory* was published in 1915, and it created a considerable stir. His friendship with the Poet Laureate, Robert Bridges, whom he had met in 1912, developed during the First World War. Despite ill-health, Williams managed to get himself accepted by the army, and he became an exceptionally fine Gunner. In 1917 he sailed for India with the Royal Garrison Artillery. While he was away, his mother died and Mary had an extremely hard time, with poverty, hunger and difficult relationships to endure. India excited and inspired Williams. After he was demobilised in 1919, he and Mary built themselves a house in South Marston with their own hands, an agonizing labour. He published various works: a book of folk-song lyrics that he had cycled many miles to collect from village singers; and a book about the Upper Thames; and *Selected Poems*. He taught himself Sanskrit, despite his unremitting, heroic struggle to earn a living. His last book was *Tales from the Panchatantra*, published shortly after he died, starving, in 1930. His services to literature were rewarded by a Civil List Pension, but it arrived too late: he was already dead, and Mary was on her death-bed.

Dr. Fuller looks back with the hindsight of an adult, but trying to see through the eyes of a child, as he recalls the last five years of Williams's life:

'My mother kept a small general shop, opposite the White Hart at Stratton

Park Cross Roads (the cross roads with its pub, timber yard, farm, shop and few cottages was more like a country hamlet). Alfred Williams and sometimes Mary his wife used to walk to and from Swindon, and would often call in. He would sit on the wooden bench in the shop, and I remember him eating ice-cream and on another occasion drinking cream soda mineral water. Later we moved to the house next door to the shop, but I still saw Alfred Williams.

In the summer, or even fine winter days, he used to like (apparently) to point out Wanborough Church, three or four miles away on the hillside, easily identified by its spire and tower. Then he would take our eyes along to Liddington Church, then up to Liddington Castle with its ramparts and tiny cluster of trees. He was interested to know that my grandmother, as a small girl, had helped drag a tree from that clump, which blew down, to her home in Liddington, for firewood. He told us all the folklore of the villages he could see and also those beyond our vision over the downs. I did not know then that he had written a book called *Villages of the White Horse*. I had never read it, so his story-telling was vivid.

He sometimes talked of South Marston. In those days it was possible, early mornings or late night, without traffic as today, to hear from Stratton, South Marston church clock striking the hours. Sometimes he talked of old Stratton characters he knew: he never put them into print; I wish I had made notes at the time.

I remember him as a lean, skinny sort of man, always looking as if he could do with a good meal. He never looked strong. His voice was soft and a bit high pitched.

I got the impression that Alfred Williams was more at home with children than with adults.

Sometimes we walked a bit of the way back to Marston with him (or sometimes a quarter of a mile toward Swindon if he went that way. That was still fields with ditches and hedges and trees). He would point out all the wild flowers and grasses and hedgegrove shrubs. He knew all the local birds. He told us of the days when the A420 (Swindon/Oxford) was a gated road – I doubt whether he remembered it, but had been told about it when our age. He also told us about the old Wilts-Berks Canal.

Just before his wife died – the only time he would not stop to talk was when he was battling against the wind on his bicycle to go and see her in Victoria Hospital, Swindon – I realised that my parents had most of his books, having bought them at a cheap rate when first published. For a while I found it difficult to not hear (in my mind) Alfred Williams saying what I was reading – his piping Wiltshire voice seemingly to come through the printed word.

It was much later that I began to enjoy the works of the somewhat reserved man I had known as a child – a man who at that time gave me the impression more of an informed farm worker than a country writer or poet. But a man who could inspire the confidence of children, and converse with them without seeming condescending.

Nowadays, if I can find a spot where I can see the Downs and Liddington Castle, and put the built-up area of Swindon and Stratton behind me, I can still hear his voice – "Follow the sun along to Wanborough Church, the one with the spire and tower." '

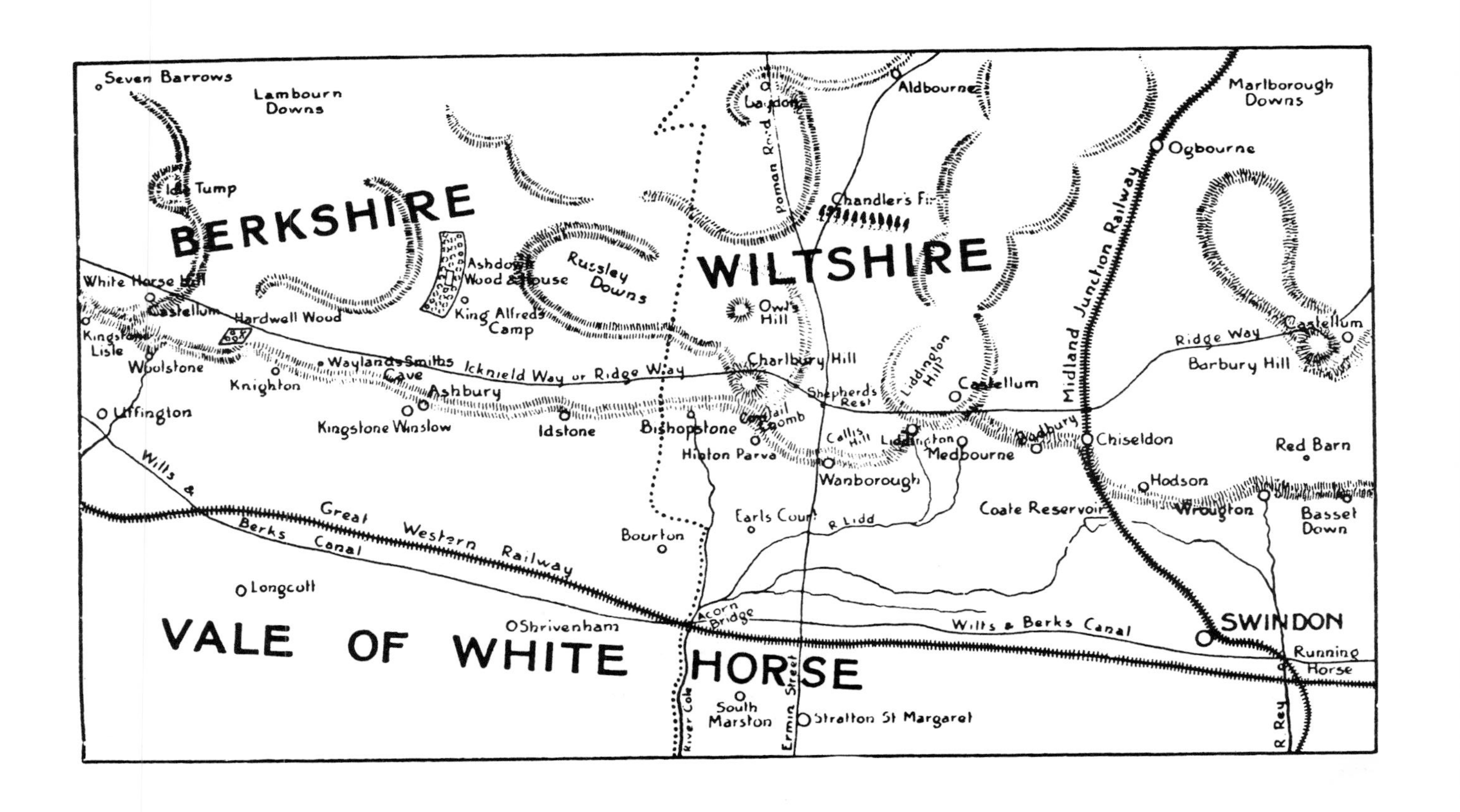

Seven Barrows
Lambourn Downs
Idle Tump
BERKSHIRE
White Horse Hill
Castellum
Kingston Lisle
Woolstone
Hardwell Wood
Knighton
Waylands Smiths Cave
Uffington
Ashdown Wood & House
King Alfreds Camp
Russley Downs
Icknield Way or Ridge Way
Ashbury
Kingstone Winslow
Idstone
Wills & Berks Canal
Great Western Railway
Longcott
Bourton
Bishopstone
Hinton Parva
VALE OF WHITE HORSE
Shrivenham
Acorn Bridge
River Cole
South Marston
Ermin Street
Stratton St Margaret
Roman Road
WILTSHIRE
Owl's Hill
Charlbury Hill
Chandler's Fir
Aldbourne
Shepherds Rest
Callis Hill
Wanborough
Earls Court
R Lidd
Liddington Hill
Liddington
Castellum
Medbourne
Badbury
Midland Junction Railway
Chiseldon
Hodson
Coate Reservoir
Wroughton
Wills & Berks Canal
SWINDON
Ogbourne
Marlborough Downs
Ridge Way
Barbury Hill
Castellum
Red Barn
Basset Down
Running Horse
R Rey

LIST OF ILLUSTRATIONS

1

SOUTH MARSTON AND WEST MILL

South Marston, or Maason, as it is commonly called, is a straggling village. There is, really, one main street, if such it can be named, very close and narrow, consisting of a single row of houses, plain in appearance, the doors of which open almost on to the road. At one end stands a bakery and post office combined; at the other an inn, modern and conventional, known as the Carriers' Arms. A little way below this stands a cottage where dwells 'Grandfather' Bridges, who plies his trade of market gardener and general carrier with great energy, although past the age of eighty-five. His better-half supplements the income with the sale of sweets and sundries, and is noted for the possession of a ready wit and a hard business faculty. A little brook crosses beneath the road just beyond, and tittle-tattles all through the shade of high elms and willows till it emerges wonderingly into the broad meadows, and is received into the Cole just opposite a large clump of hawthorn that stands by the side of the old weather-beaten hatches. Hard by is a cluster of white-flowering chestnuts, shading the highway. From these trees a large bough was cut every year, till recently, to grace the signboard of the neighbouring inn at the anniversary of the old village Benefit Club.

The narrow road, bordered here and there with old-fashioned mud-built cottages, leads away by the north to the ancient town of Highworth, or Hyvuth, as a good many of the local inhabitants persist in calling it. Another track, known as the Green Lane, or Gipsy Lane, branches off and conducts you through the fields and under a magnificent avenue of elms till you strike the main road opposite Kingsdown. A footpath brings you past Hunt's Copse Farm and Broadmoor into the road leading through dense lines of beech to the pretty village of Stanton Fitzwarren. At the other end of the street are roads which bring you, on the one hand, to the downs by way of Ermin Street, or straight on to the industrial town of Swindon; on the other, to Sevenhampton, or Sennington, by footpaths through the fields, or to the Berkshire villages of Bourton and Shrivenham by highway. A short way west, across the fields, is the more considerable village of Stratton St. Margaret, of early foundation. This also is reached by footpaths through the meadows. To the north lies Highworth; to the east Shrivenham; to the west St. Margaret; to the south an expanse of richly fertile and luxuriant country, mostly pasture-land, extending to the foot of the downs, where nestles the peaceful hamlet of Hinton Parva. These complete the boundary on each side of the village.

The name Marston is of Saxon origin, and is derived from Merestane or Merestone, which meant Markstone. It is certain that Marston existed before the Domesday survey, by the very constitution of its name; and we know, furthermore, that it was a place in the time of the Roman occupation, because there are Roman remains not only all around, but in the very midst of the village, though unfortunately they have been ploughed over now, and razed quite out of view. These remains were situated in a field on Rowborough Farm, some distance from the main thoroughfare of the village, and about two miles to the east of Ermin Street.

Old 'Jacky' Bridges, or Dart, the road-mender, knew the place well before the ground was broken up by the plough, and he has told me over and over again that there was a 'fortification', and that it was a square, of quite an acre within the mound, that it was level inside, and that the walls were four feet high or so, and that he had kept the cows in that field many times when he was a boy. And I remember, too, that when I was a boy I kept cows in a part of the selfsame field; and when the fogger came to do the milking in the afternoon, driving the cows up into one corner, I used to drink milk from the pail, sucking it up through a wheat-straw plucked from the rick built of corn grown over those very ruins.

In respect of the ruins, furthermore, Jacky Bridges, whose old dad was born in the village years and years before, and who worked here all his life declared that there was no doubt whatever among the old folk but that the place was a Roman encampment, and all the old people said that it was coexistent with the *castellum* on Liddington Hill and also connected with it; to use Dart's own expression, which he had heard his father say: 'There was one lot o' sowjers yander at Liddinton, an' another in thase field, lookee; an' both an 'em belonged to one another." According to this it would seem likely that the entrenchments on Liddington Hill were a base, or central garrison, and these ruins were once an outpost, one of many which were scattered about the valley in olden times, but which have disappeared now.

Old Jacky's father used further to declare that relics were found in the vicinity of the camp – bits of pottery, perhaps, and parts of old arms; and there was a very earnest belief among the villagers that if excavations were made, there would be discovered large quantities of these things concealed.

The cottages are scattered along the roads and lanes at intervals, and the farms are dotted here and there in the rich green fields. Winding round the

Hayfield at Fyfield Manor Farm, when farmed by Mr Herbert Jeeves (in white coat). His horse and cart were used for Chapel outings and picnics on Pewsey Hill

lanes, bordered with magnificent elms, which stand in lines along the hedgerows and down the orchards, suddenly you come to a farm which, but a moment before, had been invisible. There are trees to the right of you, trees to the left of you, and trees all around you. The chattering rooks build in the high boughs above; the farmyard cock crows lustily, perched upon the ivied wall; the ducks waddle to and fro; the geese crane out their necks and hiss at you, or cackle, and pluck off the tender grass; the dog lies on the sward beside the gate; the red-and-white cows graze near, or lie down, chewing the cud, while the tiny calf, but two days born, with the star on his forehead, scampers grotesquely about the close, with tail straight up, snorting and puffing; and here comes the carter, with the young mares in the wain, off down to the meadows, the younster walking beside them, hempen halter in hand, whistling cheerily.

This is not the only farm possessing these attractions; it is the same whichever way you turn. Just now I was thinking of the Priory; you will find it so, too, at Burton Grove, Hunt's Copse, Nightingale Farm, or the Manor. All these are picturesquely situated, are rich in timber, in pasture and corn land – does not Farmer Westell derive fourteen sacks of prime fat wheat to the acre from his field? – in herds of fine plump cattle, and thrifty workpeople as well.

The farmhouses are chiefly old buildings, stone-made, large and rambling, not designed with any special view to ornament, but intended rather for use, yet entirely picturesque. Away in the fields to the south is the Elizabethan farmstead of Earl's Court, in a truly delightful situation; and near by is one known by the less pretentious name of Bodge, not as interesting and ancient, but in the richest of rich surroundings, and out of the beaten track of civilization. The land is low, and greatly under water in the winter, so that accounts for its richness in the summer months. There are several streams in the vicinity, which flow down from the hills, and a great number of fine willows, in lines and avenues. The hedgerows are very high and dense, composed of wonderful hawthorn, and full of unspeakable beauty in the early summer. There is an abundance of game and wildfowl in the meadows and about the brooks, and the place is haunted by spirits, as the villagers confidently believe.

I have spoken of the wattle-and-daub cottages, which are similar to those the old Britons used to make. Till recently there were many of these in the village, and though they were extremely rude and simple in structure, they were not dirty or squalid, for that is a quality, not of the house, but of the occupier. Betsy Horton's cottage will serve as an example of this, though it was taken down after the old woman's death. The building was of one floor, and consisted of two large rooms and a small pantry, with a woodhouse outside. The fireplace was very broad; it was formerly the mere hearth, and afterwards a tiny grate had been built up of bricks, and fitted with several iron bars. Betsy's old people used to hang the sides of bacon up the chimney in the smoke, or lodge them on the wooden racks affixed to the beams of the ceiling for that purpose. The roof was thatch, of many layers, very thick and warm. The walls were whitewashed, sweet and clean, without and within. The floor was of large and small flat stones, of many shapes; these were scrubbed every week, and then whitened over with freestone. There was not much furniture inside – a rude dresser for the plates and dishes under the wall, several straight-backed chairs, and the regulation round table. In the winter it was warm and in the summer-time cool; there was nothing to retain the dust and filth; it was never stuffy, like so many modern buildings. A tiny spring of water ran down imediately behind the house. Beyond was the Great Field, as it is called; the banks and hedge were always full of primrose in the season. A little strip of garden extended from the house each way; three or four apple-trees clustered around, the hedge was neatly kept; and there, in the evening, stood quaint little Betsy, four feet high, wrinkled and weather-beaten, with old-fashioned net over her hair, and her arms folded, wearing a pretty blue print apron, and nodding to the passers-by.

Jemmy Boulton worked in the fields and was independent; sturdy William Eldridge did the same; so did Dudley Sansum, Johnny Bowles, and Jacky Bridges, and many more that I know. They lived in plain stone or plaster houses; had little furniture, but sufficient; brought up large families; had good appetites, ate, drank, and slept well; laughed, sang, danced a jig occasionally; were simple, open, hearty, spontaneous, and generous. Their clothes were artless, inexpensive, strong, sensible, and serviceable. They wore the billy-cock hat, trousers of stout corduroy, waistcoat of the same, a woollen scarf or cravat about the neck; and strong holland smock over all, home-made and curiously worked, reaching below the knees, to be tucked up around the waist when there was anything to be performed requiring greater freedom of the body. Their boots were heavy and thick, of very best leather, made to measure, and well-fitting. The Sunday-best pair was the same, and was kept cleaned and well greased. They wore the billy-cock hat and smock to church – when they went – and nailed boots; they had no other propensity for finery; their whole accoutremént was, in fact and deed, made, not for ornament, but for use.

Their food was very plain, too – in keeping with their times, character, and appearance. They lived on bread, bacon – mostly killed from the home sty – pure lard from the same – not the adulterated fat such as you get now – milk and cheese from the farm, the very best obtainable, at sixpence a pound; sweet whey butter at the same price, or good wholesome salted stuff; suety or

A team of milkers

bacon pudding; vegetables from the garden; and eggs, the gift of the farmer's wife. They drank weak tea, whey in abundance, skim and new milk, and thin ale, or 'swanky'. This was served out at the farm, or they kept a cask at home; that was their one and only indulgence. As for amusements, such as we understand them, they were either unknown or unheeded. In the evening, or at week-ends, they worked in their gardens, or walked out and viewed the cattle and crops, and praised So-and-So's drilling, or cutting, or hedging and ditching; or visited each other's stables, and admired the horses and harness and cracked with each other's whips; or went to see the sheep and lambs, the milking cows and heifers, or the little foal galloping in the paddock. Or perhaps they went to the village inn for an hour or so to learn the latest news, and cheer the soul with a cup or two of 'fourpenny'; then home to bed, and up at four or half-past in the morning, strong and hardy, cheerful, vigorous, and optimistic. Their shoulders were broad, their bellies round, their legs short and stout, their faces round too, robust and red, and jovial-looking; not pinched and thin, haggard and ghastly, like the townsfolk. and, mark you, they were independent with it – village folk never were so generally abject and slavishly obedient to every precept and nod of the 'maaster' as is usually represented; it is an insult to the rustic population ever to suggest it.

Their wives, even where there was a large family, went out to work in the fields, too, along the summer and autumn, winter and spring as well, when it was dry and fit; or they assisted with the milking and in the dairy.

The mother took the infant out with her into the field, wrapped it in her shawl, and clapped it down under the hedge while she went on with her work, giving it a rattle or other toy, or flowers to play with; Johnny led the horses for his father, and Jane and Nell kept the cows or sheep, or picked up stones or couch, or pulled charlock, or hoed with their mother. Grizzling children received a smart slap or two, and were quickly cured of the habit; every member of the family was hardy and industrious. Did not Granny Bowles, and Patty Titcombe, and Betsy Horton spend their whole lives, till they were nearly eighty, at work in the fields? and was any woman more robust and healthy, physically fit and vigorous than they? Or can you imagine any more strongly principled and virtuous?

I admire these grand old characters and honour them. Stark, stern simplicity alone has the quality of true freedom. The old people with a small house, hardly any rent or none at all, little furniture, healthy bodies and willing minds, robust children, ready to rough it at all times, and no knowledge or need of superfluous equipment or amusement, were far more independent than we are. The difference is, we are happy in bondage, and they were happy out of it. I would far rather live in Betsy Horton's or Jacky

Bridges' bare old plaster cottage, eat simple food, dress poorly, and be free with it, than to wear away body and soul in the senseless effort to keep a fine house, to strive to be that I never can be, to ape my taskmasters and superiors, or to excel them in style and dress with my small means – in a word, to live a life of extreme discomfort, of foolish self-sacrifice, and endless misery.

The village is bounded on two sides – the south and the east – by the River Cole. At every three-quarters of a mile or so there is a hatch, or hatches. The gates of these are lowered in the winter and spring to flood the water-meadows. A very rich supply of pasture is the consequence; the grass is often as high as your waist. Sometimes the hatches are kept closed in the summer-time too, especially in the upper reaches of the brook. This is to bay the water up for the cattle. When the bay is full the water spouts over in jets, or flows in small streams, and accumulates again at the next hatch. Behind the hatch is a pool, often four or six feet deep, and generally teeming with fish of various kinds, especially lower down, where the stream is wider. Here you might have been sure of taking roach, dace, and pike, and sometimes trout, less frequently perch. These come first of all from the reservoir, and are carried down the stream with the floods. When the water subsides, a great many remain in the still pools under the trees and bushes and propagate there, if they can escape the many creatures that come to prey upon them.

Presently the river, swollen with the addition of several other tributaries, reaches the canal, and passes beneath the aqueduct. Here also the highway crosses, and a stone set upon the greensward is graven with the words: 'Here ends Marston Road.' Crossing the stream, you are in the royal county of Berkshire. Just beyond the highway is an osier-bed, and then the railway, situated on a high embankment. Just through the railway-arch are some large hatches, and on either side of these, deep pools of water, called 'back-cuttings', from which clay and stone were obtained to construct the railway-bank. The spot where the highway crosses the river is named Acorn Bridge; the locality is called simply Acorn, and sometimes Hackerne.

The land here lies low and damp, and is remarkably fertile. The pools are very deep, and teem with fish – roach, tench, perch, and pike. The roach are of a very dark colour, almost black on the back, and the pike attain to a great size. A few years ago one was taken from the water over thirty pounds in weight. Its mouth and jaws contained several large steel hooks with which it had been entangled at different times, but it had snapped them all. In the winter, in the shallower water, you may sometimes take pike through the ice. They are then numbed and sluggish by reason of the extreme cold, and this renders them incapable of studying means necessary for their safety.

The river was narrowed in slightly to form the hatches; they are about sixteen feet across. There is a flood-gate each side, before the hatch, to turn the water off into the adjoining meadows. A large main trench, about six feet wide and four feet deep, receives this at first; numerous other small channels branch off and distribute the water here and there. finally, there are tiny furrows, about half as big as those a plough would make. These are made by a man with a breast-plough. This is an implement with a small share attached to it, and a strong crosspiece at the other end. This end is applied to the breast, and so the operator forces it along and cleaves the trench. By this means the water from the stream is conducted entirely through the field; though when the floods are heavy, the waters do not trouble to flow in the channels, they inundate the whole banks and fields to the extent of several feet; the whole course of the river is flooded half a mile wide; it is like an inland sea. Enormous crops of grass follow these inundations — the yield is often three tons to the acre. The custom of flooding the meadows is extremely ancient.

The walls and gates of the hatches are old and crumbling now. How long these hatches have existed here I could not say, but a small boy from the farm in search of 'catties' among the loose stones in the water the other day found a George III penny, bearing the inscription 1792. Perhaps this is about the date of the last new walls and gates; if so, they have worn very well, and might easily claim the indulgence of a pound or two spent upon them.

There is a hole in the bed of the stream behind the hatch, six feet deep or more. The water, after passing through the gates, glides down to this over a floor of iron, and falls below with a medodious sound, quite untranslatable into the human language: it is the language of eternity.

In the winter, provided there is frost enough, there will be abundant skating and sliding on the pools, and often in the water-meadows as well, though the ice there will not be as stable.

The country boys do not often possess skates, but content themselves with sliding instead. Their heavy nailed boots are very well adapted for this; they glide along over the smooth surface for a long distance. If one of the nails in their boots should happen to be sharp and cleave a long white line in the ice, they call this a 'streak of fat bacon.' He who can effect the longest streak is counted above the average among the juveniles. The farm youngsters often meet with accidents in sliding and skating on the ice, and frequently get severe wettings at it. Sometimes they attempt the ice before it bears properly, or slide into a spot sheltered by trees or bushes, or, if it is in the water-meadows, they may be deceived with a current which has retarded the frost, and come to grief that way, but they do not care very much about it, and continue with the sport. Once, in my boyhood, when I was in the habit of coming home from the farm by way of the ice on the canal several successive nights in the starlight, I suddenly found myself struggling in the middle of the water nearly to my shoulders. While I was in this predicament the testy old farmer at the house near by, being warned of the accident by his man-servant, who was in waiting for me, hearing that I had slid into the hole, thrust his head outside and cried: 'An sard un devilish well right, too; a no business an ther.' The ill-natured old man had had the holes broken on purpose to entrap the skaters.

The best skating and sliding takes place on the pools called the back-cuttings. The whole village, old and young, turns out to join in the pastime, when it may be indulged in, though the exceedingly mild winters of the past few years have not offered many facilities for this kind of sport. Sunday afternoon is the liveliest period; there are then big crowds upon the ice. The men and youths play 'bandy,' the young women and children slide up and down over the shallower waters; there is no fun more hearty than rollicking on the ice. If there is a little snow on the ground, and a clear sky overhead, the joy will be heightened; everyone will be happy and lively and gay; the maidens' cheeks will be rosier than ever.

The water in the brook seldom freezes unless the cold is very intense; even then it remains open by the hatches. The wild-ducks and moorhens generally manage to keep an open space, however; by constantly swimming to and fro under the thick bushes they prevent the ice from forming there.

Years ago, Acorn Bridge was a noted rendezvous for cock-fighters, and for prize-fighters as well, especially before the railway-line was made. Challenges were issued in distant parts of the country, and the combatants used to come here to indulge in their inglorious sports. Happily civilization has gone far to stamp out this relic of brutal barbarism; I should grieve to think that such scenes could be enacted in our own day. Cock-fighting was indulged in by the villagers here regularly until forty years ago, and in all parts of the village beside, but this is no longer the practice; fear of the law, and that alone, has stifled the passion for it.

After leaving the hatches, the river winds down in and out through most delightful meadows, past the covert, towards the little hamlet of Sennington. In the spring and early summer there is an abundance of large watercress growing in the stream, and about the trenches of the meadows as well. The boys and men from the farms know where to find this; almost any Sunday morning you may meet one or other of them bearing a bundle tied up in a red pocket-handkerchief.

Years ago there were professional watercress men, but these are not so much in evidence here lately, since old 'Patsy' died. Patsy was a familiar figure about the village, and in the town too. He had been the local watercress man for many years, and had grown old in the occupation; he was well over seventy when he was forced to retire from it. Patsy was short and slight in stature, bent and stooping; his clothes were ragged and rough, his coat-sleeves long, and his trousers short; his boots were very old, and full of holes; his feet were naked within them; his hair was long and grey; his weather-beaten old face was clean shaved and sharpish looking. He wore an old cloth cap, and carried a large flat-shaped open basket at his back, slung with cord over the shoulders. As a rule, he was only visible in the mornings and evenings; during the daytime he was lost in the far-off fields, and about the brooks and ditches. When he had obtained a sufficient quantity of cresses, he used to take them to the town and dispose of them to the small shopkeepers, and so eke out a precarious living.

At night he slept in the fields, under a haystack, or in the cattle-stalls, during the greater part of the year; in the dead of winter, he was forced to take refuge in the workhouse. He was well known to all and sundry round about, though he was very reserved in manner, and seldom conversed with people. His general conduct was above suspicion; he was trusted by all, and was never known to interfere with any; he was a lonely and solitary creature. The last time I saw him was one morning in late October some fifteen years ago. As I was passing through the town on my way to work at an early hour I saw Patsy standing underneath the wall of a house on the pavement, in a most abject condition. The morning was cold and raw; there was frost in the air and some fog. He had his basket at his back, as usual, with a few cresses, and his old hands were thrust deep into his trousers pockets. His neck was open and bare; his feet and legs were very wet. I could tell by the mud on his boots where had had been. He was shivering with the cold; it was enough to give a stronger man than he his death. I can still see the crowd of workmen staring contemptuously upon him as they passed along, smug and comfortable enough, to the warm workshops. I can even now feel the hot blood mount up, as it did then, in indignation and sympathy for the old man. I loved him then for his utter abjectness, and because he knew and had frequented all those little nooks and crannies in the meadows I took such delight in. I never saw Patsy after that morning. I think he went to the workhouse, and soon after died there. His was a hard life, in some respects, and a cruel ending, but he loved the brooks and the fields.

Over a mile past the covert stood the old mill named Friar's, the first you meet with on the stream. Here is the house, too, known as Friar's Farm – Fyas, the country folk will call it — but the mill has been demolished these five years now. The all-conquering steam-engine has greatly superseded the water-mill, though it has not yet extinguished it, as we shall see, and there

Flour Mill, operated by the Howse family, Hight Street, Pewsey. (Now the Southern Electricity Board showrooms)

was not enough work locally to employ this, so in time it fell into disuse. The meadows alongside the brook are very rich; it is no wonder that old Peter Westell and his kin, who lived at the farm, made a big fortune in cheeses. That, too, was years ago; there is very little cheese made in the neighbourhood at this time.

The little valley continues for about a mile, winding round; the river follows the centre of it. This brings you to West Mill, which, though dilapidated, is still in use, and does much grinding, though chiefly grist work, with a little wheaten flour beside. West Mill is situated in a sequestered yet delightful position, solitary enough in the winter, if anything ever could be solitary to rustic people, but beautifully green and cool and pleasant in summer and autumn.

The mill-dam is close under the grinding-house; there is just room to pass across by a small bridge. An old grape-vine adorns the west wall; it is laden with fruit in the season. Here is a door, and just within a small hatch which admits the water to the wheel. It is remarkably simple; you merely draw the hatch up gently, and secure it with an iron pin; a few inches merely will afford the necessary power. The wheel is within the building, immediately beneath you, and is very heavy, of iron throughout, just like the paddle of a steamship. The first contact with the water starts the wheel; in a moment or two it increases in speed; very soon it is revolving at a good rate; its momentum is considerable. To view the process you go round the building, and enter on the other side. On the ground floor are large bins to receive the flour from the shoots, or sacks are hung, as behind a thresher. There is a trap-door above your head, through which the heavy sacks of corn are hoisted up. The pulleys are operated by power from the wheel; the water does all the labour. The grist, as you catch it in your hand falling from the shoot, is warm through contact with the stones. A wooden stairway conducts you aloft to where the machinery is. There are two sets of stones, one for grist, the other for flour. The corn is fed on top, and enters to the stones evenly and regularly. Near by are the 'silks' for refining the flour. The chief power is conducted to the stones from the water-wheel first by an iron shaft beneath; above, all the pulleys, spindles, cogs, and everything, are of apple-wood, strongly made, exactly in keeping with the locality and industry.

The revolutions of the water-wheel are increased to suit the miller's convenience; he can generate as high a speed as he thinks fit. The belts flap smartly from pulley to pulley; the wooden cogs run in and out, communicating their power almost without noise; the floors and machinery oscillate gently; the old building trembles sensibly; the fine impalpable dust of the flour settles everywhere; there is no other sound audible from the loft. The water, as it turns the wheel, flows out at the mill-tail with a musical note –

the river sings at its task – and the foam is carried down and swims away through the bridge beneath the road, and out into the meadows.

What an interesting character the miller is, and how important he is, and the position he occupies! He ranks almost before all the agricultural community. Nearly all millers seem to possess similar charcteristics. Perhaps the nature of the craft is responsible for this. Its genialness, natural simplicity, and quiet; the refinedness of it, the handling of and contact with Nature's most precious produce, the sense of being concerned in one of the oldest and grandest employments, have an effect on the individuality. The soft musicalness of the water and the absence of all harshness of sound are formative agents too; all this together helps to make the miller a genial character, and to give him a philosophic cast.

Our miller is a comparatively young man – thirty-eight or forty. He has worked here from a boy; his old master, just deceased, was eighty-four, and had lived at the mill for sixty-two years. He is medium in height, rather thick-set and plump, very healthy in appearance, agricultural in type. His face is round and bronzed, tanned with the sun and wind, for he is much out of doors; his features are regular, he is neither striking nor intellectual looking, but reflects a genial dispostion, a quiet and homely wisdom and intelligence. His voice is low – almost as soft as the waters that murmur beneath his wheel – his eyes are kind and sympathetic, frank and honest. He does not speak very much, he is sparing of words – to strangers, at any rate – but you will easily perceive the affection he has for his wheel and machinery.

He delights to show you over the mill, and make you acquainted with the several processes, and is not afraid to inconvenience himself. If he is otherwise engaged and you require him, he smiles softly and acquiesces pleasantly. Yes, he will show you round. Down go yoke and pails, or any other paraphernalia he has; he seems eager to oblige you, stranger though you be to him. Without another word he proceeds to the hatch: you follow. Here he turns on the water. That is eight horse-power. Could he increase it? Yes, he could pretty nearly double it if he wanted to; he could lift the hatch up to here, look, but that might break the mill. Then he enters the building, you behind, and while you wait before the bins, he sets the mill going, mounts upstairs and feeds it, then comes down to you again. As the grist falls through he catches a handful and shows it to you for your opinion; you catch a handful, too, and turn it over and over with your fingers. Then the miller mounts up the stairway again, and you after him. He goes to the sacks. All this is for gristing, look. They do a lot of gristing, but not much flour now. None at all? Oh yes! We grind our own, but not for sale, you know. Well, someone may come and buy a peck now and then. This machine here is the refiner, and here is some of the 'firsts.' What do you think of it? He likes you to praise it, of course, which you do, and mean it, too; for it is deserving. It is not as fine as that produced by elaborate plant, to be sure, but it is good enough for me at all events, and might be so for others. It is a little brown in the hand, it is browner still when it is cooked, and very sweet. The loaves made from it are deeply rich and nutritious, not light, dry, and chaffy, like the starvation stuff you purchase at many of the shops, where everything is prepared for the eye, or the pretended refinement of the palate; the needs of the stomach and body come last – but that is the present fashion. Puddings and pastry made from it are as brown as the bread, but very wholesome. The puddings are very glutinous, and adhere well to the cloth. You need very little sweetening with it, and cannot eat much at all, it is so satisfying, but it is excellent for the stomach and body.

So the miller takes you from point to point, and shows you everything there is to be seen, full of a quiet enthusiasm. How carefully he handles everything! The gear is wooden. He sets it in motion so that you may see all, then, when you are satisfied, shuts it all off and makes everything secure. Now you go down the steps and out into the open. He lowers the hatch. The water still spouts through underneath; it does not shut quite tight, he says. The wheel still turns, then slackens and stops. The foam on the water in the mill-tail floats out and disappears. All is silent. The miller must go now, for it is late afternoon. It is time to serve the pigs and collect the eggs in the sheds, which is his work; sometimes he does this while the mill is running. Then he goes indoors to tea – his cottage adjoins the mill. After that, he may take a walk around the fields, or do a little fishing, or grind a little more corn for pastime. He need not do this, oh no! and he is not paid overtime, but he likes it; it is a pleasure.

2

CHARACTERS OF FARM AND WORKHOUSE

This morning is a sharp frost. Close in the field is a sheep-fold, barricaded all round with thick walls of warm straw, and divided into numerous sections and compartments like a little city, for it will soon be lambing-time; and this is the shepherd coming with his dog. The old man is of average height, robust and healthy in appearance, tanned with the sun and the wind, with a fine nose, regular features, and most kind expression. His top lip is clean-shaven, he wears a grey beard under the chin, his frosty old brow is topped with a billy-cock hat, well soiled; he agrees well with the hoar frost on the grass and the rime on the branches. He wears a strong brown holland smock, well patched-up, heavy nailed boots, and thick leathern gaiters. In his hand he carries a stout staff with an iron crook at one end. His flock is of best English ewes, tegs, and wethers. His dog is a large stocky animal, black and white, very old-fashioned-looking. He walks behind his master most respectfully, and observes a moderate distance. When you address the old man, he does not thrust himself into your notice, but stands or sits some way off, and looks sagely at you, or turns his head towards the fold. Doubtless he is thinking of the flock, and where he shall lead them to-morrow – among the swedes there or along the clover patch.

The old shepherd is pleased to speak to you. 'Yes, 'tis cowld; but a nice marnin, a know. Chent so cowld as 'twas.' He has been up a long time, and is off home to breakfast now. He is getting ready for the lambs. Will the cold hurt *them?* 'Bless ee, no, 's long as 'tis dry. Don matter 'ow cowld 'tis, 's long as chent wet; tha do get the rot so, then.' The iron crook looks cruel and out of place. 'Do you not hurt the poor sheep with it?' 'No, bless ee, not if ee be keerful. Some people do say as 'ow it do, and 'ow it breaks their legs, but I never hurted one in mi life, as I knows on. A okkerd fella might do 't, a know.' How sweet the baby lambs look when they are first born! They lie in a little nest made for them, and are nearly all ears and legs. Their pretty little noses and eyes are very quaint; when they are lying down they are like little figures in china or porcelain. The shepherd used to receive a bounty for lambs, but not now; that is included in his wages. On the downs there are

Westbury White Horse. This postcard shows sheep in pens made from hurdles

sometimes as many as a thousand ewes, and these yield on an average eleven hundred lambs; but Shepherd Smith's flock is not nearly as big as that. A shepherd with a large flock of ewes is possessed of considerable skill, knowledge, and feeling too. See the life in his hands! He is father of a large family; he is physician, nurse, and guardian combined; he is the Providence of the fold. He is sometimes the Nemesis as well, for he must perforce play the butcher from time to time, and supply the house with mutton; he can kill and dress a sheep with the best of them.

Formerly the shepherd lived at Hangman's Elm Cottage. This elm received its name, not as one might imagine, from an execution, but from a suicide there. Now he dwells in the village, at the foot of the hill. His old wife is dead; his sons and daughters are grown up; he is in the evening of life, near the sunset, but he is bright and cheerful and optimistic. The old shepherd lives in the present, and lives well, if severely; he does not trouble very much beyond that.

South Marston, upon which we are again steadily converging, lies deep below in the valley, completely hidden from view by tall, dense trees. The steam of the railway engine, dazzling white, is visible a moment right away to the left of you over Acorn meadows; then it dissolves and disappears altogether.

Climbing up the highway, along the hill, you come to several series of tall elms, which are visible all round for many miles, and especially from the tops of the downs facing you in the distance. At the farthest end of these a road leads through the fields to Queenlains Farm. Here, for a great number of years, lived one Richard Chillingworth, bachelor – 'Uncle Dicky' he was always called – together with his sister Maria, an elderly maiden lady, conspicuous for her kindness to the farm-boys. When young Strawberry, of Round Robin, came to the farm one day, and had been asked into the kitchen to have a bite and a sup, she surprised the youngster by bringing in a monster roly-poly pudding, smoking hot, and saying: 'Which end will you 'ave, the crutton end, or the carrot end?' The pudding was made of cruttons and carrots.

Uncle Dicky was an old man a quarter of a century ago. His farm was very extensive – some hundreds of acres – lying around in every direction, though he was only the tenant of it, not the actual possessor. He and his ancestors had occupied that holding for nearly a century, and had made a good pile out of the bounteous old earth. Those were the palmy days for agriculture, as it is frequently said; wheat fetched a good price, there was not so much imported from oversea, and, consequently, not the same amount of competition; and the Crimean War, though it cost much blood and treasure, conferred a not insignificant benefit on corn-growers in these islands, and Richard Chillingworth, with many others, became the richer for it.

Uncle Dicky was of slight stature, middle height, and gentlemanly appearance. His features were clean cut – fine nose, kindly eyes, very thin lips. His hair was shot and grey; he wore a cloth suit, and a white felt bolero hat. He seldom walked about the fields of his farm, but rode a very quiet chestnut that went jiggetty-jog, jiggetty-jog everywhere. His lands extended right down to the village. Every day he visited there. At a certain hour of the morning and afternoon you would see his white hat bobbing up and down over the hedge-tops. When he came to a gate, he opened it without dismounting; his chestnut understood the operation, and cantered close up; the old man leant over, and opened it with the handle of his whip, and closed it up again securely; then jiggetty-jog away as before. If a small boy happened to be anywhere about the fields bird's nesting, or getting nuts or blackberries, and the old man came up unexpectedly, and the youngster did not run away at first sight – for they were all mortally afraid of 'Old Dicky' – but stayed and opened the gate for him, he might escape without a good scolding, but he never received a gratuity. Instead, the old man would very likely look at him pleasantly enough and say: 'Wha's thy name?' and, on the youngster's telling him, would reply: 'Come yer, an' let I hit tha one on the head wi' my crab.' Hereupon the youngster would take to his heels and scamper off in a great fright as fast as his legs could carry him.

There was one person who lived down in the village that was a constant source of trouble and irritation to the old man. This was an old woman named Blunsdon, otherwise known as 'Barley Nuggin,' by reason of her acitivity at leasing up the barley and wheat in the harvest. The two were often in contact; there was generally a little disagreeableness resulting somehow or other. Not that the old fellow objected to leasing in the least; he liked to see the women and children gathering up the ears in the stubble well enough, and never interfered with them. Nor did he mind their going blackberrying, or gathering rotten wood under the trees in the meadows, as long as they did not interfere with the mounds, but he would have all the gates securely shut after they had gone through. And this is what Barley Nuggin never would do. Moreover, she used to take a hatchet into the old man's fields and go 'chumpon,' as she called it – that is, getting chumps or stoles of wood out of the hedges, and take them home to burn.

Barley Nuggin was a long, lank wrinkled old dame, very thin and stooping. Her nose was long and sharp; her chin pointed, too; her lips pressed tightly together; her eyes sunk and watery; high forehead; shrunk, withered cheeks; very grey hair, confined in the old net. She wore a faded blue print sun-bonnet; her whole appearance was sharp, sour, and disagreeable. She generally wore a little woollen cross-over, a black threadbare skirt, and heavy nailed boots. She was the first woman to go leasing in the autumn, and was not at all particular as to whether the field was cleared or not. If there were sheaves remaining, she would pluck handfuls of corn from them with no compunction whatever. As soon as she had made a hasty run over the piece, she decamped elsewhere, always afraid lest she should come second anywhere, and so miss the first gleanings. She was frequently talking about making 'barley nuggins' with the leased corn: that is how she acquired the nickname. The old man Chillingworth knew of her propensity for theft, and sometimes lay in wait for her. He was sorely troubled about the 'chumping' business, too, and, what was more, she never would close the gates, but left them all wide open for the cattle to wander through. At last, one day, he caught the old dame red-handed, with hatchet, wood, and all; she was just passing through a gateway. So he rode up to her, and told her to put it all down, but she answered with: 'Thee go on with tha. Who dost thenk's afraid o' thee? I wunt do no sich theng.' This was too much for Dicky. He lost his temper, and struck at her with his stick. Nuggins vapoured and spat at him like a wild cat. 'Ya owld devil,' she screamed, 'I 'awp I shall meet tha in hell, I do.' With that the old man turned his horse and cantered off. He had met his master, or his mistress, that time, at any rate.

Leaving Queenlains you come immediately to a highroad, leading to the town of Swindon, five miles away. Presently a small by-road branches off and brings you through delightful avenues of beech to the quiet little hamlet of Stanton Fitzwarren, noted for its pretty, old church, its lake, and woods. A little distance farther along is the site called Cat's Brain, the home of old Joby Lane, and the working ground of Josh Hughes. The field opposite Stanton turn is called Four Docks. If you had walked down Green Lane, from Cat's Brain, some years since, you might have seen a large notice-board affixed to an oak-tree in the wood telling you to 'Beward of the man-traps.' These relics of a semi-barbarism are exactly like a modern iron rat-trap, with very sharp teeth and strong spring. It must have been an unpleasant experience for the sporting individual who chanced to get caught in one; I should think he avoided the woods by night for ever after that adventure.

There are some stone quarries in Four Docks field, and ten large chestnut-trees standing along the other side. Harry New, the old quarryman, was employed here all the year round, when I was a boy; and here my mother used to bring us to glean up the wheat in the harvest holidays. The spot is very lonely by night; it was not an uncommon thing then to be stopped by thieves, and forced to hand over your purse or other valuables. I remember we came to the field once immediately after dinner to lease up some wheat there. The sky was dull and leaden, there was no wind, and the air was humid and oppressive. Little white clouds – 'messengers,' Josh Hughes always called them – stood out in relief against the darker background, and floated across the sky – a certain sign of wet among rustic people. We stowed our small bundle of clothes and provisions beneath a fine large chestnut, fastened the linen bags for the ears about our waist, and went into the stubble.

Very soon the large drops of rain came, steadily at first, then thicker and thicker. We kept on gleaning for a little while, then all took shelter under the chestnut, and in the deep ditch. The old quarryman stowed his tools and wheelbarrow, and, taking his dinner-basket, prepared to leave the field. 'No more dry to-day,' he shouted, and pointed to the solid, leaden sky above. 'No more dry to-day, I says,' he repeated, then trudged off across the stubble into the roadway and disappeared. We stood under the chestnut and watched him go, my mother in dismay, we with feelings of pleasure and delight; we liked the storms to come and confine us in the shelter of the trees now and then. The rain swept in clouds across the valley from the south-west, almost blotting out the other part of the field; the hedges and trees were soon dripping with the moisture. We children climbed the high boughs, and ran all along the ditch among the tall docks and thistles, or played hide-and-seek. Presently we ate the afternoon meal, squatting around the trunk; then, as the rain showed no signs of abating, and the large drops from the leaves were making our clothes very wet, we packed up our small belongings and tramped off down the long road home to the village.

Following the way down by Cat's Brain fields, a short distance brings you to the workhouse, which, though a mile from the village, is yet very closely related to it: it is the last home of the poorest and most unfortunate. Many have gone there to end their days, to die out of sight of all that is kind and charitable, doubting of life, doubting of love, of truth, fidelity, and friendship, doubting sometimes even of Providence itself – alone, forgotten, deserted for ever, forlorn and solitary. The workhouse is not one building; there are many sections and departments, a great many of them modern, newly-built, indicative of the times. Fifty years ago the place was considerably smaller, but there was not so much poverty about in those days, and what is more, a good many of the old folk were not so readily inclined to accept of its barren hospitality as are very many of this generation; there is a deplorable weakening of character creeping in all round upon us. Modern local industries and conditions, too, have vastly increased the need of a refuge; it is surprising how many 'cast-offs' there are here from the manufacturing centre. Once admitted, these soon became acclimatized. The atmosphere and environment of the place prevail over whatever moral courage they may

Pewsey Union Workhouse

otherwise have had; they accept the condition, and think no more of battling with life themselves. If they were not paupers before, they are doubly so now, physically and morally too.

The general aspect of the place from the entrance is very gloomy and forbidding; it is enough to make the stoutest heart quail to behold it. Old Mark Titcombe, weak and infirm at eighty-five, his last bit of savings spent, would rather have been butchered in bed than taken from his cottage and carted off to 'that place over yander, to the 'firmary.' That is a smooth hypocrisy, used to beguile the simple and ignorant. 'It is not really the workhouse you are going to, you know,' they tell the old people, 'but only the infirmary.' As if that were not an integral part of the system, and one of the most distressing at that.

The workhouse, dingy and drab-looking, lies off the road somewhat, sixty or seventy paces. The entrance to it is barred with stout iron gates, which are generally fastened and locked, day and night as well. High elm-trees overshadow the entrance, and continue in a line along the hedgerow there. Just within is the porter's lodge – a little hut big enough to contain two persons – fitted with a stove for use in cold weather; to the right and left, before the house, are some shrubs and evergreens, which look almost black from the road. On the one hand, going in, is a patch of turf with goal-posts, where the juvenile paupers forget their situation in the excitement of a game occasionally; on the other, are gardens for flowers and vegetables. Farther down on the left are outhouses and buildings where the tramps and roadsters, who are admitted for the night, pay off their score the next morning with a little healthy exercise with the saw and hatchet, or other implement. Beyond that is more ground for vegetables, worked by the permanent 'staff' of the place. Here is the school play-yard, walled round, and fenced in with iron railings like a prison; this is the shoemaker's, and there is the tailor's shop. In the front part are the master's quarters, the Board-room, and the offices; adjoining these is the workhouse proper, where the paupers are confined. The infirmary is a new building, and is situated at the rear.

The greater portion of the tragedy is here, for those detained in the other parts, though poor and unfortunate, are able-bodied enough; these are doubly wretched, in that they have no possessions of any sort, and are afflicted with diseases as well, more often of a permanent kind: there is no hope of escape for them. 'What is that man there?' I asked one old fellow, well over eighty. 'Is he going out again?' 'I dunno; I dun expect so,' he replied. 'A lot as comes in stops here till they dies.' That is it precisely. The old fellow was there waiting for death to relieve him, too; but though he could see and dimly understand the fates of others, he had not fully grasped the position in regard to himself. Other people's misfortunes generally strike us more forcibly than our own.

There are all sorts of people in the infirmary, afflicted with many and various complaints, and a few with none at all beyond that of extreme old age. Very many of them are old roadsters, who have tramped, and tramped, and tramped, until their legs were quite worn out, and they could go no farther on the journey. Their friends are dead – if they ever had any, that is; their kindred dead too. A great many of them never had a home; they have drifted and drifted about from place to place, town to town, village to village, from one county to another, workless, aimless, and careless, happy enough, no doubt, until Time clapped his hand heavily on their shoulder and cried to them: 'Hold! you have gone far enough.' Henceforth no more highway, white and dusty under the summer sky, or brown and muddy in autumn, or frozen in winter. No more lying down in green fields, and under shady trees, or camping in the lanes, with wallet crammed full of provisions begged from house to house along the road through the village. They have entered here for the last time now, and will leave no more, until their old bones are haled away to the churchyard.

A great many of these are confined to their beds, and do not move about the ward; and while, here and there, you may induce one to talk a little, others are moody and sullen, and will have nothing to do with you; it will be best not to interfere with them. The tramp's habit of life invests him with a certain amount of reserve, and even of defiance; that is his characteristic. Most likely it was the early quality that determined him to adopt that manner of life, too; so we must expect it to be no less in evidence at an advanced age. You cannot break their spirit of independence: they maintain this to the last. Some of them, to be sure, will talk with you, and tell you all about themselves; but the best way to effect this is to take them on the road. Here, if you have leisure, and a few pence to spare, you may easily obtain your value back again in narrative.

The other night, coming home from work in the dark in January, a voice hailed me out of the mist and shadows, and inquired the way to the 'house,' and the distance. Drawing near, and halting, I could see it was an old man with a long grey beard, and billy-cock hat. He had no wallet or bundle of any kind. His voice was low and musical; he was evidently town-bred; he spoke very courteously; you liked him immediately. His name was William Lines, age sixty-nine and a half, by trade a tin-smith. 'How far have you come?' 'From Nottingham, sir.' 'And where going?' 'To Bath, sir.' 'Don't "sir" me, there's a good fellow. Got any friends?' 'No! Well, not that I know of.' 'No sons to help you?' 'I had two, but I don't know where they are. They were both in the army at the time of the war; but I think they enlisted under other names. I have never heard of them since.' 'Where have you lived all this time?' 'I was born at Bath, sir; then worked at London for a time, after at

Worcester, and since at Nottingham. I have not done a lot for some years now, but have wandered about from place to place. You see, I thought if I could get to Bath, my pension will be due in six months' time, and I might rub along then a little. How far is it to Bath from here?' 'About thirty-five miles.' 'That will take me three more days, for I cannot get along very fast.' I gave the old man what money I had, with many apologies – it was no more than three-farthings, if I must confess a personal matter – shook him mightily by the hand, and wished him good luck and his pension. He took the small gift generously, thanked me profusely, and with a 'God bless you, sir,' and a kindly 'Good-night,' went on his way. I hope that by this time he has received the coveted weekly allowance, and has fallen in with some one or other of his boyhood acquaintances, and is moderately comfortable, at all events, for he seemed a most genial and affable character.

The other occupants of the infirmary are a miscellaneous lot. Of the genuine agricultural class there are very few; that is a matter for congratulation. Here and there, of course, where a man outlives all his relatives and friends, and becomes bedridden, he is forced to come into the 'house'; but the superior health of the rustic stands him in good stead, and if he has any children they usually see to it that he is spared the disgrace of the 'union.' If they do come here at last they will not live very long. Old John Lane, who clung to his little cot at Cat's Brain till he was eighty, and was fetched inside, only survived a week, and Mark Titcombe died in three months. The man of independent spirit is deeply wounded at being brought to the workhouse; he is struck to the soul with it; it will be most likely to prove mortal.

Albert Trueman, exactly seventy, whom I met in the yard as I was going in, was pacing up and down like a caged beast. 'Here,' thought I, 'is one ill at ease, who cannot be reconciled with his condition.' A little conversation with him soon verified my conjecture. He was a most diminutive man. He was scarcely four feet high, with the tiniest of features. In one eye he was stone blind; he could only see a very little with the other; by raising his head and turning it on one side he could just discern you. At first he thought I was an official. I soon set his mind at rest on that point. Where was he born? 'At Highworth.' 'What! just out here?' 'Yes, sir.' 'And what happened afterwards?' 'Then we went to Wanborough. That's where I went to school.' 'Yes.' 'Do you know Wanborough, sir?' 'Oh yes, I am often there.' 'Then we went to live at Bishopstone.' 'Yes, I know Bishopstone too.' 'I knows every inch of they hills, sir.' I felt drawn very near to him. 'But what did you do after that, and how did you lose your sight?' 'After that I went to London, sir, and kept a coffee-shop at Vauxhall, and then a little hotel, and done well at it too.''But your eyes?' 'I got a cataract, and underwent an operation. The same doctor done it, sir, as took the one from Mr. Gladstone's.' 'Yes.' 'But they got bad again, you know, and I can't see at all on this one, and only a bit with the other.' 'What did you do then?' 'Lost everything, sir, and got my living selling matches.' Here he took an empty vesta-box from his pocket, and showed me the kind. 'But how did you get here?' 'Walked it through Hungerford last fall. I wanted to see the old country. I hadn't see the Shepherd's Rest for fifty years. But I wants to get out of here. Bless you, sir, I can't rest like some of 'em. I wants to get my living. You see, I am seventy, and if I can get my pension I can earn some more beside and muddle along. But I can't stop in here; there ent a bit of peace night nor day. Remember me, sir, and do what you can for me. I am going to see the pension officer next week.'

Tom Chamberlain, or 'Chamblin,' as they say, the Crimean veteran, also of the village, need not have come to the workhouse at all, but he applied for admittance, and pays for his keep into the bargain, which is quite unique, and a revelation of character, regrettable though it be. He could not get on with his people, and he could not stand the children. The martial spirit is strong in him. He is not disagreeable, but he is extraordinarily restless. He cannot be still, not he! The tramp, tramp, tramp of the regiments still sounds in his ears; the motion of the armies took possession of him; he will never be at peace this side of the grave. After fighting in the Crimea with the French and Turks, at Alma and Inkermann, he came home and worked on the farm again. The contrast of the fields, the quiet and isolation, preyed on him somewhat; he developed this spirit of unrest, sternness, testiness, if you will have it so, but he remained strong, courageous, military, and patriotic with it. True virtue does not consist in mere affability. The finest metal is the toughest and hardest; that will cut a way through everything. It is the same with the human temper. The soft edge is easily blunted, the rigid character overcomes all things.

The old man is a true type of the army veteran. He is tall and medium built, though he stoops slightly now. He has a fine face, even features, red cheeks, and thin, pointed nose. His hair is grey. He wears a moustache, which is continued around his mouth and underneath the chin. This is grey too; he is the picture of what we like to think an old soldier should be. How proud he is of his medal! Every Sunday he wore it, pinned on his coat with blue ribbon. He worshipped it almost. When he came to church with it, he walked up the nave in veritable triumph; it was just that pardonable pride in the possession of a trophy that pleases so well. If you converse with him, he is full of the sights and experiences of battle; he is white-hot with it. 'I fowt in blood up to my knees,' he declares to you solemnly. He hated the 'Rooshans' like poison, and scorned the French soldiers: 'The dirtiest devils alive,' he styles them. The Turks were the best of the lot, in his estimation. He can tell you of many hardships, the horrors of war, the suffering, the bitter cold of winter, piercing frost, and famine. He was happy to return back to old England. He received a pension for his service, and is really very well-to-do. It is a pity he cannot be settled out of the workhouse, but he protests to you that he is quite happy and satisfied, and if that is so, he may as well choose his own dwelling, for satisfaction is the general goal of life, though few indeed are they who ever succeed in attaining to it.

There is an interesting character in the old men's ward. He used to be gatekeeper for many years, and was a schoolmaster by profession. He was surprised that anyone should be interested in him. 'This place is a hell to me,' he said fervently, 'there is no one at all to speak with, no one at all.' He looked round on the others: 'The best time they ever had in their lives, most of them,' he declared; 'they love it. Oh, if I had only known it, if I only had! But there, it's no use now.' He was born in Oxfordshire. They were well-to-do. 'I hear you were a schoolmaster.' 'Yes.' 'Now, tell me all about it.' 'My first school was near Marlborough; that was in '64. I have spent many happy hours in the Forest at Savernake. Then I went on the *Indefatigable* in the Mersey.' 'Yes.' 'After that I went to Wrexham, then near Snowdon, but I did not get on so well among the Welsh. After that I had a school in Surrey, that was my last.' 'And why did you leave that?' 'Disagreed with the parson over High Church matters, and was forced to quit. My dear mother died at that time. I spent all my money. Father didn't want me. My brothers were well off, but they didn't want me either. I tramped about from place to place, came to Swindon, got a job, clerk to an insurance agent at twelve shillings a week, and lost it, and that's how I came to be here.' I forbore to ask him of the future, for he has great sensibility, and that is pretty obvious. He is seventy now. What hope is there remaining for him in that place – what hope, I say?

In the ward with the old veteran were a little lad of ten in consumption, waiting his turn at the sanatorium; another of about the same age with skin troubles; a blacksmith who had been operated on for spinal disease and pronounced incurable; one in bed with hopeless rheumatism; another with heart and lung disease, who, when he breathed, lifted himself half out of bed, and whose days are certainly numbered, though he spoke to me very cheerfully; and another lying like death itself. Several times I asked him, as kindly as I could, what was the matter, but received no answer, or thought I did not, though his eyes met mine, then he turned them aside. Stooping still closer to him I repeated, "What *is* the matter with you?' Then his lips moved, though very faintly – no sound came from them – but I could tell from their motion it was 'Heart.' His dinner, a large cup of stew and a thick chunk of bread, stood on the locker untouched beside him; the other inmates went on with their meal, and took no notice of him.

Here we are in the village again, on our way to Burton Grove – Beerton, a good many of the folk call it – the home of old Launcelot Whitfield.

Burton Grove is a large farm-house, with much land attached, pasture and arable too. It is surrounded with sheds and buildings and provided with a huge barn. Here is an orchard, well stocked with apple-trees and filberts. Adjoining this is a spacious garden, two handsome black beeches shade the house on the western side. At the rear is the entrance to the dairy – many cows are kept – and here is the old brewhouse, with the wide hearth, the scene of many 'harvest-homes,' teas, and suppers, in times gone by. What games have been played here! What blazing logs, and flames leaping up the chimney! How the old roof rang with the songs and laughter! The rick-yard – rick-barken, the old people called it – is farther away, and surrounded with elms, too. The neighbourhood swarmed with owls. Every night you could hear them, to the right of you, and to the left of you, before and behind; in the trees high up over you, and close by your very head they seemed to come, and startle you with their loud screams and the familiar 'Tu-whit, u-whoo-oo-oo!'

3

OLD LAUNCELOT AND HIS STAFF: HAYMAKING

The chief thing about Burton Grove was old Launcelot himself and his staff. The principal of these were Jemmy Boulton the carter, the fogger, the shepherd, and Betsy Horton, the little quaint old woman who lived in the tiny wattle-and-daub cottage by the highway. These were not all the farm-hands. There were Grubby and Scamp, and Smithy, the under-carters and ploughmen, day men and women, 'half-timers' from school, and a troop of young girls beside, who helped with the hay and harvest; for if Launcelot was odd in some respects, he was a great believer in labour; and though he exploited the young people, perhaps, it was no more for cheapness' sake than because he just liked to see them about, and have them with him. During the greater part of the year there were seventeen hands employed in one way and another, whereas nowadays you would see no more than six or eight at the outside, though the same quantity of land is in cultivation. But the arable land is not kept as clean now as it was at that time. Women are not employed to 'pick the couch,' or to pull docks, charlock, and thistles, as formerly; what the machine cannot do is left undone. For one thing, the women of the village would not be seen doing the work nowadays; and as for the young girls, how it would soil and blister their pretty fingers to use the hoe or paddle, and how stained and browned they would be with the milk of the dandelion and sow-thistle! But you should have heard the girls sing at work in old Launcelot's fields years ago, when I was a boy and toiled with them; it would have done your heart good. They were as happy as all the birds in the air, and did not wear that look of superiority and self-consciousness which is becoming more and more general everywhere throughout the land. Nell Smith, the old shepherd's daughter of Sennington, used to help her dad with the sheep and lambs, and work like a man on the land, and was healthy and strong as anyone alive; and a good, honest young woman, too, into the bargain, a sound, useful wife for any working man in the country.

Launcelot was tall and square, strong, and well built. His head was

Haymaking on Stanley Haines's farm, Milton Lilbourne

massive – broad forehead, beetle brows, small, ferret eyes, rather fierce looking; high cheek-bones, thick nose, mouth pursed up, top lip clean-shaven; short, iron-grey beard under the chin; stern and severe in general appearance; hale and hearty-looking, every inch a yeoman; in uniform he would have made a good 'beef-eater.' In cool weather he wore a velvet coat and flat-topped boxer hat; in summer and autumn a loose holland jacket, and broad-brimmed straw. Wherever he went about the farm he carried a paddle – less often the gun. As soon as he caught sight of a thistle-root, or dock, or any other weed, up it had to come in a moment; he was certain destruction to noxious and parasitic plants. Where the master set such a good example, the workpeople were sure to follow; if they saw anything 'maaster' had missed they quickly pulled it up; that is the reason the land was much cleaner than it is now.

In manner Launcelot was variable. In the first place he had a temper, and when that was roused he looked at you as black as a thunder-cloud or went livid with passion, and shouted out, and called you wooden-head in a moment, though he was immediately himself again, and did not bear any ill-will, no matter what offence you had given him. He was generally quiet and reserved, and did not interfere very much with the work-people. He walked round the farm once every morning, and carried the paddle or gun under his arm. As he walked he had a peculiar way of raising and dropping the head and eyes at every few steps. If he did this quickly he was incensed, if more slowly he was normal. All the men sharpened up a little when maaster was at hand, and relaxed slightly when he had gone, but not much; there was no need at all to skulk, for in spite of Launcelot's small peculiarities, he was a down-right good master; hot-tempered, if you like, but broad-minded and generous, a payer of fair wages, liberal with food and beer, sympathetic and charitable. But he hated all nonsense and make-believe; Launcelot was altogether a plain, outspoken man. When he addressed the carter it was sometimes as 'Boulton,' and sometimes 'Jemss.' Jemmy usually replied with 'Ya-as, sir,' or 'Naw, sir,' or plain 'Eece.' He was the master's lieutenant, and worthy of the confidence, too. When Launcelot wanted the stable-lad, he generally shouted loudly for 'Grubb,' or 'Grubby,' or 'Grubaxe,' or 'Peckaxe,' or 'Stick-in-the-Mud,' according to the humour he was in. The latter came cloutering along the pitched way from the stables, quaking in his boots; he dreaded to have to face the maaster when he was not pleased. Even old Betsy used to get it occasionally. One morning, by mistake, she got among some young corn, and Launcelot, coming to the field, fell in a towering rage. 'Hi! hi!' he shouted, 'what bist thee at ther?' Come off o' that.' But the wind was the wrong way, and she could not hear. Then, waxing hotter, he turned round and roared out, 'Go and tell her to come off. If 'a dwunt come off quick, damn if I dwunt shoot the old bitch.' But he was good and kind to the old dame, for all his temper, and she almost worshipped him for it in return.

Jemmy Boulton, the carter, was an ideal character. He was nearly as broad and thick as he was long. His face was round and red as the rising sun almost. His shoulders were round with fat, too, and his belly was like a barrel. The old fellow's head was thick and chubby, the face shone; thick Dutch nose, merry twinkling eyes, top lip clean-shaven; broad, smiling mouth; thin fringe of beard under the chin, the ends of which, viewed sideways, projected upwards in a crescent like the new moon; his was a hearty and jolly countenance, the expression of good health, fair living, a contented mind, a jovial spirit, good-nature, and good-humour, wit, intelligence, frankness, simplicity, and honesty; he was as fair a man you would ever wish to meet. The top of his head was bald; he wore the billy-cock hat; in height he was about five feet. You seldom saw him without the short, white smock, reaching nearly to the knees. On Sundays he wore a new one, which his wife had worked for him. His trousers were of corduroy, his boots strong and thick, made to measure by the village shoemaker. In the winter he wore leather gaiters that reached up the thighs. He carried his dinner in a broad, flag basket, and usually bore a long whip with numerous well-polished brass ferrules up the handle, of which he was greatly proud. He knew the roads for many miles around, and had gone with his team in every direction within a radius of twenty miles, which was a considerable world for a carter to be acquainted with thirty years ago.

As to Jemmy's character, it agreed precisely with the description I have given. He was very shrewd and witty, hard to beat, and hard to teach, where he could not grasp a thing naturally; well versed in his profession of carter; able to plough and sow, reap and mow, milk, or anything else; ignorant of books – he could neither read nor write – and fond of a good large mug of ale. He and Dudley Sansum were bosom friends well met, both jovial and convivial; and both were members of the old village Benefit Club. You should have seen Jemmy carrying the big flag, and waving it to and fro at the head of the procession on anniversary days round the village! How very proud he was of that blue silk with gold letters and fringe! That was the happiest day of all the year to him; and then the big fat dinner at the club-room, washed down with plenty of foaming ale, and the band playing. When the old carter was somewhat over sixty, he came home from work one night, kicked his boots off at the foot of the stairs, and said bluntly, 'I done now,' and went straight up to bed and never got up any more.

Betsy Horton was very tiny and insignificant in stature; she was not more than four feet high. Her face was very wrinkled and sunburnt, like leather almost, for all her life had been spent in the open fields, and chiefly upon the corn-land, summer and winter too. At one time she picked couch, or pulled docks and thistles, hoed the young roots, made hay, tied the corn after the reapers, fed the threshing machine, cleaned and pitted the swedes in autumn, and helped the shepherd all the winter. Her nose was straight; she had large brown eyes, strong features. Her general expression was most quaint; she was an old-fashioned little body. Her grey hair was parted in the middle, and tied up in a little wisp behind, or contained in the net. She wore a blue print sun-bonnet and a coarse brown apron to work, with thick boots. When it was too wet to work out of doors she helped 'Missis' at the farm, or Launcelot found her employment in repairing the sacks. Her cottage being so small, and her furniture small too, she had but little housework to do; it could all be performed inside an hour. At half-past four or five o'clock Betsy came home from the field; you soon saw the smoke going up from the chimney; she generally carried home a small bundle of dry wood from the field to kindle the fire. Then the old-fashioned blue cups and saucers were forthcoming, the table was set, and tea was brewed. Bread and butter was the usual fare, or a little cold boiled bacon; she drank her tea without milk. On Sundays she wore a black gown, and a tiny bonnet perched back upon the head: she looked quainter than ever then.

Betsy was very simple in manner and behaviour; how could she be otherwise? She could not read or write. When her 'bwoy Tom' went to Australia the neighbours had to read her the letters. She was slavishly obedient to Launcelot and his interests, and never spoke of him but with the profoundest respect; it was 'Maas Whitful' this, and 'Maas Whitful' that, to every one. The neighbours had much fun at her expense, for Betsy was very absent-minded, and often made ridiculous answers to questions. But she was kind and true; her heart, rough as it was, was of pure gold; she had lived a hard life, and yet was remarkably cheerful and happy at the end of it.

As for all the others about the farm, 'Missis' and 'Miss,' 'Vogger,' old Reuben the shepherd, 'Grubby,' 'Scamp,' and the rest, I cannot stop to tell of them. First as to 'Missis,' she was an invalid. 'Miss,' the only child, was sharp, clever, and tactful, and full of business, riding with Launcelot to market in the high trap every Monday, and assisting him many ways, and waiting on the farm people beside; drawing the ale, cutting up the bread and cheese, and sometimes paying them their wages too. 'Vogger' was son to Betsy, and was full of fun and mischief; Reuben was old and quiet, Grubby was as stolid as a pillar, and Scamp as fat as a porker, and mischievous, as his nickname implies. The other men were day-workers. The girls and young women, ranging in age from twelve to eighteen, were as full of sparkling fun and gaiety as youth could ever hope to be, and could sing like thrushes. The time passed quickly in the fields where they were; work was easy; they were laughing and singing or prattling away all the time, brown as berries, but happy, fit, and well. I was a small boy of eight years when I worked the first summer among them.

I shall never forget those early days in the fields; that was my first experience at real work. Old Launcelot had sent down to the school for boys and girls to help with the haymaking. I was one of those chosen to go forth and put my shoulder to the wheel, or my hand to the implement. About all I really did do, though, was to lead the horses, carry the wooden bottles of ale to and from the farm, or rake up the hay with the girls; but I felt very important, especially when the time came round to receive my wages for the task – a bright two-shilling piece every week-end. How strong the sun shone in the meadows! How strange and far-off the hills looked to be! And how beautiful the trees, and copses, and hedges were to my boyish eyes! I can still see the far-off corn-fields quivering with the heat, the near meadows trembling too, the tall elms like spectres, everything in nature stock still, as though it were painted so; not a breath of air, not a sound but the tinkle of the mowing machine half a mile away, the rattle of the waggons, the voices of the pitchers and loaders, and the young girls laughing and talking as they raked away behind. The dense hedges were covered with wild-rose and blackberry bloom; here the boughs were thick with sloe or wild bullace, crabs or wilderns, but there was hardly any shadow. Old Jemmy's face was red as fire; he was stripped to the waist, all but his shirt, and the sweat rolled down his nose and dropped on to the ground, but he laughed and talked and chaffed the girls, and shouted 'stand firm' to the loader all the time; he was just in his element, and the hours passed like magic. How different it all was from the long dragging day, the smoke, and filth, and fume, the foul stench and suffocating dust and atmosphere of the factory! The sweat of the open fields is clean and sweet, yielded naturally; that of the other place, before the furnace, is wrung from your very heart and soul in anguish, leaving you faint, weary, powerless, and exhausted. The other is gentle, medicinal, corrective, and salutary.

The grass crops were fit to be cut about mid-summer, though a little depends on the season. If the milky showers drip well in the beginning of June, they will soon produce a good bottom growth. A few day's sunshine then will have a magical effect; you can almost see the grass grow with the eye.

For several days old Jemmy had been preparing the 'sheen,' cleaning and oiling the parts, sharpening the knives, and getting everything ready to begin the mowing. He had his headquarters in the carthouse; there he filed and

Local haymaking scene, from a lantern slide taken by the father of a friend of Mr Doug Martin

filed, and hammered and tinkered till all was in perfect order. The special harness for the mares was cleaned and oiled; he made a cushion for himself, to fix on the seat, out of a sack stuffed with hay; his long whip was ready; he used cords for reins. When the tops of the grasses were turning ripe and the weather was settling down fine, Launcelot gave the word. Jemmy coupled up the two young mares and set out for the field. They were very frightened and restless at first with the rattle of the machine; Jemmy tugged the reins, struck them sharply with the whip, and scolded them soundly with 'Now then-a,' and 'Wai then,' and 'Stand still, oot.' They pawed about, then started forward, then ran back, now wheeled round, till at last they came to understand what was required. Then, nodding their heads quickly, one against the other, they half ran toward the gate leading to the meadow, nearly shaking Jemmy from the seat. So he set about the first field, going round, and round, and round the piece, sometimes halting a moment to clear the cut grass from the knife at an angle, and take a wet of ale from the bottle; then on again, with jacket and waistcoat thrown aside, and broad-brimmed felt hat; now flicking the horses with the whip, or gripping the lever which raised the knife in passing over a trench or gutter. The machine tinkled merrily; the flanks of the mares became white with the foam of the perspiration; the sun shone hotter and hotter.

About nine o'clock Jemmy stopped for lunch – a mouthful of bread and cheese, and a long pull at the bottle. This time the mares were allowed to eat their lunch, too; a pile of the sweet juicy grass was set before them, and the iron bit was removed from the mouth. Now Launcelot came strolling up, paddle in hand, and sometimes turned a swath over with it, and soon departed again. Half an hour before noon Jemmy released the mares from the machine, and took them away to the farm for water and a rest till the evening; then back to the field and on again. You could hear the tinkle of the machine till late twilight; then he came down to the farm, had his supper in the brew-house – bread, cheese, lettuce, young onions, and abundant ale; then off home to bed. The next morning he might be up at three, and have done cutting by seven or eight, to save the horses in the heat of the day, and mow the grass while the dew was in it. If he was going on mowing again at night he would take it easy in the midday; if not, he came out and joined the haymakers.

The first day the grass lay untouched. This was a general field day for the birds of all kinds, especially rooks, starlings, finches, and wagtails. They flock about everywhere when the grass has been cut, partly from curiosity, and partly because they find a great deal of food in the exposed roots of the grass. The second day the haymakers proper appeared, little Betsy and her school, the laughing girls and boys, the fogger too, and his young men. Some came with rakes and some with prongs, and pulled the swath over; others shook the thick heaps about; it was laugh and chatter, tease and prattle all the time. Betsy chimed in with the rest and interpolated a little wisdom now and then, and 'We must get an wi't, else us shan't do much.' At dinner-time the rakes were hung on the high hedge, the forks stuck into the earth; one and all gathered in the shade of the elm-trees and ate the meal, sitting on the ground. The girls had lemonade or milk for refreshment, sent from the farm; a fresh supply of ale was delivered up to the men.

About two days were sufficient to dry the grass and make the hay, if the sun was at all strong. After turning the swaths with the rake the 'tedding' machine went over it once or twice, or it was done by hand; then the women and juveniles pulled it up into 'wakes,' and it was fit to carry. The bed of the rick had been made of bushes and old thatch in the yard, and the elevator set. Then the waggons came out for gathering up the hay. There was one, or perhaps two pitchers, and there might be two loaders, though generally one. The small boy led the horse with a hempen halter; the women and girls raked the loose hay behind the waggon. How happy old Jemmy was at hay-cart, to be sure! How his old face beamed and shone! How broadly he smiled! And he kept talking away all the time, teasing and chaffing, or telling tales about this and that, but he worked hard, and kept the man on the waggon well employed. He thrust the steel pitchfork into the 'wake,' pushed it up as quick as thought, for four or six yards, inclining his head right and left at every step, accumulating a mighty heap, then plunged the fork downwards and lifted the whole lot high up above his head, and pitched it on the load in a jiffy. Then he shouted 'Hold tight,' or 'Stand firm'; the horse proceeded a few yards, Jemmy shouted 'Wai,' or 'Woa,' and gathered up another pile.

As soon as a load was completed it was taken off to the yard; there were several teams going backwards and forwards; a constant supply of empty waggons was at hand. A short rest followed every load; the loader wanted refreshment, though sometimes the jar or bottle was thrown up to him on the waggon, or a grain of the fork was passed through the ear, and it was handed up that way. When Jemmy drank he usually went down on his knees and swallowed the liquid with extraordinary relish, though it was not very strong; it would have taken a gallon or more to make one intoxicated. It was Jemmy's great delight to tell you how one year 'the maaster' laid in a stock of Devonshire cider, and kept it in the dairy. Thinking to make it especially good and tasty, he procured a large quantity of raisins and put in with it; the cider fed on this and so derived great strength, flavour, and quality. When everything was at its busiest in the hay-field the cider was despatched off in big jars, and the ordinary gallon bottles. 'Lore, ow we did get that down!' Jemmy said. And they did, in fact, too well, indeed; for long before the afternoon was out the men were all intoxicated together, and the work came to a standstill. Launcelot laughed ready to split his sides when they told him of it, and cried out 'Well done!' heartily, but he did not repeat the experiment.

In the rick-yard the work proceeded busily, too. One threw the hay from the waggon into the box of the elevator, the machine raised it, then over it turned and fell on the rick below. Two or three were there to remove it, and pass it on to the builder; he laid the layers all round skilfully and evenly, and shaped the pile. A horse operated the elevator, walking round and round in a circle; a youngster walked round with it. Sometimes I did this, and at others helped in the field. When the hay had been cleared, I led the horse in the machine-rake. A young girl, four or five years my senior, walked behind and manipulated it, drawing down the lever that raised the rake and released the hay. The old mare, a grey, had a foal, I remember, and my companion was surprised to learn that I had never tasted mare's milk. So one day, after dinner, she brought a small bottle and milked some into it, and gave it to me to drink, which I did, and afterwards I held my mouth under the teats, and she milked it into my mouth. I had never tasted it before, and I have not since, but it was very sweet, pleasant, and palatable, though thinner than cow's milk.

Haymaking generally lasted about three weeks, though it was sometimes interrupted by showery weather. At such times the men 'tucked' the ricks, and the women and girls went 'yelmin,' that is, preparing haulms for the thatchers, when it was dry enough. The haystacks required to stand a few days to settle down before receiving the thatch; then the fogger set to work and covered them over, and clipped round the eaves, making it all look smart and tidy, and so on till the whole lot was done.

After this came the 'hay-home.' This was a tea, not a supper, and was provided in the brew-house. Everyone who had helped with the hay was invited. The hour fixed was half-past five. This was after milking, and gave all the men an opportunity of sharing the meal. The old house had been well scrubbed out, the rough tables were spread with clean white covers, chairs and benches were set. We youngsters went attired in Sunday-best, the girls and young women the same. Old Betsy was there, too. She had been helping 'missis' and 'miss' all the afternoon, boiling the water, and cutting up the cake, and bread and butter. She wore a clean smart apron; her hair was most carefully brushed – for a wonder; she was full of business and bustle. Presently Jemmy, the fogger, and the others came in, smelling a little of the rich milk, as milkers do, though that is not out of place on the farm. All sat down. 'Now then, Betsy,' Jemmy cried, 'put I out a drap, come!' 'Thee must wait a minute, till I sard these young uns fust,' Betsy answered, and went on filling the cups. 'Miss' tripped off to the dairy and brought more milk, fresh that afternoon.

Oxen pulling hay wagon, elevator behind, on one of the Stratton farms in North Wiltshire

The large kettles steamed and hissed over the wood embers on the hearth; willing hands passed the viands round. There was cake, bread and butter, and cold ham, crisp sweet lettuce, young onions, mustard and cress. The girls laughed merrily; the ploughboys ate and drank till they were boiling hot. Old Launcelot looked in once or twice to see that all was well, and stood mopping his brow with his handkerchief in the doorway. He had just come back from viewing the corn. 'Ow be gwain on wi't Jemss?' Launcelot inquired. 'Aw, all right, maaster,' the other answered. When all had had enough the tables were removed, and the girls and young women sang songs, and the boys as well, and afterwards played 'tip it,' and 'kissing in the ring' till dark; then all flocked down the fields home together, singing all the way.

4

CORN HARVEST, AND THE VILLAGE SCHOOL

About three weeks after haymaking, harvest commenced, sometimes earlier; occasionally wheat is cut and carried too in July, though not often in the valley here. Here the soil is heavy and cold; the crops are consequently later, you must mount the downs to find early cutting and carrying. Old Launcelot had all his cutting done by machine, unless the crop was down flat on the ground. Sam Davis, of Rove's Farm, another fine type of the English farmer, would not use a reaping-machine for years and years, but had all his done by hand, and made a good pile. I have heard that when his father first came to the place, he borrowed money from the carter to pay wages, and died finally worth £9,000. That is what conservative methods in farming did for him. His cattle were of the very finest, and he reared large numbers of sheep, and had threshing tackle beside; he employed many hands. Dudley Sansum, and Tommy Bowles, and Jemmy Boulton's wife Martha worked for him; he was a good master, and took his time with everything. It is the quiet farmer that thrives, generally; the one who is always cutting and paring, slashing and driving, is very often poor and in debt.

When the wheat became beautifully rich and yellow, and waved like a sea of gold under the slight breeze in August, and the time was fine and dry, old Jemmy rigged his machine and prepared to slaughter the ripe upstanding crop in Footpath Field or Moonlights, as you go up the hill to Queenlains. First of all, a way was cut round the piece for the horses to walk, so as not to beat down the corn, for that is far too precious to waste. This was tied in sheaves and thrown back clear of the track for the horses. The machine was of the early type; there were no self-binders then. The cutting space of the knife was about four feet. Four huge arms swung round one after the other, with beaters between them. These beaters knocked the stalks down, and the arms, fitted with teeth like a rake, came along and thrust them clear of the machine, in quantities enough for a sheaf. Day men and women, or 'strappers,' did the tying up by the lump; five shillings an acre for binding and setting up in shocks was the price paid. There were three horses to draw the reaper. Grubby or Scamp rode the first, Jemmy sat on the machine. Round and round they went, hour by hour; they played great havoc in a short time; the pride of the field was soon laid low.

Perhaps you have not all had the opportunity of accompanying the reapers at their task, and following the machine round and round the corn-patch; the interest is of an engrossing and compelling nature. I could walk behind the wheels for hours and hours, and never be weary of it. Granted that the old method of reaping and fagging is the more purely natural and idyllic, and that the modern reaper or self-binder savours of the pressing needs of the time, all this is forgotten in the far-off fields, with the blue heavens and the skylarks; you enter heart and soul into the work, and come to appreciate and admire the clever mechanism which cuts the corn, collects it, binds the sheaves, and disposes of them with almost human touch and sympathy. What a delicious smell there is in the wake of the reaping-machine, too! The hay field is sweet, but the harvest field is far sweeter, just after the corn is cut; it is very balm, the quintessence of delightful odours and perfumes, rich and sensuous. The straw itself is fragrant. The thick white campion is sweetly fragrant, too; then there are the scabious, corn-cockle, corn sow-thistle, pink and white convolvulus twining and clinging to the straws, and, sweetest of all, the deliciously scented corn-mint, growing everywhere through the field; the whole air is redolent with it, and especially in the heat of the day; then the sweetness seems intensified many times. These are not the only flowers of the cornfield by any means; the ground is covered with pretty creeping plants of every description, to say nothing of the wonderful brilliant poppy, so much at home everywhere in the cornfields and crops.

The reaping-machine is drawn at a good rate, up and down, round and round; there are not many words spoken. The sheaves are cast far enough out to leave sufficient room for the horses to pass; the edge of the corn, after the machine has gone by, is straight as a line. The part in which the knife operates is supported by a small wheel. A long sharp iron tooth precedes this, and divides the straws at the base; other smaller teeth are ranged along the knife-board. These divide the stalks again, and bring them into compressed contact with the blades, which travel to and fro within at great speed. There is real tragedy in the cutting. As the teeth displace the straws at the bottom the heads of the stalks shake violently; in a second they are severed; for a fleeting space they remain upright, then stagger and totter, uncertain which way to fall, till the beaters swing round quickly, and knock them all down backwards. In the case of the old reaper, they accumulated till the toothed arm came and swept them aside; with the self-binder they are received on a revolving canvas sheet, and conveyed within the machine. The tall proud poppy and crowfoot are drawn in with them. Here they are collected and well shaken together to form a compact sheaf; presently the stout twine is clapped round, the knot tied automatically, and the string severed. Immediately the sheaf is released; steel fingers thrust it forward; down it slides and falls on to the ground. The 'shocking-up' is done piece-work.

The ingathering of the corn-harvest is by far the most important feature of the farm year, especially where there is much arable land, or perhaps it may be all corn in some places, as on the downs, for instance. If the weather is wet in hay-time and the crop spoiled, that may not matter very much; but in the harvest, that is truly tragic! Who does not deeply grieve, apart from the monetary loss involved, to see all that is left of the beautiful corn blackening and rotting in the fields, under the dark rainy skies of October and November, as is sometimes the case, utterly useless for anything but litter or manure, and the ground too wet and sodden to admit of collecting it for that purpose even? It is no wonder that farmers are sometimes styled 'always complaining,' and 'irritable.' Where their very all is so frequently in jeopardy they cannot help feeling suspense and concern for its safety.

So when the corn had stood in the shocks four or five days, the horses were coupled to the waggons, and there was a general exodus to the field. First of all Launcelot had plucked some ears from the sheaves, and rubbed the corns out in his hand, winnowing them with his breath, and trying them in his mouth to see that they were hard and dry enough. Jemmy Boulton and old Betsy, with several of the girls, rode in the first waggon, others came along behind. Scamp and Grubby rode on the horses' backs 'side-saddle,' or on the shafts, ready to jump down and open the gates on the way. Several pitchforks were in each waggon, and the females brought rakes, to rake up the loose straws scattered about. Generally they had an ell-rake; this required two to draw it; it was hard work to use it in the stubble, because the teeth hitched in the bindweed and other plants. Food was taken out as well – Jemmy's in the broad flag basket, the others' in little hand-bags – and big jars of ale for the men; there was never any stint of this in the cornfield; for, however generous the farmer may be in hay-time, he always excels himself in harvest. 'How much beer do you thenk you chaps drunk yesterday, Willum?' the master said to 'dad' Eldridge one day. 'Aw, I dwun know sir,' Willum answered, 'a smartish drap, I warn.' 'You emptied a thirty-sixer; and I be jest a gwain to tap another for ee to-day, look.' There were quite three dozen hands, men and women together, employed on dad's farm at Woolstone, but even then it was a huge amount to get through in a day.

Arrived in the field, the waggons were soon piled up with rich golden corn bundles. The sheaves were pitched up, two and three at a time; the loader seized them, one in each hand, and threw them in their places; he had no trouble in getting them to remain in their position. The youngster shouted 'hold tight,' and led the team between the shocks; the load was completed in a very short time. To enable the loader to descend from the pile, the pitchers thrust their forks hard into the butts of the sheaves high up, the other leant an hand on each, and slid gently down to the ground. Jemmy's face was redder than ever, and the others' as well; he continued laughing and talking all the while; he entered heart and soul into the harvest. Old Betsy and the girls, very hot and sunburnt, drew their rakes to and fro, and brought the proceeds to Jemmy; he tossed it up on the load, and went on whacking the sheaves up again like a giant.

Down at the farm the work proceeded busily, too. First of all the big barn had been crammed full from roof to floor, with a way through left for the thresher, then the ricks were built outside; several of these were often completed in one day. Barley was not bound at all, but gathered in loose; this took longer to handle consequently. If the weather was at all unsettled the thatch was immediately clapped on. Generally, after that, the outside of the rick was sheared all round to make it spick and span, though this is considered labour in vain nowadays, and is seldom performed. If the weather was bright and fine the whole harvest was complete in a fortnight, or a very little longer; then heigh-ho! for the harvest-home in the brew-house again; there was great joy and satisfaction at the safe and final ingathering of the corn crops.

As to the harvest-home, you may easily imagine what a congenial gathering was there; the round, cheery faces, the broad smile, the merry peals of laughter from the maidens, the fogger's ready wit, and old Jemmy's prolonged chuckle. A tremendous fire of logs had been blazing on the wide hearth all the afternoon and evening. The boiler outside had been steaming away, too. The fat hams and beef had been cooking for hours. There was an abundance of vegetables of every kind, and a monster 'roly-poly' plum pudding to crown the board at the finish. The ale stood in great gallon cans; the men drank from large tin cups, the women from glasses. Old Launcelot puffed and blowed like a steam-engine, bringing in the dishes. Jemmy performed the carving, and slivered off the juicy ham and beef.

'Now then, yer, what bist thee gwain to hae, bacon or bif?'

'Aw, gi' I a bit o' that ther 'am, ull ee.'

'Come an, then. Le's hae thi plate yer!' and off he cut the slices of meat, half an inch thick and more.

'Yer, 'old on. Shan't be able to mawy if ee gets that lot down,' the other replied.

'If thee casn't aat that bit thee dossn't want nothin' at aal. I could polish off two or dree sich lots as that. Now, Grubby! jump about a bit, come! Go and get I the steel Betsy, ull ee? This yer knife dwun cut a bit. Lode a massy! my old ooman's cyarvin' tackle 'ood fetch it off twice as quick. What dost thee want, Smithy? Now, you wenches, clap 'em along yer. No backin' out on't mind; ya got to get it down zomhow.' Here the steel is brought. Skeep, skawp! skeep, skawp! skeep, skawp! 'Tha's better Betsy! Now we shan't be long.' The potatoes and cabbage were piled up; a large brown loaf stood in the middle. No one thought to say grace; all fell to with a will. Jemmy sat at the end of the table with arms sprawled out, and leaned well over, his head almost touching the plate, and shovelled it in, wiping his mouth and mopping his face from time to time with a large red handkerchief.

Time after time the plates were passed to and fro for helpings. 'Tha's it, mi bwoys,' Jemmy cried, 'get it down ee; ther's any amount yet, and plenty moore wher this come vram.' Grubby and Scamp were ready to burst. Betsy ate sparingly. The girls pretended to be shy, but could not escape. 'Go an wi' tha. If thee dossn't aat that mossel thee shatent go whum to-night, I can tell tha.' After the first course the ale was poured out. 'Now, Betsy, drenk up!' Jemmy said. 'I dwun want none,' she answered. 'Come an with tha, do,' he persisted; 'thee bistn't a teetotler.' 'I dwun want none, I tells tha, so ther,' Betsy replied. 'Aw daal tha, if thee dossn't, mun, I do. Yer goes,' Jemmy responded, and swallowed the liquor in great style, and the others with him as well. The girls had milk and lemonade; there was no stint of anything at the harvest-home.

After everyone had had enough the tables were cleared and a concert indulged in. The young women came prepared to sing. The old brew-house rang with harmony; the log blazed at the chimney back; the firelight played along the black rafters overhead.

'Bistn't thee gwain to seng to us, Betsy?' Jemmy inquired, with a broad grin from ear to ear.

'Lar' bless tha, no,' the old woman replied. 'Thees knows I caan't seng, very well.'

'What, not at 'arvest whum?' he continued.

'Thee get off wi' tha,' Betsy answered; 'my bwoy Tom 'ull seng for I.'

So the evening was spent in wholesome fun and merriment. The girls sang of lovers and rivalries, several woeful ditties, in which the 'dark beauty' won the erewhile 'constant and true' swain. The forsaken one died of a broken heart, and was laid to rest.

> 'And on her grave was a turtle-dove,
> To show the world that she died in love.'

Scamp sang 'The Miner's Dream of Home'; someone else followed with 'The Soldier's Letter' and 'The Harbour Lights,' and Jemmy stood up with half-shut eyes, and, after some little hemming and hawing, provided the treat of the evening,

'The zun was zettin' be'ind tha 'ills,
Acrass yan starmy moor.'

After repeating the chorus several times all together at the close of the piece, the entertainment ended with a 'Hip, 'ip 'ooray for Maaster, Missis, and our young Miss!' and the company divided, Jemmy frequently admonishing the carter-boys 'Nat furget the marnin', mind,' and 'The 'osses be out in the whum ground.' Outside, the moon was high up over Gardner's Garn; the owls hooted and screamed. The old church clock struck ten as we came away home down through the fields. That was the end of harvest-home, for that year at least.

In the central part of the village, with its old stone houses and gardens and magnificent walnut-trees, was a little enclosure called the pound, which was used to confine lost or straying cattle, until such time as they were claimed by the owner and released. Here also stood the village smithy, where we children used to peep in to see the man at the forge and anvil, to listen to the roar of the bellows and the ring of the metal, and to watch the fiery, fizzing sparks swish out all round. Here toiled one George Fisher and his son of the same name, old George and young George, both men of great stature, tall, broad-shouldered, fat, heavy, and ponderous. The old man was a smith of repute; the younger was fonder of the knife and fork than hammer, tongs, and tools. It was seriously said, I remember, he ate so heartily, that he had to be greased and rolled after dinner. While father and son were earning their daily bread at the forge with the sweat of their brow, the wife and mother – and a rare, good, old-fashioned soul, too, a kind, compassionate creature – went about with a basket of cow-heels and tripe. Old George lived to a good age and died suddenly; young George did not long survive him. The wife and mother has long been dead, too. The old shop has been pulled down – I can just remember assisting in the operation – so that smith, smithy, and all are gone; there is not a vestige of anything left to mark where the forge, bellows, and anvil stood. Whoever wants a horse shod or a repair made to any ironwork or machinery at this time must hasten off to the next village; the sound of the hammer on the ringing anvil is heard here no more.

At the corner where the road branches off is a curious sarsen-stone full of round holes, several inches deep, let in the bank, obviously for the purpose of preventing the wheels of vehicles from wearing away the mound there. My old grand-dad, Josh Hughes, a true old rustic gentleman, very unsophisticated, but hard-working and thrifty, brought that very stone from a field on his small farm at Cat's Brain, and placed it there sixty years ago. I have always felt more interest in the old man than the sarsen-stone, and I am sure you would do so, too, from what I have heard, if you had known him, for all the old folk say that he was a most interesting character. One amusing anecdote related of him is that on being seriously advised to put his money in the bank, for safety's sake, he took the cue and promptly scooped out a hollow place under the hedgerow, and concealed it forthwith. If that is not the artlessness and simplicity which is virtue itself, I should like to know what is.

The village school stands in a field near the road, a short way down. There the little mites of children toddle off each morning to acquire the rudiments of learning, such as is deemed necessary to equip them for the struggle with life and circumstance. A few of these are farmers' children; part of them belong to the mechanic or artisan class employed on the railway, or at the distant town, but the majority are the offspring of farm-labourers. Some of these dwell in the lanes, some in the fields near at hand, and some at the cottages on the far-away farms. These bring their dinner in little baskets or handkerchiefs, and eat it sitting down under the hedgerows in summer, or in the lobbies or school-room in winter. Sometimes they exchange food with each other – children are fond of tasting each other's bread – or some child living near at hand may invite them to his or her house to eat the viands. When I was a small boy I delighted in exchanging my white bread for that cut from the brown cone wheat loaf of a companion, who lived at Owl's Roost Cottages. These children's fare is simple; bread and butter, or lard, jam, or treacle. Sometimes, when you are sitting down to dinner, a timid little rap may come at the door, and on opening it some little dot or other will bashfully ask you for a 'dop o' wato.' If you should happen to have a good large mug of lemonade or milk handy, and give him that to drink, holding it to his lips, you will be handsomely repaid with the smile of pleasure and satisfaction which beams on the youngster's physiognomy as he gulps it down, and afterwards requites you for it with a hearty 'tenk-oo.' After this you may be sure the visitor will come again, and bring others as well; but then they never dream of intrusion or imposition; there should be no end to hospitality in their eyes; they have not learned the limitations of life.

It is a pretty sight to meet the country children coming or going from school; there is so much that is exceedingly quaint and picturesque in them, and primitive, too. They are bright-looking, fresh and well-kept. Some of the little maids from the farm buildings are very quaint and old-fashioned, both in feature, general appearance, and behaviour. They put one in mind of the figures on the old willow-pattern china-ware. They are not pretty – that is, as is usually understood by prettiness, but by their simplicity of feature and

Schoolboys of a later generation with Miss Cross, their schoolmistress, in the School Garden, South Marston, 1912

demureness of expression they are exceedingly attractive. Here is no ornament of dressed curls or ribbons, beads, or fine head-wear, or frilled frock, or armlet, or dainty brown boots and stockings, gloves or mittens; the child's clothes are plain, simple, and unpretentious, just as you would expect to find it in the circumstances. The face is square, the nose shortish, eyes brown, hair straight, tied over the crown with a piece of old black velvet or braid, dress of drab cloth stuff, print pinafore, dark stockings, and stout, heavy, square nailed boots, blacked weekly. When it is fine they come unencumbered; if it looks stormy they half carry and half drag a little jacket of coarse material on one side of them. As they near you they lower the eyes and head a little, and partly turn it on one side to avoid your gaze, coyly or timidly, but when they have passed by they will be sure to steal a glance round to see if you are looking at them, and hurry along toward school. Several times, up the lane, they will turn round again to see if you are watching them; nervously if you are a stranger, sociably if you are not. Their parents are poor, and they reflect their comparative poverty; they have not been pampered and spoiled, one can see that; their very bareness and humility force you to sympathize with them. Their cheeks are rosy and firm, the eyes strong and deep, the stature short and stunted, the whole physique hardy and natural, not drawn up like a hot-house plant, and spectacles are very rarely met with in the case of true farm-labourers' offspring.

The boys are of corresponding appearance. They, too, are short in stature – Nature always rears a sturdy, hardy plant – generally thick, robust, and well-set. Their hair is usually long and bristly – sticking up for fine weather, as they jokingly say – and home-cut. Their clothes are mostly threadbare, made out of father's left-off, more than likely, often with trousers reaching halfway down the legs, ridiculous to the critical eye of the town-folk. They wear a woollen scarf around the neck in winter, and nothing at all in summer. Their boots are heavy, thick, and cumbersome, and well nailed; such as come from the farms in the fields wear leather gaiters in the winter, and keep them on during the day. The boys will not be as timid and shy as the girls, or not all of them, though the little brothers Gilbert and Jesse were most sensitive in this respect; it was amusing to see their pretty bashfulness, and how they hung their heads and retired behind the other boys. But poore Jesse is dead now; in the summer a horse in the field kicked the little's mite's brains clean out.

Some of the country boys are very rough and noisy, and ready for all kinds of mischief and skylarking, but they are frank and open with it; they are never secret and malicious. Others are sober, and outwardly dull; I do not mean that dulness which is stupidity, but rather that which may denote a retiring, yet keenly observant nature. A great many of these rustic born and bred lads prove to be very long-headed and resourceful, not brilliant with intellectual wit and cleverness, but endowed with a large portion of sound and practical common sense, which is of so much value in life. Their receptiveness and acquisitiveness are remarkable, and they will easily beat the town boys when they are brought into contact with them in their own sphere; they invariably make good workmen.

There are about eighty pupils at the school; counting infants and all together – the entire population of the village is no more than three hundred and seventy – these are managed and taught by a governess and two young assistants. I have told you already of their quaintness as individuals, if you should see them assembled in a body, this feature would be much more in evidence; they would strike you as being quite a unique little gathering, a very rustic and sequestered lot – Nature's own offspring. A short while ago someone showed me the photograph of a group taken at the school a quarter of a century ago, and my own self in it, boys and girls together, teachers and all and I could not help smiling at the figure we cut at that time, the very oddness of the whole picture; it all seemed inexpressibly funny. The long white pinafores of the girls, and patched sleeves and trousers of the boys; the round chubby faces and sturdy features; the mischievous smile, and downright irrepressible grin, this one hiding his face behind the other ready to explode with laughter; another looking so solemn and expressive; the modest and demure countenances of the girls; the consciousness of this one, the artlessness and stolidity of the other, the teachers at the rear with antiquated head-dress, and the parson on one side, presumably to overawe us with his superior presence – it was enough to raise a smile.

There is swinging in the playground for the maids, and a tumbler and bars for the boys. At the back of the school, towards the field, is a large shrubbery which abounds in blackbirds and thrushes. These sing loudly from the yews and laurels while the juveniles are at lessons, or in the play-time, and the cuckoo takes his position in the elm-tree in the season and utters his cry, so dear to and beloved of the school-children. Now and then he perches on the playground wall and sings there, too; and I have known him to alight on the ground within the enclosure and sing as loudly as ever, 'Cuck-oo, cuck-cuck-oo!'

The school-room walls were adorned with pictures, Scriptural all, and though we did not understand the whole of the subjects, from being always before our eyes, they made a deep and lasting impression. There were two which I especially remembered, from their being hung just opposite my form in the class-room: one of these was Abraham on his way to offer up his son Isaac, and the other was the fiery serpent lifted up in the wilderness to stop the plague. I can still see the youthful Isaac bearing the faggot on his back to kindle the altar, and the agonizing features of those gazing upon the serpent in the other.

The school was subject to visits from the vicar and the lady of the manor. These looked in when they were least expected, the former to correct and supervise certain points, and the latter to inspect the children, and note their appearance and behaviour. The best and tidiest girls and boys were rewarded with gifts of coins and complimentary remarks, the badly-behaved were made to feel that they were not in her favour. If the youngsters did not make their obeisance out of school, the lady visitor would very gravely address them and say: 'Little boy, where are your manners?' the reply to which generally was: 'Ain't a got none, miss.' After this, the young hopeful shot off like an arrow, not knowing whether to be glad or sorry, fearing to be punished for his daring misdemeanour.

Country children discover a great many edible things in the hedges and fields, which are unknown to those who dwell in the towns; they can usually find something or other to munch at all times of the year. In the spring they eat the large buds and young leaves of the hawthorn, commonly known as 'bread and cheese,' which are quite palatable; later they devour primrose and cowslip petals and stems, the juicy leaves of the sorrel; afterwards they dig up the underground nuts and eat them, too, and often bite a crowfoot bulb by mistake, which is remarkably hot and pungent. Then, in the summer, there is the fruit of the maple-tree, 'hatchets and bill-hooks,' crabs and wilderns; and in the autumn blackberries, acorns, beech and hazel nuts. When these are gone there remain slans (or sloes), peggles (hawthorn fruit), hipsons (the wild-briar berries), and the rich berries of the yew. All these things are gathered and devoured by the youngsters of the country-side, to say nothing of raw wheat and barley, peas and beans, with turnips, swedes, and mangolds from the field.

I remember once eating some of the brilliant crimson berries of the arum, or cuckoo-pint – 'snake's victuals,' and 'ladies and gentlemen,' we called them – and severely burned my throat with them. I wept all the way home, and went to my kind old grandmother, who forthwith gave me some hot tea to drink out of a blue basin, which did not mend matters very much; I can still seem to feel the scalding liquid going down my throat. Though I always exceedingly admire the berries now, and the finger-like stalk on which they grow – for they are most delicately ornamental and beautiful – I never attempt to break my fast with them; I have not forgotten the early experience.

All the leading boys of the school make efforts to immortalize themselves by engraving their name on the trunk of one of the high beech-trees that stand by the pool in the meadows. I have heard this practice referred to in scathing terms, and pronounced barbaric, but perhaps it is not quite as bad as that in the case of small boys; it is just as natural to them as apple-stealing. If it is really a crime to carve one's initials on the trunk of a tree, then I am a most guilty culprit, for mine is there as conspicuous as any.

As soon as the children leave school they go to work, generally starting on the farm, perhaps with their father, helping him with the horses, or driving plough, or assisting with the cattle; for this they receive three shillings or so a week, and some portion of their food. The girls go out in situations as nurse or kitchen maid, and soon become initiated into the mysteries of pots and pans and household duties. Their wages for this would be about sixpence or a shilling a week, with keep. By-and-by these see better situations, and drift farther away; some of the boys migrate to the towns; a good many of the girls are packed off to London or elsewhere, where wages are higher. Other children take their places at the school; there is a steady coming and going all the while; the number of students remains practically the same.

In dealing with the school and school-children I have said a little about my own days, but this I have done, not because they were any more interesting than those of the present time, but because I had a more intimate knowledge of them; but you may be sure, for all that, that whatever was done then is done now; all the old games are still indulged in. The boys kiss the girls and are cuffed in return; the children are whipped and kept in after hours; the teacher scolds and stamps her foot in passion; the students look ridiculously and smile defiantly, or quake with dreadful fear; there is laughing and crying, nodding and whispering, sweethearting and coquetting – all the old childish joys, griefs, passions, and feelings exhibited. However wise they may ultimately become, we cannot force the children to look at things through the eyes of sage experience; theirs is the time of glorious irresponsibility and carelessness; they are not to be measured by the standard of adult humanity. For my part, I love to see them and to be near them; I love them at work and at play, whether quaint and curious, well or ill cared for, plain, pretty, simple, or ornamental. The only distinction I do make – if I must confess any degree of partiality at all – is in the case of the very poorest of the farm-children; for something or other, in spite of other considerations of judgement, brings the balance of interest down on their side. I think, in my heart of hearts, that I care for them most of all.

5

CHURCH, CHAPEL AND ROAD-MENDERS

There is a church in the meadow opposite, facing the school. On one side of it, and slightly to the rear, is a farm-house and buildings, most picturesquely set among shrubs and trees; an orchard adjoins the burial-ground on that part To the left, farther away over the fields, studded with high elms, other buildings are visible, with thatched roofs.

The church is solid in structure and large enough. It was never intended to be pretty and ornamental, but firm and substantial.

The tower is square and very massive; the walls are very thick, of three stories, and the whole is crowned with pinnacles and battlements. The roof is flat and well leaded over. There is a little square aperture by which you may reach this if you can climb up the wall inside. We boys found the roof very convenient for making observations, and especially at festival times, when we could creep in unnoticed. On the night of Queen Victoria's Jubilee we stayed there till twelve o'clock, viewing the bonfires on the hills and all around. Sometimes, however, groping our way up the pitch-dark stairs, we accidently came in contact with the rope of the 'ting tang,' and made that sound, and so discovered our whereabouts. Forthwith the old sexton, of eighty years, with Roman nose nearly touching his chin, grey-headed, and bushy grey brows, stooping and bent, with billy-cock hat, white smock, knobby stick, and heavy cloutering boots, came shuffling into the belfry and painfully up the steps, crying out in a shrill treble voice, sounding very far off: 'What be you bwoys at up ther? Come along down. Come down, I tell ee;' to which we one and all unceremoniously replied: 'All right, gramp! You stop ther; we be comin',' and mounted up higher and higher. Irritated with our daring, the old man climbed up to the clock floor, repeating his demand for our return, and threatening to 'fetch the reverent,' until, out of sheer concern for him, we went down the steps again, this time giving the rope a vicious tug or two and making the bell ring loudly. The old man stood on one side at the base of the stairs and struck at us with his stick as we passed down; we laughed merrily at his discomfiture. It took him about ten minutes to hobble down the dark stone spiral stairs and reach the open air; we were already far away and out of sight.

There are three large bells in the top story of the tower, the heaviest of which weighs almost a ton. Then there is the middle one, on which the clock strikes, and 'the little bell.' The old wise-heads used to say that when the latter was made, a lady stood by and shot a whole lapful of silver into the melting-pot. I do not understand enough about bell-making to know how the proportion works out in metals, but, though the casting has a fine rich tone, it is not what I should call silvery. The three together emit a rather monotonous sound of 'Bim-bom-bell, Bim-bom-bell'; but, whether it is through custom and association, or a perverted taste in the musical, or want of appreciation, I must confess that I like the sound of them as well as I do of any. In the church over the fields they have four bells, the sound of which the children interpret by expressing the words: 'I'll tell John Brown,' 'I'll tell John Brown,' and 'Tommy Lincoln,' 'Tommy Lincoln.'

The bells of the village church are not rung very frequently. At Christmas time the ropes are pulled well, and on New Year's Eve, then again at Easter Sunday, and later on at Harvest Festival. All the rest of the year they are merely chimed, unless a wedding takes place. Then, if there is the possibility of a shilling or two, and a good deep draught of ale, the old tower is made to tremble for a short while, though not for long. The heavy bells want some swinging, and no one is willing to work for nothing nowadays, not even bell-ringers. Sometimes the heavy bell swings up too high, and lodges in an inverted position. In that case it must remain so till the mechanics arrive; there will be no more music from it that night.

Within the churchyard are several firs and a large yew-tree. When I was very young I thought it would be nice to be buried beneath such a shrub, but at this time I must confess that I should prefer an open position in the full sunlight, for the yew is a poisonous plant, and the little florets will not thrive beneath it.

The interior of the church is spruce and trim, all modern, new, and well kept. There are few interesting relics to claim the attention of the visitor: these were swept away at the restoration; there is scarcely anything to kindle the imagination. The ticking of the clock in the tower above you seems only to give a greater intensity to the silence which otherwise prevails, and has a peculiarly depressing effect on the nervous mind; it is a relief to escape from it into the open air. Once outside, the eyes rest upon green pastures, large elms and sycamores, and the mortal spirit is soothed and pacified. There is a creepiness comes over you standing in the belfry, beneath the high window, and especially when you open the old door to ascend the stone steps in the darkness, a strange sense of awe and fear takes possession of you for the time being, in spite of yourself. You feel in that darkness to be in the company of the spirits of those long dead, as if expecting every moment to be tightly gripped by skinny arms and fingers; the whole atmosphere is that of weird solemnity.

It is interesting to enter the church early, and see the worshippers come in, the old men first, afterwards the youths and maidens, and finally the children. Robert Brooks was a regular attendant at morning service, though over eighty-five; he is in the workhouse now. His grey beard and shaking head, as he walked feebly up the nave, were pathetic to see; he was a striking figure. Next came William Maisey, hard on four score. He wore heavy nailed boots, and gaiters of corduroy, with both hands held down by his sides. His old head was frosty white, and his short beard the same; his nose was prominent, his eyes kindly, his whole expression exceedingly pleasant. His heavy boots sounded loud on the paved floor; he cloutered along noisily, but he was welcome; everyone had a smile and a kind word for old William; and one young married woman took such a fancy to him that she went up to him and kissed him outright.

The village maidens are delightful to see. There is a town and a country beauty: the former is cultivated and derived, the latter is natural born, as artless and fresh and lovable as the wild roses that bloom about the fields in early summer. The town paragons lack this grace, this richness of form and figure; they are too spare, too thin-shouldered, lean, slight, gaunt even; they seem to me to want the very rudiments of true beauty.

The dress of the country maidens, too, where they have not been too much influenced by the town styles, is simpler, more tasteful and suitable, more becoming and natural. There is little pretence to elaborate finery. In the summer you see whites and creams, in the winter warm reds and blues. In the sunny days the cool thin muslin and large-brimmed straw hat; in the shadows, a pretty red jacket and delightful little round cap of the same colour, enclosing a face fresh as an apple, robust, and yet delicate, a perfect picture of health and beauty. All eyes are fixed on the maidens as they enter the church; old and young alike gaze at them, for beauty compels everything. There is another quality which agrees so well with beauty in the village maidens, that is, demureness; they are not self-conscious. This is bred of rusticity, of simple life and conversation, of innocency, and is the most lovable feature of all, though it is rarer now than it used to be.

The little boys and girls march in all together, the boys cap in hand, cloutering along with heavy boots, panting and sweating very often, for they have been playing in the field, likely enough, and are very nearly exhausted. The girls walk quietly round to the transept, leading little Jacky or Tommy by the hand, who turns his head over his shoulder and looks behind him all the way with wide open eyes, astonished to see so many people together. The poor mother enters with her little swarm, and places them all along in the seat beside her, and hands them books, as many as can tell the words and letters.

The sermon in the village church is often long, and the minister severe. Knowing all his flock so nearly and well, he is pretty much acquainted with their several weaknesses and shortcomings; and when anything of note transpires – if this one is guilty of some little fault or indiscretion, or that one has been 'having it over' with his neighbour, or has been absent from his pew for a long time, and so on – some kind of reference to it will most certainly be made; everyone in the building regards the allusion, and recognizes the person for whom it is intended. There is a good deal of nudging in the pews. 'Zumbody bin gi-in ee tha wheeze, missis,' the old farmer declares to his wife, after church.

I have spoken of the originality and independence of some of the villagers. That has been illustrated in church, even during service, and in my own recollection. Old Launcelot Whitfield, of Burton Grove, liked church well enough, but he could not bear the intoning of the responses, and the chants generally; he could never understand what purpose it served, nor what it was done for; nevertheless, he put up with it as well as he was able. But one Sunday morning – perhaps he came there in an ill humour – he took the chants much more seriously to heart, and when the parson sang 'Lord, have mercy upon us,' he jumped up from his seat roughly and bawled out, 'Yer, gi' us my 'at, and le's get out o' this. I've had enough o' this. I can't stand it no longer;' and marched out of the building, frightening the ladies, and shocking the vicar and his wife. Launcelot's face was fiery red, his mouth firm, and his old eyes glittered; yet for all that impatience of his, he had an honest and manly heart. One old farmer would not go to church any more because the parson prayed for the soldiers at the war, and mentioned their names individually.

The old sexton was accredited with many quaint sayings and eccentricities. It is said that he suffered from rather astonishing lapses of memory, and was a little too much addicted to the habit of sleeping at his post as well. He lived before my own day, though, and I cannot vouch for the truth of all that is said of him. But that he slept soundly in church, and woke up suddenly, thinking himself to be in far-away scenes, and sometimes uttered rather irreverent exclamations, is beyond all disputing. One morning, for certain, he slept very soundly, all through the sermon and after, and was only awakened by the noise of the people trooping out of church. Then, suddenly starting up, dazed and bewildered for the moment, and rubbing his eyes, he exclaimed loudly: 'Damn it all, is it awver, then? Lard a massy ow!'

His son Billy, who succeeded him in the office, continued his sire's characteristic, though he was not quite as slumberous. He was an old man when I was a boy, of small stature, very much bent, with hooked nose, and pointed chin; he walked with a stout stick. He was known to the youngsters, all and sundry, as 'Bagger nation.' Whenever he saw any of the juvenile clan in the churchyard, he always hobbled after them with his stick, and shouted; 'Bagger nation sakes the bwoys, come along out.' Billy's chief glory was in funerals. One thing, they provided him with work. There was so much for digging the grave, so much for tolling the bell, and, beside this, he had to officiate and help the priest. I can still see him casting in the mould as the parson read the words: 'Earth to earth, ashes to ashes, dust to dust.' After the ceremony was over the boys used to help him fill the grave, and perform other small offices; I have more than once helped to tread the earth down upon the unhappy corpse to earn an honest penny, which was the remuneration for that toil. Once when there had been several deaths in the village in quick succession, a farm-hand said: 'Main vew vawk dyin' about lately, Willum.' 'Eece 'tis; nice vew a know,' Willum replied. Then under a happy inspiration he added: 'Must all go, zum time or nother, a know, and chent one in a 'underd as lives longern that.'

After Billy's death the office devolved upon 'old Tommy.' He is extremely deaf, you may know to what extent by this fact alone, he never hears the bells, though they are just up above his head. At a funeral the other day I was standing near him, waiting for the cortège; he was tolling the big bell. His face wore the utmost gravity; for my part, watching him there, I could not help but smile. Tommy gave a vigorous short tug at the rope; 'bom' went the bell; the vibration almost lifted you off your feet. He walked out of the belfry door and looked out for the hearse; in a moment he came back and gave the customary tug again. Then he turned to me, and said in a husky voice, 'Towls well?' I smiled and nodded. 'Can't yern, ya know,' Tommy continued, and tug, tug again. He guessed the time required for the sound to die away before repeating the operation.

Tommy is a slight-built man, not very tall, grey-headed, and with a small straggling bit of beard. His face is wrinkled and weather-beaten, for his life has been spent wholly out of doors in the fields, and with the cattle. His voice is always very hoarse, and in addressing you he leans his head towards you, and speaks very loudly, in a raucous and almost uncanny tone. You can always tell when he is near by his loudly-uttered words, though no doubt he thinks he is speaking in a most subdued manner. His hair is rough and curly. On Sundays he wears a high linen collar, the corners of which stick out in something of the Gladstonian manner, and which gives him an old-time appearance. His coat is of the swallow-tail order, of black cloth, and trousers of the same. His small head is crowned with the bolero. In the winter afternoons and evenings he is to be seen with old-fashioned horn lantern in one hand, and a bundle of large keys in the other. He visits the church at all times of the day and night; he is not a bit nervous. Besides being sexton, he sees to the lighting of the lamps all round, and in the porches, too, as well as to the fires for heating. Very often in bright moonlight nights these show conspicuously; but when it is pitch dark they are out. Everyone then passes humorous remarks about the lamps, and cries aloud for Tommy. It is either the wicks or the oil at fault, or the wind has blown them out, or something else, but there is no complaining.

Tommy is intensely proud of his graves, and regards them all with fatherly care and affection. Sometimes he is deputed to renovate a mound, and keep it in order permanently. Then, whenever you meet him, he is certain to be full of the matter; all he can talk about is the clipping and paring and tidying up of the turfs. Notwithstanding his great deafness, if you should happen to ask the old man if he would like a drop of whisky, though your voice be ever so moderate, he hears well enough then. 'Jest a leetle drap,' he says.

Tommy had to attend an inquest one day as witness, concerning an unfortunate son who died suddenly. Of course, he understood nothing at all, and could not be made to do so either. The coroner was furious; he was raging mad almost. Poor Tommy was an object of extreme pity. As soon as the coroner handed him the Testament to take the oath, he began rummaging forth the spectacles and opening the pages; he thought he had to read a chapter. Several times the coroner tried to make him understand; then the storm broke. He shouted, raved, roared, and bullied the old man most shamefully; he was livid with passion, but Tommy was unperturbed. He kept giving his unsolicited evidence with child-like simplicity. 'Listen to me!' the coroner shouted, with his mouth in the old man's ear. 'LISTEN TO ME! LIS—TEN TO ME!' You could hear him fifty yards away outside. Then, in a fit of desperation, he concluded; 'Take him away! TAKE HIM AWAY! TAKE HIM AWAY!' So the old man was led outside, and the testy coroner proceeded with his business. There was not much of the milk of human kindness in him, at all events.

Just down the lane, a short way from the church, is a tiny dissenting chapel. It is no bigger than a poor man's dwelling, and is almost out of sight, hemmed in with apple-trees on one side and a quaint thatched cottage on the other. I have known the time when quite a crowd frequented the place, but it is almost deserted now.

But there have been rousing scenes in the chapel in times gone by. Then conversions were a common occurrence. There were mid-week services and open-air meetings. Pressing invitations were sent round to the poor folk, and a good attendance was the inevitable result. Preachers came from all the villages and towns in the neighbourhood; there was great and endless variety of sermons and doctrine. William Keen was the superintendent then. He was a stout champion of Nonconformity, and a stalwart progressive politician as well. His work lay in the manufactory at the railway town. All day or night he slaved in the rolling-mills amongst the blazing white-hot iron, and walked to and from the village. This he did for nearly fifty years, and after that procured an old tricycle, as heavy as a wagon almost, and trundled that along. His hair and side-whiskers were grey, and his face very red; it was said he was fond of a glass, but what of that? His work was abnormally hot and exacting, and whatever he took, he earned it. I have no patience at all to listen to those who would damn a man for taking a glass of beer, whether he be Christian, Turk, or Infidel.

There was no music at all at the chapel in those days. William Keen started the singing, and the others joined in, young and old together; it was a very homely crowd at all times. Grandfather Bridges was there, and his wife Letitia, both very devout indeed. One old lady declared she felt so light she could jump over the housetop; and another worshipper's frequent and fervent expression was that they would sweep the enemy away 'with the beesom of destruction.' He also hoped the Almighty would amend the ways of the Anglicans, or otherwise 'bring them all pell-mell into a whip (heap) o' stwuns.'

I remember one old local preacher, named Maslin, who used to come to the chapel now and then, clad in a white smock reaching halfway below the knees. This old fellow was an agricultural labourer, and lived far away over the downs. He was very short in stature, with grey hair, and exceedingly bronzed and sunburnt; he had toiled among the sheep and lambs, the wheat and oats, and had heard the lark sing in the blue heavens thousands of times. He had also felt the cold nipping wind sweeping up the valley and over the hill-tops, and had trudged through the deep snow to the village over and over again. When he came to preach he carried his dinner tied up in a red handkerchief and hung on a blackthorn stick over his shoulder. His fare was very simple – bread and cheese, and he must have a glass of ale with it from somewhere or other; he did not indulge in hot cooked food that day. A great number used to go and hear him preach; he could always command a congregation, he was so sternly simple, outspoken, and comical. He was a firm believer in the devil as a personality. Once when he had been called to see a sick man, and had not been able to make a very deep impression on the unfortunate, he attributed it all to the actual presence of the Evil One. 'I know'd 'a was ther,' the old man declared most gravely, 'for I could smell the brimstone; the house was full on't.'

One Sunday evening, in late autumn, he was down to preach, and there was the usual full attendance; the little chapel was packed; a great time was expected; they were not all disappointed. Old Maslin was beside himself, and preached vehemently. As the sermon proceeded – it was half sermon and half prayer – he waxed hotter and hotter. Now he leaned far forward over the rails of the pulpit, now jumped backward, stamped hard with his feet, and swayed from side to side. The congregation perspired, and trembled in their pews. Louder and louder the old fellow's voice pealed out; he stamped harder and harder; everyone felt something was to happen, and happen it did. There was a large iron stove in that chapel; it stood in the centre. The pipes from this went up and then passed horizontally to the wall some distance away. Moreover, they had not been swept out for a long time, and were become very foul. The storm raged with increasing fury. The old folk were getting uncomfortable; the young girls tittered. The preacher shouted at the top of his voice, and stamped mightily with his feet. 'Send the power, and send it now!' he cried. One more moment, and it came. The joints of the pipes could stand no longer. With a shuddering crack the whole lot of the horizontals toppled down. A loud yell went up from the people; the youth exploded; but there were no heads broken. There was a prompt young man sitting just underneath that pipe. At the first crack he leapt up and caught it falling; but he made a sinister use of the opportunity. Receiving the pipes in the middle, with a dexterous movement of the hands, he twirled them round, and shot vast clouds of soot over all the people from one end of the place to the other. The result may be better imagined than described; it was like a pendemonium. All Maslin's preaching faded beside that night; that was his veritable *coup d'éclat*. The old man has been dead this quarter of a century.

I have spoken of Jack Bridges, or Dart, the road-mender. He lives in the little old original cottage at the corner of the lane as you turn to go up to Nightingale Farm, beyond the Roman ruins. The tenement is his own, and was his father's before him. It was really a kind of squatter's cottage. Someone or other, not very ambitious, came along, admired the spot, obtained material, built his house, and settled in it, there and then.

The little cottage is of one story, and contains three fair-sized rooms – one for living, and two for sleeping. The roof is of thatch. There is a fireplace at each extremity. The pantry is a small 'lean-to' at one end, without the house. The original front was of rubble, but it has been modernized; brick has been substituted. A short while ago a part of the front was nearly falling down, but after the old man got the Old Age pension, he was able to get a few bricks and have the repairs executed. 'Times be lookin' up, a know,' the road-mender said; 'must do summat to't now.' The back wall of the house is built close against the bank, that is almost level with the eaves. Large elm-trees grow in the hedge there, and wave their tops high up. There, in the season, sing the thrush, the blackbird, the linnet, and the cuckoo. When the tempest howls through the elms and shakes the tops of more pretentious dwellings and mansions, it leaves the little thatched cottage unmoved; it is too humble for envy, even for that of the winds; they rage and fly along high above it. A small strip of garden is attached, protected by a box-hedge, and running down the lane. The line of elms continues down the bank.

Jacky's father lived here before him. He worked on the highways too. When the old people died, the son took up his residence under the paternal roof, and here his family of four – two boys and two girls – were born. These are all grown up, and scattered to the four winds almost, and one is dead. He committed suicide. Entering the army, he served through the South African War in the cavalry; but as is so often the case, he contracted habits of dissoluteness, from which he could never free himself afterwards. At last, out of work, disheartened and penniless, baffled by fate and fortune, and overtaken at length by that worst of all weaknesses, he gave way to the impulse of self-destruction, and so ended his life. Happening to be near the railway one afternoon, and seeing an express coming towards him, he ran down the steep bank, clapped his hands together as a swimmer would do in taking the water, and dived straight under the wheels of the engine. The old man, living alone – his wife had been many years dead – was stunned with the news, and overwhelmed with sorrow. The old villagers shook their heads. 'Ah! he come to a bad end. Know'd a ood. That sowjerin done summat for ee.' His name is there, carved on the bark of the beeches that stand by the pool.

The old road-mender is nearly eighty now. He is very small in stature, but just over four feet high. His features are small and regular; he is fine-looking – well-shaped nose, taper forehead, blue eyes, grey hair, moustache, and side whiskers. His shoulders are bent a little – they have borne many a heavy sack of corn from the thresher to the granary – and he is half a cripple. His left leg is in the shape of a bow; in walking he swings this round somewhat, and especially if he has imbibed a glass or two of fourpenny; then he will have great difficulty in maintaining a dignified gait as he totters off, stick in hand, and basket on arm, down the road to his cottage. The old man is his own master, servant, and everything combined. He lights his fires, prepares his food, washes up and cleans the house, makes his own bed – is cook, chamber-maid, and scullery-maid together. Often in the summer months he rises at four, and lights the fire to cook the sweet green peas and young 'taters.' After that he potters about till seven or eight, then goes to view his vegetable crops in the allotment; he has acquired great local fame as an horticulturist, and he usually tops the list for fine produce in the garden. After due inspection of the onion-bed and potato-patch, and comparing them with others in the field, he may visit the inn for a morning glass and a chat with the landlord; then, if it is fine, he lies down in the shade of the withy-tree, or elder-boughs, till dinner-time, and very often all day, then loads himself with produce, and goes home to his cottage again. Here he cooks for tea or supper, eats the meal in silence, and retires about eight. The great problems of the day and hour do not disturb his manner of living; in spite of his losses and misfortunes he is happy and satisfied.

Grandfather Bridges, the old market-gardener, who is eighty-six, is brother to him, and cuts about like a young fellow of forty. 'Bless you, mister,' he says, 'I eats well, and drenks well, and enjoys life as well as ever I did; the only difference is, I gets tired a leetle quicker, you know.' Every morning he rises early, lights the fire, takes his wife Elizabeth up a cup of tea, and has breakfast ready by the time she arrives downstairs. His patriarchal face and beard do not seem to have changed this thirty years.

'Master' Kemble is everybody's man, and the old road-mender's in particular. He does work for everyone in the place almost, but is chiefly at home as a drover. He is the one homeless person of the village. All make use of him, but none own him. He does a job here and a job there; takes cattle to market and sells them, and brings back the cash; deals in faggots and firewood, sticking-wood for peas and clothes-props, watercresses and mushrooms – anything to get an honest copper. He is very rough in appearance, as drovers often are; yet he is a farmer's son. His father got into low water, and when the old people died, several of the boys fell away, and would not be bound to a master. This is common in the agricultural fraternity: they are proud in misfortune, and will not forget their former circumstances: they will often remain bare and destitute rather than cringe to another. Whether such a course is compatible with wisdom or not – as the world knows it – is questionable. At any rate, it is characteristic, and many will admire it.

Kemble serves all, quarrels with all, and is reconciled with all in turns; for, though poor, he is independent, and will not be put upon. He is frequently told to 'get out of here, and never set foot on my premises any more;' but in a few days he turns up again, and solicits food, or a drink of ale or cider, and is not refused. Perhaps he presents himself at the kitchen door, wet and cold, and half famished, but cheerful as May, and begs for his breakfast; no matter what the offence has been, the farmer takes compassion on him, and serves the meal. For dinner he visits someone else, and another for supper, or he may share the road-mender's hospitality, and afterwards help him with his garden. His bedroom is chiefly the open air, his canopy the heavens, his candle the stars. He is often warned as to the perils of the course of life he leads, but he laughs at all advice, however sincerely proffered. 'I be all right, naybur, dun you fret. Lode bless tha, I be as 'appy as all the birds in the ayr.'

'Ah! thee remember old Ryder, and what he come to; and take an' get tha a constant place, an' a bed to lay on,' the other replies; but he might as well speak to the air for all the attention Kemble gives him.

Ryder was a castaway, too, an odd man of the village; a poor, simple fellow, as harmless as a lamb to all but himself, whose failing was merely a fondness for a glass of beer. His old father was shepherd at Rove's Farm; he had brothers and sisters well-to-do. When they shifted he could not be torn from the locality; he had a real love for the old scenes and faces. Part of the year he spent in training with the county militia; at other periods he went haymaking and harvesting, and doing odd work. It is even useful to have such a man about the village; he is sure to be wanted from time to time. As to his military career, he came to be sergeant there. In the hay or harvest field he was always 'shoulder arms,' 'right about face,' and so on, and wanted to drill every youth he came in contact with. He slept under the haystack, or among the sheaves, or in a shed somewhere or other. But when the years crept upon him he found the life beset with hardships; poor, destitute, failing in health, an outcast, no one wanted Ryder any more. One morning – there had been a sharp frost – he was found on the towpath under the hedge, dead; his face was upturned, his clothes were frozen stiff. He had not been well, but was seen about the night before. It was thought he was faint with weakness, and fell into the water, but got out and dragged himself under the hedge, and died from exposure. Perhaps no one mourned for him, but that is the fate of many poor.

Bill Brittin was as hard as flints. He lived in Pigeon House Cottage, and had relatives in London, whom he sometimes visited. When he went there he wore a corduroy suit, coloured kerchief round the neck, billy-cock hat, and heavy boots, with ground-ash stick in his hand. He carried a turnip watch, with silver chain dangling down. A good many of the cockneys stared hard at him, nodded and smiled, and many addressed him, very often to their sorrow. 'Morning, John,' this one said. 'Is that you, John?' 'Come again, John?' 'How do you do, John?' and so on. This one hailed him as an old companion, another tried to show him something; many dodges were tried to befool the old rustic, but not for Brittin. 'You 'old on, mate,' 'No you dwunt, mate,' 'No thenk ee, mate,' he replied to everything; and often his answers were too forcible to be repeated. 'Does your watch go, John?' this one inquires. 'Go? aa coorse a do, ya vool! goes when I carrs un,' Brittin replies; he was not to be caught napping. His favourite stopping-place was the Load of Hay, at Paddington. 'A pint o' ale and a pennoth o' bren cheese,' was his fare, 'and ther went dripence.' He was one of the old type.

There was another old fellow who used to be employed about the village, road-mending with Jacky before mentioned. He was known as 'Baby, dear.'

This was Johnny Garret, who lived in the little old thatched cottage that stood by the church, but which is demolished now. His chief vocations in life had been those of hedge-cutter, haymaker, and harvester – three of the very finest trades since the days of Adam. When these failed or were out of season, he 'snopped' stones by the roadside, pared the borders, cleaved trenches to carry off the water, and so on. He was small in stature, very thin, long nose, fierce ferret eyes, heavy brows, and thick grey hair. He brought four hammers to the stone-breaking – a sledge, a middle-sized one, and two smaller. After sledging the heap, or a part of it, he knelt on an old sack and 'snopped' away. We children helped, or hindered him, taking a hammer each, till one or the other received a clout, then the old man sent us all going. Johnny's failing was the ale; he must have a drop of the liquor, though he did not imbibe much – a pint would make the old fellow tipsy. After partaking of a drop he became very serious and talkative, addressing himself most pertinently, and answering the questions with great ceremony. The matter was usually cut short by the appearance of his wife Amy, who hauled him off roughly, and slammed up the cottage door with violence. Both lived to a ripe old age and received the parish pay – two shillings a week, and two half-gallon loaves of bread with it.

6

GRANNY BOWLES, VILLAGERS AND TRAMPS

Farmer Tull was one of the very old school, who had done fairly well in his time, but had not the faculty of making the most of his earnings. Moreover, he was altogether too easy-going, and too generous to make a pile on his small farm. He lived well, paid high wages, cared for no man, and was fond – perhaps over-fond – of little drops of gin; he would have done better if he had lived more frugally, but he was not going to starve himself, not he! and he had no relatives to leave anything to. In the end he had to partake of charity himself.

The old man was tall and stout; his shoulders were round with fat, his face rather sour-looking and flabby, his eyes were grey and steely, the flesh hung down like little pockets beneath them; square forehead, heavy brows, thick nose, mouth pursed up disagreeably, double chin, frosty pate. He always wore a suit of light, large check, and hobbled about on two crab-sticks, for he was afflicted with gout. That is why he came always to ride to the fields. Wherever he needed to go he had to be hoisted up in the old high cart, for he could not walk. In the hayfield and harvest-field the same, he drove up and down, and in and out the shocks of wheat or among the hay, giving orders, grumbling and scolding; he seldom approved of much in later years, but that was pardonable, for he was grievously tormented with his complaint. But the old man was wondrously good-natured. There was a hot cooked dinner for the men and women every day, tea in the afternoon, and supper at night; bread and cheese and ale in abundance. He used to pay the women nine shillings a week, besides food. His old wife – as kind a body as ever lived – was so stout she could not walk straight through the doors in the farmhouse, but had to negotiate them sideways.

'Tis main dull yer this marnin', chaps. Bistn't agwain to seng us a bit of a song to liven us up narn a bit, Jimmy?' the old man said one day in the hayfield. So Jimmy, the boy, struck up with lines from an old agricultural song, used in the time of the riots, and handed down to that generation:

'O you working men of England,
Take heed to what I say,
And have no rest, but do your best
To get a fair day's pay.'

'Yer, that 'ull do, that 'ull do. Dwun want to yer no more o' that. Casn't thenk o' nothin' else no different to that?' Jimmy thought a minute, then broke out again:

'O you big-bellied farmers, you pot-bellied farmers,
Your pride and ambition shall soon be brought low.'

'Damn tha, shet up! Tha's ten times wuss than ever. Begad, if I yers any more o' that I'll fetch tha one wi' my crab. Gee up, Tom, and le's get out o' the rawd an' 'em. Zend the jar in and ha'n villed when a's empty, and dwun go adry. You wimmin come in to the varm a' dinner-time, missis 'ull gi' ee zummat to aat.' The springs of the cart went down bump! at crossing the trenches, and nearly pitched the old fellow out on his head when they rose again; he made his way across the field and round into the yard. There was a little stone platform with several steps, which reached level with the shafts of the cart; here he mounted and dismounted from the vehicle, assisted by his wife and one of the workmen; it was quite a ceremony, and lasted nearly ten minutes.

After the old man's wife died he fell on evil days. Having a manager did not pay; he was confined to his house, furthermore, and his business went 'all to pieces.' At last everything was gone, every penny; so the owner of the farm gave him the use of a cottage, supplied him with all the necessaries of life, and a housekeeper as well. Here the old fellow lived for some years, almost blind; you might have seen him hobble out of doors in the sunshine now and then, wearing a brightly coloured smoking-cap, and walk in the garden, that was all. He was very testy and sharp at times, and hated the parson like poison.

Granny Bowles lived next the old man, and used frequently to look in upon him and minister to his needs; and when he died she performed the duties usual in such cases. She had been midwife and nurse for many years. She presided over births and deaths, too. She both helped a man into the world and helped him out of it; swaddled him in the beginning and shrouded him in the end; laughed at his birth and wept over his funeral; made him comfortable in each case, or tried hard to; at any time and all times, day or night, Sunday or weekday, she was at everyone's beck and call. She left her own household to attend to the needs of others; did many and various acts of kindness and real self-sacrifice without ever knowing it or caring about it, for she was not covetous of people's favour; whether you praised her or blamed her it made little difference; she was firm and unmoved through all, short and curt, strong-willed, and very individual.

She was very tall – six feet, or thereabout – lank and lean, stooping a little toward the last, of robust appearance. Her forehead was deeply grooved, her cheeks wrinkled, but fresh-looking; nose long, slightly Roman; high arched brows, grey eyes, lips thin, strained together; pointed chin, silver-grey hair carefully combed. She wore a woollen crossover, blue print apron, old-fashioned sun-bonnet, with a heavy pair of boots. She had lived a hard life, and brought up a large family. When she was young she worked on the farm in the fields, with a whole troop of girls beside. She was delighted to tell you all about the early days spent with the old companions – hard times they may have been, but pleasant they certainly were; it always is a joy to look back on past labours. It is work and hardship that brings out all that is finest in us, male or female. Those who do nothing have precious little retrospect; there is nothing to remember.

After she married Bowles – she always spoke of, and addressed her husband as, Bowles – she still went out to work, and while she had infant children, too. As soon as these were big enough she took them out in the fields with her, wrapped them in a shawl, and set them down under the hedge while she worked away, as they did in olden times. Her husband worked on the farm. He was cowman and general hand, and an excellent hedge-cutter. His complexion was almost blue with exposure; he was a hard worker, of strong principle, a dutiful husband and a stern parent. When the boys had been guilty of any offence, off came the belt, and they had it, buckle-end if the affair was serious. But the husband and father ranked second in the house; 'Nance' was the predominant figure there. It was not till middle age that she adopted the profession of mid-wife. Jacky Bridge's mother fulfilled the office before her. They had no certificates in those days, nor were doctors often called in to attend at births in country places, and accidents were rare. I have heard Granny Bowles declare she never had a bad case in her life.

Granny was very conservative in idea and method, and stuck hard and fast to the old times; she had no patience with the new-fangled ways and means of modern people. 'Lar, what wonderful things they moticas and cycicels be! Oonder who fust pervented em?' She could not bear to see ladies riding bicycles; she said it 'wasn't natteral.' If you were talking of a person at whose birth she assisted, she broke in with, 'Aa, mun, I knows what a is; I borned un.' Her patients suffered from various complaints, such as 'popilation of the heart,' 'conjection of the lungs,' and the 'winsywensy' (influenza). 'Poor Bowles! he did remire that chayr so.' 'Pon mi sinny, if chent a girt bwoy!' 'Code struth a mighty, if thee dossn't come yer when I tells tha!' 'Come an hae thi vittels yer, do, wi' tha.' 'I dun want none.' 'Hev it agenst tha dost, then.' 'He byet that bwoy unmassiful.' Her family was scattered far and wide, one here and one there; one in Australia and another in Canada. Very often, when the members of a poor family depart oversea, they never come home any more. Granny's son was drowned in the floods in Australia, and Betsy Horton's 'bwoy Tom' the same; there the wives and families remained; there was no one left to bring them back to the old country.

The village shoemaker lived in the little stone cottage near the canal, and carried on the trade he had inherited from his father. Formerly he used to make many pairs of boots for the villagers: good, strong, substantial footwear, just the stuff for country places, and especially to wear about the farms in the wet and cold of winter; but this is at an end now. The village cobbler, at any rate, as far as the making of new pairs of boots goes, is very nearly extinct. All the villagers now obtain their clothes and boots from the town – boots at five or six shillings a pair; shoddy cloth trousers, and jackets at a small figure; it is an age of cheapness all round. The boots are worn out in a short while, and the clothes, too. A few soakings with wet betray the former; they drop all to pieces when placed before the fire to dry; and if you come in contact with the slightest projection, or strain your trousers or coat, the falsely-woven fabric rips and tears, and might easily put you in a quandary. A good pair of men's boots, made of best leather by the village shoemaker – 'bucks,' as they were called, from the old fellow's nickname – cost sixteen or eighteen shillings. When we were small boys and went to school ours cost eight shillings and sixpence, as I remember, and were securely water-tight. This we soon ascertained, because we made haste to try them in the first ditch or pool we came to.

The old shoemaker was of striking appearance, of fair height, and well-built. His head was massive, broad forehead, heavy brows, strong fierce eyes, prominent nose, thick long hair, moustache, and abundant beard, decidedly patriarchal. To my boyish and unsophisticated mind, he seemed exactly to correspond with the ideas I had conceived of the old prophets; a figure expressing dignity, gravity, profound intelligence, philosophy, and wisdom, though, of course, he did not possess these qualities, or only in a small degree. But he was shrewd enough, and grave enough, and blunt enough, with plenty of common sense, and experience of life – a hard nut to crack, argumentative, self-opinionated, out-spoken and independent. In the spring of the year he went sheep-shearing with Dudley Sansum; these two were expert hands in cutting off the thick fleeces; they visited all the villages round about, and on the downs as well. At such times, if you wanted any repairs done to your boots, you had to take them somewhere else, to the town, or otherwise wait till a wet day came. That kept the shoemaker at home; then he set to work with hammer, awl, and wax-ends again.

His wife Ann was a kind-hearted old creature, and as deaf as a post. She was as thin as a shadow, a hard worker, and a hard liver; her old face was wrinkled and brown; she had worked her fingers to the bone almost in trying to eke out enough to supplement her husband's earnings, for week in and week out his profits were very small; it was a great struggle to live. So Ann went out washing and charing, and did sewing as well; from early morning till late night she was toiling and toiling to earn an honest shilling. Poor they were, and poor they were like to be; the better day did not actually dawn for them; hoping and hoping, they died before they were aware of it, in the midst of their poverty, as happens to so many deluded creatures who have not the power to grasp the disposition of life, and realize the future in the present.

The shoemaker and his wife lived happily enough together, though he was often harsh and unfeeling towards her, and called her 'an old fool,' and shouted at her at the top of his voice, and spoke of her to everyone as 'my owld ooman'; but she bore it all very patiently, and nodded and smiled, and winked now and then, and shed a few tears, and was most slavish in her attendance on him, denying herself the necessaries of life to procure things for his comfort, though she was nearly broken-hearted at the end, for he fell ill with cancer, and because of her deafness would not have her at the bedside, but motioned with his arms, and told the others to 'keep her away; he didn't want her there.' After her husband died she continued in the cottage a little while on parish pay, and finally went to the workhouse, where she died at eighty. In her young days, as a girl, she worked about the fields for the farmer, minding the pigs and sheep, and received a piece of bacon in weekly payment. If everyone had as kind a heart as the old shoemaker's wife, how much better a great many of us would be, and the world about us as well!

The next building up the highway is the old lockhouse, converted into labourers' cottages now; and just beyond that, over opposite in the field, is a picturesque farm-house and buildings surrounded with tall elms, an orchard on each side, and a large garden. The chattering rooks build in the boughs above, the blackbirds nest in the hedgerow and apple-trees, and the railway runs along at the back. It was to this place I bore the milk with yoke and pails from The Priory, and afterwards worked here as well.

Farmer Ody was alive then; to-day the farm is conducted by his widow. He was short, fat, and corpulent. He would have been better and might have lived longer if he had worked harder.

If you had occasion to call at the farm you would have been almost certain to find the master in the yard somewhere, hatless, and in his shirtsleeves, both hands thrust deeply in his trouser pockets, giving instructions to the men, or conversing with someone or other. About the first words he said to you were, 'Come along in an hev ee a bit o' bread and cheese, an a drap o' beer, look;" or if you happened to be a juvenile, he would promptly put you to do a small job or two: brush out the stable, harness the pony, carry a pail of water for 'missis' in the dairy, and so on. After you had done this – he often delayed you a considerable time – he told you to 'go down to the door, look, an see missis, an er'll gi ee a bit o' puddin';' both master and 'missis' too were well noted for kindness and hospitality. When a new boy from anywhere called, the farmer asked him his name, where he came from, who he worked for, and what his wages were. Then he requested him to say if he had a knife, money, and string. If the youngster had all three he laughed loudly and cried out, 'Then you be a lucky fella; for you can cut, buy, or tie, look!'

The farmer's wife made butter and cheese, and baked all their own bread. We heated the oven with faggots; when the walls were become white, that was hot enough. Then all the ashes were raked out, the floor cleaned with a damp mop, and the loaves inserted. I have never tasted such sweet bread since, nor such rich butter. There was a big family of children. When any of these had got into mischief they were tied up to the posts in the yard with a loose cord all the afternoon. They feared their papa very much; if he only looked at them severely when they were young they burst into tears.

There was no ploughed land attached to the farm, so the master used to purchase a few acres of standing corn – wheat, oats, or barley – away up on the downs, on Wanborough Plain, at the foot of Liddington Hill; that is how I first came to go there. That was twenty-three years ago this very autumn, and two years after the death of Richard Jefferies, the great Nature-writer, of whom, peculiarly enough, I had never heard till a few years ago, and none of whose writings I had seen till I was several years past thirty. Then by chance a new friend, a Londoner, an enthusiastic admirer of Jefferies, and a poet, sent me one of his books to read, and introduced me to that wonderful personality who was born, and who lived, in such close proximity to the village. The world, and especially this corner of it, has not been quite the same to me since; it is fuller and richer, more wildly and riotously beautiful than ever.

After the sheaves had been brought home and the ricks made – we fetched it down by way of Kite Hill, about six miles by road – came the harvest-home, for the farmer would not be less than the others in this respect, though the crop was a purchased one. The food in this case was cooked in the boiler; the brew-house fireplace was not big enough. Master came and stirred the fire now and then, put on more coal with the shovel, and afterwards thrust it in the boiler and shovelled the meat and vegetables over all together. This brough 'missis' out in a furious rage, who scolded him soundly, and called him a 'nasty bagger,' and declared she 'wouldn't touch a bit an't now;' but master laughed out and said, 'he was clane anough,' and 'us all got to aat a peck o' dirt afore us dies,' which is proverbial with the villagers. Presently all the men and boys came in, and master and 'missis' too, and the meal was served about six o'clock. No one thought of the coal-shovel, and if they had it would not have made much difference; it was a hearty and happy company that sat around the improvised long table in the great farm-kitchen.

Many tramps and unfortunates pass along the main road leading by the farm at all times of the year, but chiefly in the drier seasons. These beg their way along from house to house through the village. They are of all sorts and conditions; those who have been 'tinkers, tailors, soldiers, sailors, rich men, poor men, beggar-men, and thieves.' There are some of other nationalities too – black and white, French, German, Italian, and others as well. There are many seafaring men who miss their boat east or west, and walk to meet it at London, Bristol, or Cardiff. Some of the travellers are very impudent, others are quiet enough. Some tramps frequent the village periodically. Where they have been well treated they may contrive to set a mark for their mates who follow to recognize a hospitable house. Many beg food, some money, and others merely drinkables. A common visitor is the one who meekly asks you first for hot water from the kettle, next a pinch of tea, then a spoonful or two of sugar, and finally food to eat with it. One old fellow called on Granny Bowles, and on being given bread and meat, would not go till he had obtained salt and mustard, too. I have often been asked for my newspaper by tramps as I was coming home from work in the evening; they wished to be informed of current events.

Once a tramp asked me for money, and I afterwards gleaned some information of his life from him. He was about forty, tall and fine-looking, with black hair, intellectual face, a long scar halfway round the forehead over the ear, and another on his thigh, which he made me feel through his thin trousers; it was like a piece of cord four to six inches long. He was a clever talker, keen and shrewd, and it struck me very forcibly that he might be a villain, too. He said he had been in the navy, and had served abroad in West Africa, and at cable-laying in the Pacific. The scars were from sabre-cuts, received on expeditionary service, he said, which may or may not have been true. He was a very independent and devil-may-care fellow, and pleased me well enough, till, lifting up the flaps of his old black coat, he showed me two murderous-looking knives, which he carried suspended in sheaths from a leathern belt round the waist. He had never had occasion to use them in this country, he said, and perhaps he never would, but if he ever came in a tight corner he should not scruple to employ them. After this confidence my boyish heart quaked a little, and I felt nervous of my vagabond companion; then, as it was fast getting dark, I wished him a brave 'good-night' and retreated. The sight of those weapons, and the man's determined behaviour in the twilight, made an impression on me; I can still see them plainly to this day. How timid the cottagers' wives would have been if they had known of this! They would have closed the door upon tramps and beggars for ever afterwards.

7

MARK TITCOMBE, NELLIE AND OTHER CHARACTERS

See that old cottage there, dark and gloomy and dilapidated, with the thatch half blown away, the chimney toppling down, shutters up at the windows, and padlocks on the gate and door? This was the home of old Mark Titcombe of whom I have several times spoken, and of his father and mother before him. There is a tiny porch over the door, clustered with ivy, which afterwards clambers up the wall, and an old-fashioned creeper with it. Everlasting peas bloom each side of the porch. Just beside the door is a flower-bed, with a box-border a couple of feet high around it. In February this was white with snowdrop; in the summer it contained a large cluster of brilliant flaming peony. Before the window is a small garden, which used to be bright with primrose and lenten lilies, tulip, azalea, and an old-fashioned fuchsia. Years ago this was most neatly kept. When the old man became feeble and could no longer attend to it, it became overrun with weeds, and now it is quite desolate.

The old man was a rather eccentric person. By some he was termed a hermit, by others a miser. The fact of the matter is, he was both and he was neither. That he lived in seclusion, granted; that he was exceedingly frugal, and cautious of spending his money, granted also; but he was too sociable to be really a hermit, and misers hoard their gold just for the sake of possessing it, while he stored his because he was provident, and wished it to be enough to carry him quite through life's journey. He was just disappointed in this latter wish, however. As to how he came to possess money, who had been nothing but a farm-labourer, that may be interesting to some of you, at any rate. In the first place, his old dad before him had been careful and thrifty, and had saved money, so the quality was hereditary. This had been done by sheer courage and – I might as well say it, though it will scarcely be understood by very many, I fear – that which is called sacrifice and self-denial, unhappily so rare in this generation of ours. The old father had worked hard and lived hard, had been sober and natural in his habits of life, and the result was an independent old age and several hundred pounds to be divided among his sons. Mark came in for at least a hundred of these, and soon added more to the pile. Where such an example had been set he could not help but profit by it. He followed faithfully in the course mapped out by his agricultural parent, and thrived apace.

The old man was of average height, and very round-shouldered; he looked to be almost hump-backed. He had a fine nose and features, an intellectual forehead, beetle brows, restless, evasive eyes – he was very suspicious of strangers – pointed chin, a wrinkled and withered face, pleasant-looking, pate as bald as a basin, and one solitary tooth in his head, like a minor gravestone. His old hands were as hard as wood, drawn into a shape nearly inhuman, and his finger-nails were abnormally long – like birds' talons almost. His legs were feeble and weak, his old knees knocked together; when he walked he clutched a stout stick with both hands, and leaned heavily on it. His trousers were of corduroy, waistcoat of the same; he always wore a short white smock over all. If it was cold, he muffled himself up in a thick warm pilot coat, or wore a sack round his shoulders, with billy-cock hat, or one of the vicar's left-off. On Sundays when he dressed himself up – if he ever did – you might have seen him with a top-hat nearly a yard high, which gave him a most quaint appearance, though he seldom walked out in it, but pottered about indoors and round the garden adjoining the fields. As for a bath, he had probably not had such a thing for sixty years; yet he was of most robust health and constitution, and kept himself clean enough externally, at all events, and his cottage as well.

His dwelling was simplicity itself. There was one very large room downstairs. This was kitchen, parlour, and sitting-room combined. The floor was of large and small flat stones, which the old man smeared over once a week and whitened the whole with free-stone. The fireplace was very wide and old-fashioned, simply the original hearth, with a few bricks and bars which he had built up himself. Halfway up the chimney, on one side, was a bread oven. There was a cupboard adjoining the fireplace. Here, in a little stone pot, the golden sovereigns, often amounting to a considerable sum, were kept, and the bank-book as well. If it had been suspected that there was so much money there, someone or other might have been tempted to break in and obtain it, but only one beside the old man knew of its existence. There were three small deal tables, and three straight-backed chairs. On the mantelpiece were half a dozen old-fashioned painted clay figures – of dogs, cocks, and other animals. On the wall opposite the window were shelves for the crockery-ware, containing a little good china, the property of his mother, an ancient clock that had long been silent, and two little coloured prints, entitled 'Peace' and 'Plenty,' which the old fellow one day gave to me with much ceremony, together with his antiquated silver watch, for a keepsake, and which I still have in my possession, out of kindness for his memory.

There was a stout rack affixed to the huge beam that supported the ceiling. This formerly contained the flitch of bacon, and is to be met with in most old farm-houses and cottages. Adjoining this was a good-sized pantry. A broad stairway led to the bedrooms, two in number. The old thatch roof was as full of starlings as it could be. His food was of the plainest kind – bread and a little butter, lard, cheese, or boiled bacon, and potatoes. He drank tea once a day, in the evening. For many years he only had two meals a day – breakfast and dinner combined at noon, and tea about six. After that he made up a good fire of wood, and sat dozing in his chair, looking into the flames, thinking of his old mother and father, and times of long ago. Sometimes when I was sitting with him, very often half asleep myself, warmed with a good glass of home-made wine – a quantity of which he brewed every year with fruit from his garden – he would suddenly wake up with a start, and nearly jump out of his chair, then rub his eyes and laugh, and tell me what he had been dreaming. He was generally off on the road somewhere with his team of horses – perhaps it was to Hungerford, or Marlborough – or was out in such and such a 'ground,' along with his old dad. Once he began talking to his mother, and another time was 'runnin' aater the bwoys at ploy.'

There was one remarkable and deplorable thing about the old man, and that was his almost incredible superstition; he had sold himself to the devil, and the compact was sealed for ever and ever. It was absolutely useless to attempt to reason with him on the point, or to show the impossibility of such a thing; it had not the slightest effect, he had sold himself to 'Old Nick,' and there was an end of it. How did it happen? Ah! that I could never tell. I often questioned the old man to know how the bargain was conducted, but he would never tell me that; he simply declared that he 'selled himself to Old Nick out in Maaster Pingedar's (Pinnegar's) ground, by the canal yander,' when he was a young fellow. Oftentimes I tried to correct him from the error, and taught him to pray, and to think of Christ, Who came to save the world from sin, but he always burst out in piteous tears, sobbing like a child, and saying: "Tis all right for t'other people, but nat vor I. Chent no good vor I. Old Nick got I right anough. He's allus along wi' ma, a waiting' vor ma, a swerin' and blerin' against God A'mighty; he won never let ma aloan no more.' And this delusion he continued in right up to the end, for, though many came to see him, clergy and others, and prayed no end of times, it made no difference; he was fully persuaded that he was bound to the Evil One, nothing could shake his belief in that. To say that the old man was deficient in education, that he could not read or write, and had led a somewhat isolated life, is scarcely to explain away the superstition, for there have been many thousands exactly so situated, who have been reasonably intelligent, healthy in mind, highly receptive, and rational in disposition and character.

You have seen that he lived alone, or nearly so, and perhaps you have wondered why he did not marry a wife, and have someone to care for him, and brighten his hearth and home, as all sensible men do, especially since he was courting a sweetheart till he was over seventy; but the fact of the matter is, Nellie Kempster, for that was her name, would never consent to the match, so the courtship continued from childhood almost, year after year, right up to the old woman's death.

Nellie lived in the little cottage on the opposite side of the road, but a stone's-throw from Mark's door. The building was very old and shaky, covered with ivy, and the roof was of tiles, green as the lichen on the tree-trunks almost. A little straight poplar grew exactly by the porch – it is still standing in front of you there – high elms grew at the back, and stretched their mighty arms out over the roof, as if to protect it from the raving winds, and destructive seasons. Here she had dwelt from childhood; it had been her old mother's cottage before her; she held it in indisputable possession. Singularly enough, her means and condition were identical with those of the old man. Her father was an agricultural labourer, who, somehow or other, had managed to save a pile. Nellie went out in the fields to work as a young woman, and saved, too; when the old people came to die, she was left with a considerable stock of golden sovereigns, enough to keep her for half a century, and still leave her with a balance of two hundred pounds at the bank on her death.

Nellie had been a handsome girl, and was good-looking to the last, though she became very untidy in her later years and could not be induced to adopt a more reasonable mode of living. She was not very tall, with a perfectly shaped nose, well-moulded face, bright eyes, rounded chin, even features, beautifully shaped hands and fingers; and, in contradistinction to the old man, she was intelligent, very well read, able to converse on a host of subjects, was keen, light witty, laughing, or serious, as circumstances demanded. Her old people and Mark's had been neighbours all their lives; that is how they contracted the intimacy. Jacky Bridges and others used to torment Mark and say: 'Why ever dossn't take and marry Ellen, and live wi' 'er, nat kip trapesin' up and down yer from one place to another;' to which the old man replied: 'Her won hae ma, tha's knowst, tha's how that is.' 'Then be jiggered if I shouldn't lave er alwun, an' let the contrary bagger look aater herself,' Jacky responded; but Mark shook his head, and kept up his attendance on her. He fetched her wood for the fire, and water for the kettle, locked her in every night with a padlock on the door, then went home to sleep, and came back in the morning and unfastened it again, and prepared his sweetheart's breakfast. After that, he pottered about in the fields, or in the green lane, picking up dry wood under the trees, and came back to dinner, tea, or supper; year after year he continued the duty.

The old cottage was in a great muddle. There was only one small room downstairs, and Heaven only knows how many up, for no one ever went there to see beside the old dame, and the stairway did not look very inviting. The downstairs room contained a fireplace, a lattice window with several broken panes, stuffed up with rags and paper, and piles upon piles of furniture, and rubbish of every description; you could scarcely get inside for it. The mantelshelf was full of old-fashioned candlesticks and ornaments; a grandfather's clock stood by the stairs door; on the other side was a dresser, full of crocks, and some fine old china-ware, thick with the dust of ages. Every chair was piled up with books, newspapers, bales of dress-material, blankets and sheets, muslins, laces, calicoes, etc., rotten and rotting. A large pitcher for the water stood just within the door. The porch was of rustic work, thickly covered with ivy. Here we children used to gather and peer inside at the old man and woman, as they sat at table. Nellie called us to go in, and made us sherbet and ginger-pop, or helped us to tea from the pot, and amused us with tales and storyettes, or asked us to sing to her, which we did, especially Sunday afternoons. After we had sung, she would say: 'Tha's it, my dears; run along home now, and come and see poor Ellen again to-morrow, after school.' There was a widely prevalent belief that Ellen was a witch; many people came from quite a distance to take a peep at her, if possible, but that was the merest nonsense. She was not a witch, and she was not superstitious, or cunning, or crafty, or vicious, but only unfortunate. Friends she had, and relatives, living not far away, but they never came to see her; they were shocked and offended at her untidiness, and gave her a wide berth, but on her death they ran forward eagerly enough, and grabbed all that was to be had; but that is human nature all over.

Toward the last, the old woman cut a most sorry figure; she became more negligent than ever. Her clothes were nothing but rags from head to heel; her legs and feet were naked in a pair of old shoes; her arms were naked, too, and a great part of her body beside. The busy-bodies ran from house to house and whispered, and peeped about whenever they passed the door, in the hope of seeing something or other more to gossip about; but old Mark was as faithful as ever. At last she fell sick, and had to keep to her bed. Neither had the moral sense or energy to send for a doctor; no one attended her but the old man. In a day or two she died. The circumstances demanded an inquiry. Everyone was indignant with the old man. At the inquest he was severely censured; they told him he ought to go to prison. Mark stood shivering and shaking like a leaf; he had only carried out Nellie's wish, not to let the busy-bodies in; he did not understand the law; he had been faithful to her every command. So the old woman was put away. The cottage was ransacked; there were about twenty gallons of sparkling wine discovered, and several lots of gold, poked about in different places, with a good fat bank-book, as already mentioned. The cottage was immediately sold and razed to the ground. Every vestige was carted away; only the little straight poplar-tree remains now to point the place where the dwelling-house stood.

And what of the old man, after all? He crept about like a ghost for years afterwards, and was inconsolable; he was all alone in the world now that Ellen was gone. Most people looked on him with suspicion, and all with contempt, which made him feel more solitary than ever; he shrank from people as though he had been a hunted criminal; it was truly a pathetic condition. It had always been the old fellow's most devout wish that he might be able to end his days in independence, and not be forced to go to the workhouse. That is why he screwed and pinched and lived hard, for he had a mortal dread of 'that place over yander,' the walls of which he could plainly see from the field behind the cottage. So he parcelled the money out, and frequently computed the number of years remaining, and spent accordingly. About ten pounds a year kept him. Four pounds of this were for rent, and the other for food and firing. The seasons slipped along like magic. Four score came, and found the old man well enough, except for being 'main tottery' on the feet. Then fourscore-one, fourscore-two. The little hoard was dwindling, but there was no reason to fear. Then an accident happened. One day he was missed, and on the neighbours breaking in the door he was discovered lying helpless under the wall, too sick and feeble to move. So several of his acquaintances stepped in; as he was circumstanced he could not refuse any terms they made; he was bed-ridden for nearly three years. The little pile melted more quickly away, and at last all was gone. The old man was broken-hearted; he knew what it meant; there was nothing else remaining. He had toiled in vain; all his thrift was for nothing. The long dread he had entertained, vague and uncertain for years, had assumed a monstrous shape; it grieved and it maddened him to think of it; perhaps he was not a philosopher, though prating is cheap enough until you yourself are afflicted with an immoderate misfortune; then, as someone has said, 'counsel turns to passion.'

One night when I called to see him, coming home from work, he burst into tears. 'Tha be gwoin' to take ma awoy, an I dwun want ta go,' he cried. I tried to comfort him, as well as I was able, but all to no purpose; he was beside himself with grief. And was it any wonder? Would *you* like to have gone, if *you* had been in his place? After living within those old walls, hallowed with memories of his mother and dad, his childhood and many things beside, for nearly eighty years, working and slaving, and sweating and stinting, for what? for what? But I have told you already. Of course he did not want to go; and quite right too. It was natural and manly, honest and brave; it is only the coward that thinks otherwise; and the spirit should be commended, not blamed and stifled down, and quenched out of existence. Several times the officers called and asked him if he would go to the 'house,' but each time he answered defiantly, 'No, I wunt.' The old man shrank into the bed-clothes, and peered out at them over the top of the sheet. 'I'd soonder starve, an' die in mi bed fust, than go to that place,' he protested. Then the officers went away. The next day a conveyance stopped before the cottage, in came the officer again, and two men to carry him off. At first the old man wept like a child, then bawled and shouted at the interlopers: 'Lave ma alwun.' 'I wunt go.' 'Let ma die in mi bed.' 'Get a hatchet an chop mi 'ed off;' but all to no purpose. They dragged him out of bed, pulled a pair of woollen stockings on his shrunk shanks, clapped a blanket and an old coat around him, hauled him out of the cottage, slipped him in the conveyance, banged the door, and drove off as hard as they were able.

He did not live many weeks at the workhouse. Once I saw him there. A smile lit up his features when he recognized me, and the big tears rolled down his cheek. How he clung to my hand! He looked years older. I tried to be bright and talked of old times, of Ellen and the cottage, and told him to cheer up, though I knew it was only make-believe. I felt the biggest hypocrite alive. Then the time came to leave. I promised to come again soon, but there was no need any more. A fortnight after he was taken in the night, and was dead in an hour. They brought him to the village for burial, past the cottage. It was quite a grand turnout; a black horse in the parish shillibeer, and artificial flowers for decorating the coffin. It was an insult to worthy old bones; but what matters! The very grave was cold and uncharitable, too, for that was nearly a foot deep in water, and a hard storm of rain and sleet came on as we gathered around to hear the Burial Service. 'Earth to earth, ashes to ashes, dust to dust,' said the parson. Somebody answered 'Amen.' The mourners left the graveside; the big bell clanged out; that was the end of Mark Titcombe, as far as I can tell you, though I doubt not there have been hundreds of others who have lived and died in very similar conditions and circumstances.

So much for the tragic side of life. Dudley Sansum was of a totally different nature altogether, quite unlike old Mark, though he lived beside him for some years. He had worked for Farmer Davis of Sennington, and his father before him, all his life, and had won fame as a mower and fagger, a shearer of sheep, and many things beside. In addition to this, he and Tommy Bowles of Sennington also, went about with the steam threshing-tackle all round the neighbourhood; perhaps he was better known in this capacity than in any of the others. How proud he was of the engine and machine! He worshipped them almost. I can see him now, standing with one hand on the driving lever, his face red and black together, expressing perfect joy at the task. Sometimes he stood like this for nearly half an hour at a stretch; he liked to be close to his engine, and to feel the oscillation of it.

Old Dudley was one of the happiest mortals alive, and one of the simplest, too. He cared nothing for the sorrows and troubles of other people, and had very few of his own. Life to him was a thing to enjoy; no riddle, no puzzle, no obscurity, and no hardship; it was as easy and plain as the nose on his face – he lived. He knew there was seed to plant, sheep to be sheared, hay to make in summer, and whole fields of golden, waving corn to be reaped or fagged in harvest, and after that, the threshing all round, year after year the same. He rose early. Every morning, about five, you might have seen him with corduroy trousers, short white smock, and billy-cock hat, with broad flag basket slung over his shoulder, and all through the summer a little jar of ale, which he took from home; there was plenty more of this at the farm. He was short and stocky, plenty fat enough, a little bow-legged, and of great strength. His face was round and jolly, red as the sunrise almost, with good features, top lip clean-shaven, a little beard under the chin, and the merriest of twinkling eyes; he was full of jest and fun, and great good-nature. And how skilfully he mowed the grass down and fagged the corn! It was a real pleasure to see him at the task, and he made as light of it as if it had been the simplest matter in the world; but that is the mark of good workmanship. In the harvest his wife and the children used to go in the fields with him, and pull bonds, and tie up the sheaves. No one could touch old Dudley at harvest-work; he could cut an acre a day, if it stood well.

In the evening, after work, he pottered about in the garden, or else strolled down to have a glass of fourpenny with Jemmy Boulton and Jacky Bridges, and talk about the hay and harvest. At festival times Dudley indulged a little more freely, though in nothing stronger than ale. Then he would get exceedingly merry, and dance with the old mates all the evening. *He* did not go to the workhouse in *his* old age, not he! When he could no longer work, he lived with his son and grandchildren in the lane, and died, as a good old rustic should, at a ripe age, surrounded by his family.

Henry Love, a less colourful character, farmed Rowborough field. He was a bachelor. His dad lived to a great age, and was nicknamed 'Totty,' because he used to 'tot out' the gin, it is said. When I was very small I used to mistake him for Josh Hughes, my grandfather, and used to address him as such. Henry was very quiet and unassuming. He was tall and fine-looking, and wore a top-hat to church every Sunday morning. The school governess, an elderly body, said he was the finest gentleman in the place, and fell desperately in love with him, and pressed her suit with some persistence, but Henry was really too shy. All he could say about it was: 'Aw, the dooce! the dooce!' and 'The devil!' He was altogether too phlegmatic to burn with the grand passion. Whenever he went to the fields he wore a buttoned smock and rode a grey pony. An old woman over ninety was his housekeeper. He was a noted lover of small drops of gin. One day he said he hoped he should never have a long illness, and two mornings afterwards was found dead in his bed.

Daniel Lewis was a dissenting parson – a strict Baptist; and, together with his wife Elizabeth, kept the village bakery and stores. He was rather tall, very grave and sedate-looking, with prominent nose, kind eyes, clean-shaven top lip, thin white beard under the chin, projecting in the shape of a crescent – an excellent physical type of the preacher. He never preached in the village, but always went away each Sabbath, somewhere or other. Away from home he was held in high esteem; among his everyday acquaintances he was ignored – of no account at all; a man is always despised most among his intimates and kindred. Grandfather Bridges drove him out to preach every Sunday. At such times he wore a black suit, round felt hat, and always, when it was cold or damp, a large white or plaid woollen scarf, wrapped several times around the neck and mouth. He always took a large umbrella, and if that was not enough, there was grandfather's monster blue one, big enough to cover a haystack, almost.

The old couple lived very simply, even severely; trade was bad at the shop, and scarcely anyone paid for what they had; he had not the heart to demand the debts. He was also skilled in herbs, and used to make all kinds of strange drinks and mixtures. An ointment made from 'jack by the hedge' (garlic mustard) was one of his favourite healers; we children used to make this as well. The old man brewed his own beer in a large pot, which he boiled in the bread-oven. In his old age he had a cup of hot beer with bread in it every night before retiring, and when he was dying he called for the same – it was the only nourishment he could take. Formerly the whole premises were his own, orchard and all, but even he could not thrive by being lenient, and giving his bread and goods away. So it happened that when he became old, and wanted rest and a competency, he found himself with nothing at all, in debt, and ruined. His house and all was mortgaged and sold; there he was, a helpless and poverty-stricken old man, trembling lest, after all, he should be forced to enter the workhouse. But how patient and gentle and uncomplaining he was! How bravely and philosophically he bore with everything! And he was so poor and feeble; he often fell down in the passage, tottering to answer the bell in the shop. Elizabeth was not so calm, and more than once scolded the old man; but he always answered her with perfect affection and

William Maisey, grandfather of Jack Maisey JP, who wrote the Foreword to this book

humility, and said: 'But I love you just the same.' When he died – he simply slept his last hours away – his fellow-worshippers came over to the village and buried him according to their own particular rites and custom, and the business passed into other hands.

There used to be a great many more 'characters' about the village. The old Thatcher and his wife were a unique pair. He was at one time an agitator, and secretary of the old-time branch of the agricultural union in this district, but that has long ago died out here. He was very hearty and independent, unconquerable in spirit, and fond of a glass; 'Must ha' drap beer,' was a frequent saying of his. He did not believe in the Divinity, and never went to church but once a year, that was on Club-Day. He would not have gone then if he had not been compelled, but on that festival each member must attend the service or be fined half a crown, and the old thatcher could not afford to lose such a large sum of money as that. He was in constant work all the year round, for, though almost every farm has its rough thatcher, they are not capable of performing skilled work, such as covering cottages, and farm-houses and buildings.

William Maisey is another veteran of the field, as frosty as midwinter in appearance, but as genial as May in disposition and temperament. He is a typical rustic, rude and unlettered – I will not tolerate the word 'ignorant' as applied to agricultural people – knowing and caring little or nothing for books and studious pursuits, but well-versed in the trade of the country-side; pigs and horses, and cattle, cocks and hens, ploughing, sowing, reaping and threshing – that is the proficiency you want in the village. The old man is feeble and tottery now, especially since the old sow with the litter knocked him over in the sty, which surprised him very much; she had always been so quiet before. His health is good, however, and his endurance remarkable; he has never kept late hours, has lived simply, and never wasted nature. Only yesterday I saw him in the field at bush-harrow, and he is over eighty now. His white smock was tucked up around his waist; he held the hempen halter in his hand, and was striding along like a youngster of twenty. His expression is wonderfully kind; he looks to be nearly always smiling. But everyone felt a shock when he took the carving-knife and cut the throat of one of the horses that had fallen in the ditch recently. The ditch was very deep, and the poor animal had fallen in on its back; it was impossible to extricate it, and no one had a gun handy. So William took a big, sharp knife and slit the poor brute's throat. 'Bin an polished un off,' he said. It seemed cruel; but perhaps it was better than allowing it to suffer long tortures.

The manor-house was held by an elderly maiden lady. She owned half the parish or more; all the prime farms were in her possession, in which she took a most active interest to the last, for, though well advanced in years, she was very acute and business-like. There were several agents to supervise details, but she always directed the general scheme of operations. She was very strict and severe in rules and regulations as touching the farms and cottages, prudish and conservative in method, but sterling in motive and just in principle. Her life-long effort was to maintain a 'clean' village, and though she often failed in her endeavours, she went a long way towards being successful. At her death it was said there was 'not a bad debt in the place,' which is a great compliment to any village community.

She was very private and secluded in habit, and guarded her age jealously. None of the villagers could attain to a knowledge of it, which was a source of real concern to some of them. The wives especially like to know these little matters, for humanity, and especially feminine humanity, is much engaged with trifles.

When the lady of the manor died, the villagers thought they should know the extent of her years then, at any rate, and came in great numbers to the funeral on tiptoe with expectation, but they were once more disappointed. The old lady understood the matter perfectly, and was determined not to gratify the curiosity of the villagers; there was no record of years on the name-plate, to the vexation and chagrin of the busy-bodies, many of whom had inconvenienced themselves in order to be present to read the eagerly expected announcement.

8

THE RAILWAY, CANAL AND CELEBRATIONS

A railway crosses through the village. This enters on the west side through a deep cutting a mile and a half long, passing beneath Ermin Street, and afterwards emerges upon a high embankment which continues past the River Cole, and enters another cutting opposite Bourton. A substantial stone arch conducts the historic roadway above the iron track, and is known as the Roman bridge. Presently you come to a signal-station and a level crossing which connects the fields of a farm. This is an extremely dangerous spot for cattle and traffic; several accidents have happened here, serious ones too, which really and truly concern the actual life and interest of the village. Once an old man was driving his herd of milking cows over on a foggy morning, and a train dashed into them and slaughtered no less than seventeen on the spot. This happened on a Sunday. A neighbouring butcher carted the poor crushed carcasses off to his sheds; beef was very plentiful in the locality all the following week.

Once after this a similar accident occurred; eight beasts were killed this time. The poor farmer was in dire distress, but the railway people came to his assistance and helped him bear the loss. Once again a young fellow was crossing with a manure-cart, and a fast express dashed into it. Happily, the horse had just cleared the rails; the impact quite severed the body of the cart from the shafts, and, while the animal and driver escaped, that was forced along the line in front of the engine for nearly a quarter of a mile. All these things furnish the villagers with much matter for excitement and discussion; they can think of nothing else for weeks and months afterwards.

The railway has been built about seventy years. Before that time the village was much quieter than it is now, in 1911; the long, heavy thunder of the freight trains, and the sharper sound of the expresses, did not echo through the lanes and meadows and all up the valley; there was little to be heard then but the old coach rattling along the highway and the lowing of cattle about the farms. The dismal noise of the motorhorns is of recent date,

Widening the railway from one to two tracks, in the cutting between Pewsey and Milkhouse Water. Extreme right: Alec Bryden, later landlord of the Phoenix

too, and the clouds of thick dust trailing two miles long with it; the old folk would be amazed if they could see what we have to endure nowadays.

Old Mark Titcombe could very well remember the village before the line was made, and could tell you the names of the meadows which were enclosed to make the track. It was in one of these he was haymaking on the 20th of June, 1837, Queen Victoria's Coronation Day. Farmer Pinnegar held the fields then, and at five o'clock in the afternoon the horses were unhitched from the waggons, and all the farm hands trudged off to Swindon to the fête and gala, and afterwards stopped to see the fireworks. Mark was a young lad of eleven then, but he had lively recollections of the 'crowndin' affair,' and liked to tell you about it from time to time. There was another annual festival he was fond of talking about, too, which has long been abandoned now; that was the autumn fête held upon the top of White Horse Hill at Uffington. There was a brass band and fiddlers, and all kinds of sports. There was walking the tight-rope, climbing the greasy pole for the legs of mutton, catching the porker by the tail, which had been well greased – this was usually effected with the teeth – ploughing-matches, prizes for the best kept harness and team, foot-races, and I do not know what beside. Large crowds of people came from all parts, and Mark had eight miles to walk home at night. It was a favourite sport of ours, years ago, to slide down the steepest part of the hill, a distance of seventy or eighty yards, sitting on the long grass. After a start you obtained a great speed. The grass was very slippery; there was no stopping till you reached the bottom of the slope.

Most of the men who work on the railway – plate-layers and others – belong to the village. These are somewhat superior to the agricultural population, or at least a few of them – the gangers and signalmen; the labourers can scarcely claim to be better off, except in the matter of hours; they have a little more leisure than the farm-hands, that is all. The platelayers' wages range from sixteen to eighteen shillings a week, and many of the agricultural labourers obtain as much, though they have Sunday work to perform. There is a gang on the railway to every two and a half miles. Formerly this was of eight men; now it is reduced to six. There was a little more labour required to maintain the old permanent way than is wanted now though. Then the rails were laid longitudinally on single balks, and the metals were packed up with thin pieces of wood. There was rather more displacement of the rails, too, then, and consequently more labour to get them in shape again. The men used to carry a long heavy wooden lever with a rope attached to the end, with which to raise the balk and rail. Every day you could watch this operation from the highway. The iron end of the lever was placed beneath the timber; three or four men hung on the cord and prised it up, while another 'packed' it with ballast. The ballast used then was shingle brought from the sea-beach. When the boys wanted a new pebble to play marbles they always went along to the footway across the line to obtain one. Several boys used to lie down between the rails of the track and allow the express trains to fly along above them, and enjoy the excitement of it, but that would not be possible now, or it would be very dangerous, at all events. Now the rails are laid on sleepers placed transversely, and instead of clean, bright pebbles brought from the side of the rippling ocean, you have blackstone, slag, and other dingy-looking material.

Years ago the railway was bordered by two hedges of hawthorn, one each side, which were always beautifully kept, and an ornament to the embankments, but these have almost totally disappeared to-day; they have been destroyed and wire fences set up in their place. The hedges required cutting every year, which meant labour, and no return; the wire fences do not need this. Appearances do not count with the railway folk; everything must be reduced to the utilitarian standard. Formerly the line through the village was bordered with magnificent beech-trees as well, but these, too, were doomed; in some cases the trees were cut down altogether, in others all the branches were lopped off and the trunks left standing, like dismembered giants; it would have been better to cut them down outright, as they are all dead from the mutilation.

The railway provides a useful time-table for the toilers in the fields, and the good-wife in the cottage as well; the farm-hands, for the most part, count their time according to the running of the fast expresses and the 'stoppers.' As nearly all the farmers of the place send their milk to the Metropolis, this necessitates a journey to the nearest station once or twice a day. This affords an opportunity for all the milk-boys round about to meet and form acquaintances; great is the fun and many are the games indulged in about the station premises morning and evening.

Watching for the trains and noting the names on the engines is a further interest for at least some of the boys. I remember how long and carefully I used to wait behind the hedge to catch the wonderful names and store them up in my memory. How inexpressibly and mysteriously great some of those titles seemed to be to my boyish mind, even at that early age – Agamemnon, Hyperion, Prometheus, Ajax, Achilles, Atalanta, Mameluke; they fired my imagination, and filled me with strange feelings of pride and joy. It was years before I came to learn who those lordly personages were – if they really ever were, that is – but I surely and certainly received an intimation of their august greatness at the time I first saw their names as a small boy about the farm, and I doubt not but many others have been similarly interested and affected.

The signalmen are the élite of the village railwaymen. Their wages are better, their work cleaner and brainier – it is genteel by the side of that of the platelayers and farm-hands – but there is great responsibility attaching to the post. Good reliable men only are retained in the signal-boxes, who have been tried and proved, who are unhampered with exterior business, able to concentrate their whole thought and mind on the signals and instruments. One lapse of memory would be sufficient to bring about calamity; they would be ruined as far as their life on the railway is concerned.

Fogs are the dread of the signalmen, as well as of the drivers of trains; it is an anxious time then for the man in the signal-cabin, and the one on the foot-plate, too. As soon as a fog comes on, the signal-cabin in the village is closed, and the operator calls out the fogmen, who place detonators on the line, and signal to the engine-men that way.

The night is long and lonely for the signalman in the winter, and the wilder the weather the greater need there is for him to be on the alert. A short while ago, just after midnight, the signalman on duty heard a strange and unaccountable noise, as of someone scuffling about outside, and coming slowly up the steps to his doorway. Puzzled for the moment, he opened the door and found a man on his knees halfway up the stairs, with his clothes all torn, and fearfully cut about the head and limbs, and covered with blood. It turned out that the man was a traveller by the midnight mail, who, somehow or other, had mistaken the door of the carriage, and had fallen out of the train going at full speed; it was a wonder he was not killed outright. There was a freight-train due at the time, so the signalman stopped this and got the man aboard, and thence to the hospital at the neighbouring town.

The Priory Farm, a large stone house and buildings, stands immediately by the railway, alongside the cutting. This was formerly occupied by a small gentleman farmer of very limited means and scarcely any practical knowledge of agriculture, though at the time I worked for him – this was my first place after leaving school – he was possessed of a fair stock of cattle, and a vast herd of pigs. These he allowed to run everywhere – over garden, lawn, flower-beds, roads, fields, and all places beside, at their pleasure: they were very often lost for weeks together, especially in the autumn, when they decamped to the far-off coverts in search of acorns. On their discovery, well fattened up, they were promptly converted into bacon. The old sows were very artful, and knew their way about well enough, and could open all the gates, if they were not securely chained. They caused great mischief with their snouts, ploughing up considerable patches of turf, and ravaging everywhere. One day the farmer brought home a large bucketful of horse-fat for greasing the cart-wheels, and, happening to leave it a moment, an old sow came along and swallowed the lot in about half-a-dozen gulps: it is amazing what a quantity of filth they eat. The farmer sold me a little pig for five shillings, which

I carried home in a sack over my shoulder, and which my mother cared for and fatted up.

My master was a young man, under thirty, fond of balls and parties, and a member of the Yeomanry – a good, easy-going fellow, but doomed to certain failure, and almost to a state of absolute want. He was lacking in all those qualities which go to make the successful farmer – shrewdness, caution, hard-headedness, sound judgement, and business faculty. In the first place he was a late riser – that alone spells failure in agriculture. 'Early to bed, and early to rise,' is the invariable rule in successful farm-houses. You must be up with the lark to keep pace with things. There are the cows to be milked at an early hour, and the churns to be got away to the railway-station, or the milk attended to in the dairy; after that the cattle must be fed and watered – in winter at least – or the teams must be got off to plough or drill, mowing or reaping, whatever there is to be done about the fields: it is useless to lie in bed dozing and dreaming after the sun is once well up above the hills in the south.

Farmer Chaplin generally thrust his head out of the bedroom window towards eight o'clock, and shouted loudly across the yard for me to have his boots cleaned, or to go and drive the pigs out of the garden, or 'tell Harry to put the horse in the trap,' and have it ready by such and such a time. After breakfast, if he did not otherwise go out, he sauntered round, with spotless white shirt, and threw maize about for the poultry, or he might perchance put on a smock and help feed the pigs, but at best he did not do very much. We used to boil up Indian corn grist in vast quantities for the pigs, and any amount of horse-flesh as well. This seemed a most unnatural thing to me, and I did not like it, but they laughed and said it was 'good stuff, just the sort to make them fat.' Another practice, which I thought most foul and horrible, was to lodge great pieces of raw horse-flesh in the boughs of the apple-trees about the orchard, and let them rot there. This was to provide choice morsels for the hens. The putrefying flesh was soon full of gentils: the hens flocked round, and devoured these with great avidity. People said it 'made them lay well.' Perhaps it did, though I would not have eaten eggs produced from such a diet if I had known anything about it. It is only fair to say, out of respect for those whom I know to be particularly fond of eggs obtained in the village, that the practice is quite obsolete now, in these parts, at all events.

We received our wages fortnightly, which was productive of great complaining in my workmate, and then very often master was 'out of cash,' or 'had no change'; sometimes it was a month before we could be settled with. So one day my companion tackled him on the point. 'Sir,' said he, 'do you know how we sort of people live?' The master looked surprised for a moment, and then responded with, 'N-o! Not hardly.' There are many who do 'not hardly' know how the poor workpeople live. Many there are, too, who do not care; but not all are alike. After this, the master paid us our wages weekly, for he understood then. My hebdomadal earnings were three shillings. Out of this my mother gave me threepence every week, which I saved. The first thing I bought from my savings was a telescope for eighteen shillings; with this I wanted to view the hills for I had never been upon them at that time.

Perhaps the chief factor in my young master's ruin was his friendship with a farmer who lived in the fields not very far away. This latter was a gamester, a fast liver, and a dangerous customer at all times; one who smoked all cigars, drank whisky, and spent half and very often the entire night in card-playing. Such an intimacy was bound to be productive of ill-results in one so young and inexperienced; very soon you could perceive something had gone awry. After losing heavily in money the stock began to dwindle; first a pig was driven off to the other's premises, then two; by-and-by the farm implements went as well; now a horse-rake, at this time a nearly new cart; finally it came to horse-flesh; and one of the very best mares was taken off to pay a debt. After I had worked with him about a year he left the farm and soon came to the ground. The last I heard of him was that he was fulfilling the office of cowman, at a farm away up over the downs, which is distressing to learn. Happily for agriculture, gambling is not very frequent among the yeoman class; wherever it exists there is a depreciation in the management and general conduct of the farm. He who would thrive well and save a pile quickly, must needs shun the card-pack, the whisky, and the habitual cigar; an honest pipe, a draught of plain ale, and an early ascent of the farm staircase, will be the better course for him to take.

The old canal runs parallel with the railway throughout the village. This is in disuse now. It was made some twenty years before the line, and was formerly crowded with traffic, chiefly corn, coal, stone and timber. Even after the railway was constructed it continued to be utilized down to a dozen years ago. That was before the pace became so hot; patience was a common quality then; as far as commerce goes it is extinct now. It is the same with canals everywhere. Even the fine waterway that passes through Devizes and Savernake is out of use now, though the locks and bridges are good. Here everything is old and ruined and useless. In a few years the bed will be quite full of mud and earth, and level with the meadows.

The old walls and gates of the locks are very dilapidated now; the pounds are dry, the whole is half-filled with a mass of gross vegetation; the smell is not pleasant.

Years ago there were many teams plying up and down the tow-path. These passed along at all times of the day and night, Sundays as well. Some of the barges were drawn by horses, some by mules, and some by donkeys.

The pace of the donkeys was very slow; they could not have gone more than two miles an hour. The boatman and his family lived aboard. The good-wife plied the tiller; the youngsters poked their bare heads out of the hatchway, or ran along the deck with naked feet. There were many wooden bridges over the canal, swing-bridges they are called. The driver crossed over and raised them for the barge to pass, then let them down again. These are all to pieces now. A steam traction engine, in trying to cross one nearby just recently, fell through into the bed of the canal. The woodwork is old and decayed; they have stood for nearly a century.

Formerly the waters of the canal abounded in fish. There were few weeds then. The steam dredger worked away every year, and kept the middle clear; the lock-keeper attended to the sides, and cleaned the obstructions out with a heavy iron rake. He caught many fish by this means, especially tench, which lie near the bottom. The chief fish beside tench were roach, perch, pike, carp, and eels. The eels are caught with night-lines. A dead bait is set, weighted to the bottom overnight; if an eel should chance that way, it might find the morsel and be caught. I have been up as early as two a.m. to attend to the lines. Very often the men used to attach nets to the stern of their barges, projecting each side. As the barge floated forward the water swam back, and the fish with it; it was an easy matter to take a large quantity by this method. Very often the canal was netted by farmers occupying the meadows each side, and sometimes it was poached. A common way of taking fish was to empty the pounds. Here you procured an iron bar, and prised the paddle-doors up a little, sufficiently to drain the water out, but not high enough for the big fish to escape. This operation took several hours; but when the water became low you could be sure of a good haul of fish from the paddle-holes.

Beside traffic in corn and minerals, there were pleasure craft as well – steamboats, canoes, and sailers; and every year the children from the neighbouring village were conveyed to Uffington in barges, on their way to White Horse Hill for the annual school-treat. How pleasant it was to slide along through the sweet green fields, away from the noise and dust of the highway! These started betimes in the morning, and returned late; drawn by strong horses, they easily covered four miles an hour. All the boats paid their fees at the lock-house. In the winter, when the canal was frozen, hundreds of skaters passed through the village; now it is deserted. In the severe frosts of 1891 I crossed the ice to work at the farm every day for seven consecutive weeks.

Old John Ferris lived at the lock-house at that time. It was his duty to superintend the locks, and receive the tolls, to see that everything was in good repair – this he performed himself, both helping to build up the walls, and replacing the heavy timbers – to clip the hedges, mow the grass on the

Donkey-wheel in use in Broad Hinton. It was dismantled in 1908

tow-path, drag the canal for weeds, and regulate the water by hatches in the feeders. This came from the reservoir at Coate, which belongs to the canal authorities. The old man had three sons: Shadrach, Meshach, and Frank. His only daughter's name was Phoebe.

Of the old lock-keeper's sons, two helped their father with his duties, and the third, Shadrach, was blind; but, as is so often the case, where Nature has withheld one gift, she has bestowed others even more wonderful; and here, though she had refused sight, she had compensated the loss by the addition of a remarkable taste for and skill in mechanics. Accordingly the blind man had a lathe and benches fitted up in the workshop; here he did wood-turning and carpentering, and all kinds of repairs to agricultural machinery.

What a day the old club anniversary used to be in the village years ago, before the little society became enfeebled and crippled by other more powerful and national institutions! It was quite the event of the year; Christmas and Easter were nothing to it; it was, in truth, the red-letter day of all, young and old alike. There were about thirty members in the society altogether. These contributed a certain amount per month for sickness, and the club 'broke up' every five years; that is to say, the accumulated moneys were shared out to the members, only retaining a sum for present needs. The anniversary was held on the second Tuesday in May. This comprised a general assembly at the inn – the headquarters of the club – a general procession to church, headed by a brass band in the morning, and afterwards a parade of the village, with music and collections for the society's funds, at the manor, the farms, and houses *en route*. At one o'clock all sat down to a substantial hot dinner of roast beef, and other cooked meats and vegetables, provided in the clubroom; the band played selections; the foaming ale was brought in in large two-gallon cans; the greatest good-nature prevailed. Farmers and all belonged to the gathering; it was no one-sided affair, and a great number of folk attended from the neighbouring villages; all the old people made it their business to come to 'Maason Club.' The procession was headed by three men bearing blue silk flags with tassels and fringes, a large one first, and two smaller ones, one on each side. The members wore regalia, red and blue sashes and rosettes, and walked with blue staffs with gilt heads.

Jemmy Boulton always carried the big flag. He wore a stout leather belt, with socket in front; the flag-staff fitted into this; if there was a breeze he needed all his strength to maintain it. He was just in his element then; you may imagine how his eyes twinkled with pleasure, and what delight he felt. His old face was redder than ever; his smile was ineffable. How very proud he was of that fringed and tasselled silk! If the wind blew he kept it upright and rigid; if it was calm he waved it about from side to side, and when the crowd was stationary before the farms, or near the club-room, he waved it so low as to touch the people's heads.

On club days the whole street of the village was thronged with people and traffic; the stalls and booths, shooting-galleries, swings and cocoa-nuts, were so numerous that oftentimes their owners had to retire altogether for want of space, or otherwise pitch in an unprofitable spot away from the centre. There was generally a Punch and Judy show, with the 'original dog Toby,' and once a man brought a small menagerie with a 'Rooshan' bear and a gorilla. The 'show' consisted of a drama, a very crude affair, illustrated by means of shadows thrown on a sheet from behind, a sort of cinematograph entertainment, the charge to see which was one penny.

Nearly all the villages round about had their clubs in those days, and some were quite famous locally, especially those of Watchfield, Bishopstone, and Wanborough, but they have dwindled now, or else disappeared altogether.

Another event of importance was Highworth Michaelmas Fair. This used to be a great muster; vast crowds flocked in from all the villages round; the town was quite full of sight-seers, especially in the evening – carters and carter-boys, cowmen and shepherds, with their wives and families; old and young, children and grey-beards together. All through the harvest-time the mothers used to admonish their children to 'behave yourselves, mind, and buck in to the rippin' and pickin', else you shan't go to Highwuth Fair.' We needed no other spur than this to incite us on to the task; it would have been a great punishment to very many to have been left behind at such a time as that.

I remember my first visit to the fair. We had been acorning in the fields all the morning. My mother said if we could pick up a bushel we should all go after dinner. Highworth is three miles from the village. We used to gather acorns and sell them at a shilling a bushel for fattening pigs. So, in the afternoon, we walked through the fields to the town. The fair was held in the market-place; but the whole of the principal streets were packed with booths and shows, swings, roundabouts, and other means of amusement; you could scarcely move for the crowds of people. Here were exhibitions of all kinds – of beast and birds, waxwork figures, model machinery, glass-making, cotton-spinning, picture-galleries, and all sorts of things beside. We could not afford to see everything, but my mother took us into the wax-works show, and also to see the cotton-spinning. A great Zulu and several negroes performed the war-dance outside the former of these places, and a man blew loud blasts and fanfares with a trumpet, and invited the people to 'walk up and see the great Napoleon Bonnypart, the "Dook" of Wellington, and other celebrities, very lifelike and natteral.' In the evening, though very small, I stole away from my mother and companions, and made tracks for home alone in the darkness; I did not appreciate the hubbub and confusion of the fair.

All the men and boys who went to be hired wore whip-cord in their coats or hats; by this the farmers knew they were in search of a situation, and accosted them, and engaged them on the spot. I only went to the fair once to be hired, and then I was unsuccessful, as it was past noon when I got there, and all the hiring was over by midday; if you were later than this hour, you stood precious little chance of obtaining a situation. When the farmer wanted a man – these used to stand in a line along the edge of the pathway displaying their badges of whip-cord – he walked down the street, eyeing them all up and down till he saw one that pleased him: then he went up to him and asked him a series of questions – where he had worked, and for how long, whether he was married, the number and age of his children, and what he expected to receive in wages. If the answers were satisfactory, he offered the man a shilling; if the other accepted it the bargain was considered as made: there was no setting the bond aside afterwards.

Cherry Feast Sunday is still observed by a majority of the villagers, though there is less interest taken in it than formerly. Daniel Lewis's wife Elizabeth, who lived at the little shop, was always the foremost in observing the festival in their more fortunate years. Then she always celebrated it with an extra specially good dinner, consisting of a whole leg of mutton boiled, green peas and young potatoes fresh from the garden, ending up with a choice rich 'Feast' pudding, made like those which smoke on the tables at Christmas. It was usual for Elizabeth to be down with dyspepsia the week following Feast Sunday, but that was a small price to pay for the pleasure of keeping up the festival. On Feast Sundays the church itself is generally empty, or in the evening, at all events. The majority of the villagers betake them to the vicinity of the inn, where the 'Feast' is held, and buy the rich, red cherries, washing them down with ale or ginger-pop, and see no harm in the matter. The warden of the law is at hand to keep order, and preserve the peace. Everything passes of smoothly; the next day labour proceeds as before.

These village festivals served at least one good purpose, that of bringing folk together, and promoting friendliness and sociability; many a rustic met old friends there whom he had not seen since the last Club, or Feast Day. 'Mind you comes awver to feast, look ee; we shall expect to see ya then, ya know, missus an' all an ee. We can gie ee a bite an a soop o summat or nother.' Those who live at a distance borrow a horse and trap from maaster and drive over; they will be sure not to miss the invitation.

'Chick-Chack' Day fell on May 29, and it was incumbent on all the farm-boys to wear 'chick-chack' in their button-holes, or pinned on to their caps. There were three kinds of 'chick-chack' to be worn – young maple-leaves, ash, and oak. Very often, however, oak was not to be had, for that is late in

The Cooper's Shop of John King, with sign-board, in Ball Road, Pewsey; now called "Thatch", it stands beside Somerset Farm House

expanding into leaf, but you must be equipped with the other kinds; it was a dishonour to farm-boys to be without the emblem. If one wearing 'chick-chack' encountered another without it, he accosted him with an old rhyme:

> 'Chick-chack, powder monkey,
> You're the biggest fool all round the country.'

A few boys of the village still keep up the old custom.

The 'rough band' is another diversion of the village youth, though men and all used to take part in it years ago. This was intended as a punishment for such as had been guilty of immorality, especially in the case of wedded people. When any such offence had been committed, a large body of young men assembled in the evening, provided with old pots and pans, anything and everything that would emit a loud noise, and stout sticks to beat them with. Then they marched in procession to the houses of the offending parties, and made as much noise as possible, keeping up the nuisance for several hours, if they were not set upon by the enraged victims, and severely handled, which was sometimes the case. This kind of entertainment lasted for five nights. Sometimes the law was required to intervene by the offending parties, but they seldom obtained much sympathy from the man in blue. He came over as a matter of course, and watched the proceedings, but seldom interfered in it.

The fifth of November was most enthusiastically observed by all and sundry in the village. When we went to school all the children collected twigs and bushes for the fire, beginning several weeks before the 'fifth.' These we stowed in a heap on the roadside, where the fire was had; no one ever interfered with us, though it would never be permitted nowadays. A great many of the farmers used to have a fire as well, in their grounds, which was usually a private affair. Farmer Ody used to collect a large pile of bushes, hedge-croppings, and other thorny substance, and crown the whole with a tar-barrel. On the evening of the 'fifth' he invited Henry Love and others to come and drink a glass of whisky with him, and view the sport. The children from the cottages came to see the fire. Henry Love laughed as well as any, but used to think it a pity to burn so many good bushes; he thought they would have made capital beds for ricks. The beds of hay and corn-ricks are generally made with a good layer of bushes or faggots, with a little rough straw or old thatch on top.

A short while before Christmas, preparations were made for mumming. There were half a dozen or more performers required to make the company. These dressed up in costumes and wore masks. One was King George, another was the doctor; beside these there were represented the Prince,

Slasher, a fool, and the devil. First of all the players went to a house and asked if they would like to see the mummers play. If the occupants were agreeable, the mumming proceeded. The fool entered first and craved room for the players:

> 'Room, room, good people, give us room to sport,
> For to this room we wish now to resort;
> Resort and repeat to you our merry rhyme,
> For remember, good sirs, this is Christmas-time.
> The time to cut up goose-pies now doth appear,
> So we are come to act a little of our merry Christmas here.'

After this request, King George and Slasher came in and fought, and then the doctor was summoned:

> 'Doctor, doctor, where bist thee?
> King George is wounded in the knee.'

Hereupon the doctor came in, who could cure

> 'The itch, the pitch, the palsy, or the gout;
> If a man got nineteen devils in him, I'll cast twenty out.
> Here, drink out of my bottle,
> And let it run down thy throttle;
> If thou be not quite slain,
> Rise up and fight again.'

After this, others entered and fought with swords, and last of all the devil came.

> ' In come I, little Devil Doubt,
> If you don't give me money, I'll sweep you all out.
> Money I want, money I crave;
> If you don't give me money, I'll sweep you all to the grave.'

There was also a party of mummers who came from St. Margaret, and who were better taught than those of the village. Sometimes these came in contact at the farm-houses, but, though they were very jealous of each other, there was no unpleasantness. I can remember when rival youthful factions of the villages did meet and fight each other though, and set out with that intention.

Besides cricket and football, there used to be quoits, which is not quite as popular just at present, though perhaps it will revive again. Some villages still have their quoit-clubs now, though not in these parts.

'Huddle-duck' is another old-fashioned rustic game. This is played with flat stones. One large stone is placed on the ground, and the others are set on top of it; you are required to cast your stone and knock the 'duck' off. If you fail to do this you must throw your own stone back to the line, poised on the toe; or, if you take up the stone in the hand, and are caught with it, you must become 'duck.' This game was very popular in the village when I was a boy. Then there was the game called 'Row, row, rad-i-o.' To play this one had to stoop down with his head leaning against a post or wall, and the others stood round, with their hands placed on his back. Then someone removed his hand and held up several fingers, at the same time crying 'Buck, buck, buck, how many fingers do I hold up?' and this was continued all round. If the one stooping down guessed correctly the two changed places; if incorrectly, all the others beat upon his back with their clenched fists, crying out, 'Row, row, rad-i-o; row, row, rad-i-o,' for several minutes.

Besides tree-climbing and brook-jumping, there is fox-hunting as well. This is played by schoolboys and farm-boys too. One of the swiftest runners is chosen for reynard, and allowed a start, fifteen or twenty follow in hot pursuit, all around the meadows, over the brooks, and everywhere, till, puffing and panting, and unable to run a yard farther, the fox is taken. Then, if it is dry and warm enough, they all lie down under the trees, or strip the bark of the young ash or sycamore, and make whistles or pop-guns from elder, or make cowslip-balls, or plait rushes into whips, or climb up the trees to the rooks' nests, and get into trouble that way, or fall into other mischief; for the boys of the country-side are not more dull than those of the towns, only their amusements are simpler and ruder, more boisterous and vigorous, robust and hearty.

The village has its small parliament, which, if not as august as that of Westminster, is almost as important, in its own estimation; it is a very grave and solemn assembly. This is elected once in three years, and at such times there is quite a commotion in the place; there is often considerable rivalry among the inhabitants to obtain a seat on the Parish Council. This body meets once a month, and gravely discusses matters of urgent importance, and afterwards prints all its motions and doings in the public press. Here, if you really have the affairs of the country at heart, you may read how many of the allotment-holders paid their rent last quarter, and all the minutiae beside. At one time a new step has been fixed to the stile in the field, at another a hand-rail has been added to the small bridge across the stream. This farmer is served with a severe notice commanding him to crop the hedge on the roadside forthwith; that one is called upon to take up a drock, and so on – all which is set in type, and the account eagerly and soberly perused by many of the villagers. Whether it be a little matter or not, it is of great moment to them, especially if their name should, by any chance, happen to get mentioned and honoured with print.

When a real election comes round – that is, a Parliamentary one, then you may see a little more excitement, though not nearly as much as is exhibited in the towns, and not nearly as much as was shown in country places formerly, either. We have all heard and read of the riotous scenes which used to take place in the district, years ago, at Cricklade, and Wootton Bassett, but times have changed since then. Nowadays, elections, as a rule, are very well-ordered things. The farm-labourers proper, though they take a deep and active interest in political matters, and may feel strongly on questions of the hour, seldom or never exhibit such enthusiasm and hysteria as you meet with in the towns at such times. There the excitement is most intense; the very air is electrified with it.

It is a very common error to imagine that the villagers all follow the squire and parson in political matters, and vote on their side at the poll. That they certainly do not, and as for intimidating them, you might as well try to shift the church tower. 'I dwunt keer for you, maaster, nor no other man; I allus voted for who I was a mint to, an I be gwain to this time. I dwun want yer vittals an' beer.' Old Jemmy Boulton, and Dudley, and Jacky Bridges were all on the popular side, heartily and wholesomely independent in principle. At election times Jemmy was doggedly firm and unshaken by whomsoever solicited. 'I'm a yalla, I be. I never did vote blue, an' never wunt neither. I'd soodner die fust.' Tom Chamberlain, the Crimean veteran, inclined to the other side – a great many ex-soldiers are Conservative in politics – and used to argue long and seriously with the others, but to no purpose. On the day of the poll they all pinned up their colours in monster rosettes, with streaming ribbons attached, and marched proudly and defiantly to the station to record the vote; and afterwards talked over the chances of the rival candidates, sitting at the inn, with a cup or two of fourpenny. Where you do get a heckler at village political meetings, he will generally prove a trouble to the speaker, and equal to anything you can meet with in the towns.

When a birth takes place in a village, news of it is quickly passed from house to house; everyone in the parish is soon made aware of the circumstance; it is quite a public event. 'What is it; a bwoy or a girrul?' is the first question asked; and afterwards, 'Wha's ee's name gwain to be?' In due time the infant is baptized, often in the middle of a service. If it is a first-born, and the rustic husband is prevailed upon to attend, he will be extremely bashful and awkward, blushing like a schoolgirl. If the father works on the farm, his mates will expect to be treated to a glass or two of ale, to 'wet the youngster,' and 'drenk 'is 'ealth,' and the wish is acceded to good-humouredly.

Marriages of parties of the same village are rare. Schoolboy and girl courtships do not often continue after the tender age and develop into riper affection, though there are exceptions, of course. If the young woman has an attachment at home in the village, when she gets out in service and sees the world she generally changes her mind and bestows her affection elsewhere. Often it is a case of going farther and faring worse; perhaps she is taken with a smart outer appearance, marries, and shortly after repents; she would have been better advised to keep to her old love at home, but it is too late now. ''Er made 'er bed, an' 'er must lay on it,' the country folk say.

In the majority of cases, however, the girls of the village have formed no attachment before leaving home; these invariably find a husband, sooner or later, and settle down among strangers. When the 'young man' is brought home for the first time, all eyes are upon him; he has to run the gauntlet, and be subjected to a cross-fire of criticism. 'What zart ov a fella is a?' 'Is a any good?' 'Smartish swell, yen a?' 'Dwun like the looks o' ee!' 'What do a do?' 'Wha's is name when a's at whum?' 'A puts I in mind of a Londoner.' The wedding is certain to take place in the village, at which all the feminine population usually attend; after that the entertainment is kept up at the bride's home till early next morning; in a day or so they leave for their new abode – in the Midlands, or the Metropolis. or elsewhere. 'Wilt thou have this woman to thy wedded wife?' the parson asked recently in the village over the fields. 'Yes, if er's a min to't,' was the brisk reply. Then, as they left the altar, the bridegroom blurted out: 'Aa, tha bist married now mun, owld wench!' He was evidently bent upon getting the upper hand in the new condition of things. One poor fellow, a farm-labourer, on a broiling hot day in summer, came to church without the necessary documents: he had walked five miles off the hills, and had to walk back again after it in sultry weather. Though pressed for time, however, he just managed the journey, and luckily, too, for all concerned; a child was born early the next morning.

When a death occurs the bell is tolled from the tower, the little one for an infant, the heavy one for one of riper years; all the cottage blinds in the vicinity are drawn; there are many sumpathizers. A number go to view the corpse; that is a custom rigidly observed by rustic people. 'Lar, a's very natteral, poor dear an in. Feel 'is poor 'ands!' It is the rule to feel the corpse; then the villagers say you will not dream of the dead, which you will otherwise do. At the funeral the bearers are chosen from the dead person's near acquaintances, his workmates if possible; Jemmy Boulton and old Daniel Lewis both named men to be their bearers before they died. Half-a-crown each is the fee for the bearers, and an invitation to tea beside, or otherwise bread and cheese, and several mugs of beer; the funeral always terminates in a feast.

Formerly, when a farmer died, his body was brought for burial in a waggon, and the bearers, men of his own farm, wore white smocks; but that custom is rare now, in these parts at least, though old Farmer Westell, of Friar's Mill, was conveyed to Sennington Churchyard in a manure-cart. The villagers are calm and philosophic, though very reverent, in the presence of death. They console themselves with various reflections and sentiments, usually adding, 'Us didn't all come together, an' us shan't all go together. The Almighty knows wha's best for us. Chent no use to murmur. Lar! it might be my time next, or else thine; us never knows a minute.' That is the stoicism of the country-side.

9
GLEANING, COMMUNITY LIFE, AND BASSET DOWN

When June comes in, preparations are made for haymaking; the implements and machinery are drawn out from the sheds, and overhauled or sent to the blacksmith. The corn-crops must be attended to as well, and other things planted, such as rape, swedes, mangolds, and turnips. When the young roots come up they must be hoed, and then cut out to a uniform distance. These want plenty of nice showers to help them along, though mangolds may do very well in a dry season. Haymaking usually lasts for a month, if the weather is normal; if it is wet, it may not be finished before September. Farmer Wheeler, of Rowborough Lane, was entirely ruined by the failure of hay-crops. His was all pasture land, and situated by the river; excessive rains came, and the floods washed the whole of it away, and left him penniless.

After haymaking comes the harvest. Now all the corn is cut by machinery. Fagging was the universal method before that, and, still earlier, reaping by hand with the sickle. Farmer Davis, of Rove's Farm, was the last in this neighbourhood to resort to machine reaping. He employed a great number of hands, men and women too, did his land well, cleaned and manured it thoroughly, reaped great crops, and was highly prosperous. I can just remember reaping with the sickle in his fields. That was in 1882. There stood the long stubble, about eighteen inches high. This was very often mowed with a scythe afterwards for litter; it made excellent manure.

Harvest-bugs are an inconvenience of the corn-field. These are exceedingly minute, red in colour. They are very partial to coltsfoot; the under parts of the leaves of this are red with them. These burrow in the flesh and set up great irritation, though the true rustic does not take much notice of them.

As soon as a piece of corn was cleared, word was sent all round the village for the gleaners to come out and gather up the remainder. In earlier times still, before my own day, the church bell was rung to signify that the corn was cleared, though all that has passed away now. At the end of wheat-harvest it was also the custom for the school children to gather in the field and ride down to the farm on the last loads. The children were pitched up onto the load with the big fork. The fork was placed under their arms, and they held tight to it, and the loader received them safely in his hands. What joy it was to them to ride down to the farm in that manner!

The village schools were always closed for gleaning. This was the harvest holidays. Nearly all the village wives turned out, and the children went, too. We took the day's provisions in a bag, and a cup to dip the water from the little spring bubbling up under the hazels, with a clean white sheet, or counterpane, taken from the bed, for the 'nitches,' and small linen ear-bags to be fastened round the waist for the loose ears, broken off by the reapers, or more frequently 'britted' off by the heat of the sun. There were always a few to anticipate the general hive, and have the early run of the field, though these frequently fared worst in the end. My mother and we children were usually the last to enter a field and the last to leave it. Our appearance was hailed with a good-natured cheer, and often a little humorous banter, but we always bore off the fattest bundle in the end. We used to consider our harvest a poor one if it did not total fifteen or sixteen bushels of threshed grain. Gleaning in a field that had been overrun was called 'prowling.'

There were eight of us altogether – my mother and six others – ranging from five to thirteen years. All the children gathered small handfuls, then brought them to her; she put them together into one, twisted a part of the straw round several times, and thrust the ends underneath the bond, then set it down in the stubble, ears up, and went on as before. In the morning we had lunch at ten, dinner at noon, with 'little dinner' again in the afternoon, about four. We went home about six or seven, telling the time by the sun. Perhaps we gathered forty large handfuls, or perhaps less, according to the quantity of ears on the ground. We always gleaned more in dull weather; then we could see the ears better. At night, after reaching home, all the ears were cut off with a sharp knife or scissors, and then stored in sacks and kept indoors. The cottage was like a little barn, upstairs and down, too; you could scarcely move for the corn.

The fields of the village presented a far different appearance then from what they do now. The majority were surrounded with hedges of hazel, sloe, and elder; we played all kinds of pranks among the boughs at dinner-time, especially if showers came on, at hide-and-seek, and nutting in the copses. Sometimes a shooting-party came by, and we ran after them to pick up the spent cartridges, or made a bridle with our garters, and rode a quiet old chestnut in a neighbouring meadow, or waded bare-footed in the shallow stream; but we were never allowed to go home before we had gleaned a stated quantity, weather permitting.

A great change has come over the country-side latterly, however. The old

The staff of Messrs. Whatley's Foundry, on a John Fowler ploughing engine

school of farmers is dying out, and the villagers, too. The crops are cut by machinery, and the fields raked to the last ear, and afterwards given up to sheep and swine; gleaning is often prohibited, even. Moreover, the villagers are disinclined to go gleaning; perhaps that is the chief cause of its decay. The young wife thinks there is no need for her to glean corn in the field; everything is different. The children are kept later at school; they do not benefit by the changes. It is nearly ten years since I saw gleaners in the field; that was at Collingbourne, midway between Marlborough and Andover.

The old farmers used to give bacon to their men several times during the harvest, in portions of about seven pounds. If there were father and son, the two received twelve pounds. In addition to this they had a cooked dinner every day, of meat and vegetables, and ale in the field. At Michaelmas they received a bonus of thirty shillings or two pounds, which custom still continues here. Instead of giving the boys money, the farmer 'looked round' them, to see what they were in need of, and bought them clothes, boots, or a thick warm overcoat.

Very soon after harvest threshing began. The engine and machine, covered with tarpaulins, were drawn from farm to farm by strong teams of horses, three or four on each; the troops of children, boys and girls too, followed them all up the lane, greatly excited; it was wonderful to them to see the black smoke towering out of the tall iron chimney, the piston-rod shooting silently in and out, the wheels spinning round, and the long belt communicating power to the thresher, the chaff and chaving flying, and the straw rustling down behind. The humming of the thresher has a peculiar fascination as well, especially at that time of the year; it sounds so mournful and plaintive borne to you over the field; it is like a dirge to the dying year, yet it is not a depressing sound at all, but exactly fits in with the surroundings of the farm and country-side.

The engine was drawn in first, then the thresher. The latter is set in position near the corn rick, and the wheels secured with wedges to prevent it from shifting under the power of the belt. Then the engine is set, too, at a certain distance, and the wheels firmly wedged as well. Sometimes shallow holes are dug for the wheels to drop in, to prevent motion, for the engine oscillates considerably under the force of the steam. The farmer supplies coal for the boiler, and must also see to the water. This is contained in a large tub close to the fire-box. Two rubber tubes are inserted from the engine; the exhaust steam is ejected from one of these, the water is injected by means of the other. There are two men in charge of the tackle; one of these attends to the engine, the other feeds the thresher. Dudley Sansum and old Thomas Bowles used to do this in turns, and so equalize the labour; they were both exceedingly proud of their engine. Four sacks are suspended at the rear of the machine for catching the grain. One of these is for the most inferior, all kinds of seeds and stuff; one is for the seconds, and the other two for the firsts. This patters down from the fans within like hail-stones; it is delightful to catch it in the hand as it falls into the mouth of the sack.

At ten, or half-past, the whistle sounds, all stop for lunch; dinner at twelve, 'little dinner' at four, bread, cheese, and ale, which is especially plentiful at threshing-time, for there is much work to be done, carrying away the straw, and one thing and the other. 'As hard as a day's dreshin',' you often hear the villagers say. The price for threshing, to the owners of the tackle, is about thirty shillings a day; under ordinary circumstances the day's work will amount to a hundred and twenty sacks of grain.

The price for flail-threshing, in old times, was sixpence a bushel, winnowing and all. Sometimes, though, the threshers worked at the day rate, and received nine shillings and often only eight shillings a week, and no beer into the bargain, and if they 'scamped' the work, that is, did not clean the grain out, they were liable to prosecution. For instance, Dad Eldridge's father and his mate were summoned to appear before the magistrates at Faringdon, on February 5, 1834, to answer the charge of not cleaning out the barley they were engaged upon, and both went expecting to receive punishment of some kind or other. Now, they were only getting eight shillings a week, while the men in the barn next to them were receiving nine shillings, so, as soon as the case came on, the Chairman asked the rate of wages paid, and on hearing it was only eight shillings he told the farmer to 'take them home and give them nine shillings too, and if they failed to clean the barley out then, to bring them back to him again.'

Occasionally, hand-threshing was paid for by the quarter; the men worked on, drawing a weekly wage, and when the corn was winnowed up, if there was a balance, they received it in a lump sum. The winnowing was done separately with a hand-machine, in another part of the barn. Beans were paid for at the rate of fourpence a bushel. Horse-threshing followed the flail method. This machine merely threshed the corn; that fell through on the ground, chaff and all, and was then passed through the winnower. Four horses operated this machine, attached to a lever outside the barn. Beer was supplied three times a day. The steam-thresher came into these parts for the first-time in 1851. First of all it was a steam-engine to the old horse thresher, and the winnowing was done as before. Then the winnower was improved, first to single, and afterwards to double fan. The old horse-machine did about half of what the steam threshers do. Now, instead of portable engines, tractions do the work. This is more convenient altogether, as there is much time saved in drawing the tackle to and fro. These usually convey a chaff-cutter and elevator. If they are threshing oats, the cutter-machine receives the straw from the thresher and converts it into chaff straight away. Before the chaff-cutting machines which are operated with a wheel, the chaff used to be cut by hand, with a large knife. The hay was fixed in a box-like receptacle, and held in place by means of the foot. The operator pushed the hay along, bore a lever down with the foot, and drew the large sharp knife across. For this he was paid at the rate of twopence halfpenny per basket of four bushels.

Formerly a great many Irishmen came over the Channel every year, to haymaking and harvesting, and then returned in time to get their crops of potatoes in, in late autumn. These lived very scantily and frugally, and were hard workers; they saved quite a little pile before going back to the 'Old Country.' They lived almost entirely on bread and cheese, or cold boiled bacon, and drank ale, cider, and water, not much tea. There was one came regularly to the farm, old Jemmy; he used to make a good meal off bread and young onions. He was very wise and careful, and of sterling principle.

Gipsies visited the village when I was a boy, and pitched their camps annually in the Green Lane. These were very peaceable and friendly, for the most part; the village children used to mix with them, and be very often invited to tea or supper. They are very hardy and long-lived; 'Mother' Salty, a well-known local gipsy woman, lived to be a hundred. In the winter the men used to go 'hedgehog hunting,' and indulge in a tasty meal. These little animals make a warm nest in a 'stowl,' and sleep all the winter; it is then they are best for food. The flesh of the hedgehog is savoury and palatable, something like poultry. They are very clean, and well-known as an article of food.

The gipsy children wear no hats, and very often no boots, and seldom take cold. After all, these live as near to Nature as any, though they shun the bath, but a great many people attain old age without that.

The villagers' relations one with another are of a most simple nature. They live, for the most part, in perfect agreement with each other, friendly, and well-disposed, seldom exhibiting jealousy or rancour. Now and then there may be a slight disagreement among the youths, where several are engaged together, but that is natural; a very little will kindle them to white heat. Thus, Scamp and Smithy sometimes fought, or scratched each other – on the rick, or the load in the field, or anywhere else where they happened to differ – but no one ever took serious notice of the matter. Those engaged on separate farms do not see each other very much, except in the evening and at week-ends; then they smoke the pipe of peace, leaning over the gate, or with their backs to the wall, or visit one another's gardens or allotments, or discuss village affairs and gossip, the promise of crops, and other simple matters.

The wives' relations with one another have undergone a distinct change in late years, which is easily accounted for. Formerly the greater part of them went to work in the fields, or even where they did not do this regularly, they always helped with the hay or corn harvest, and afterwards went gleaning, and so had much in common to think and talk about. Moreover, they were thrown in healthier contact with each other. The fact of their working at the same task, very often for the same farmer, or gleaning together side by side, children and all, induced kindly and sympathetic feeling; they entered into each other's lives and occupations more, and understood one another better. They were for ever discussing the last year's harvest or gleaning, how much leased corn they had when it was threshed, the quantity of flour returned from West Mill, and the date of the first pudding made from it.

The village people retire early, and the farmers before the work-folk, as a rule. A great many of the farmers retire at eight, and even by seven, in the winter, after partaking of a good supper of bread and cheese, and hotted beer, or cider – wives, daughters and all. Before retiring the farmer usually takes a lantern and walks round the cattle-yard and stables, to see that everything is safe and well. Very often the farm-labourers are much later in going to bed, burning the oil till eleven and after; but this is a bad sign. In the villages farther from the town they retire much earlier.

The villagers' food, especially that of the labouring class, is plain and simple in kind, but plentiful enough. The chief article consumed is bread, and abundant potatoes; where there is a large family of six or eight, the household requires eight or nine gallons of bread a week, or more, and then the wife and mother cooks potatoes for dinner and tea as well. The chief trimmings are Canadian bacon and cheese, butter or margarine, lard or dripping. The children eat bread and lard, with pepper upon it. When I was a child, my mother used to buy dripping of an extra special quality, which the dealer pompously informed her came from Marlborough College. This we ate with solemn reverence and an awe amounting almost to superstition, though the aristocratic stuff was no better than any other.

Bacon-pudding is a tasty meal, though waning in favour. The old carter may have a fried rasher – without the egg – for breakfast, or fried vegetables, or toasted cheese. Fresh meat is only indulged in once a week, Sundays. That is generally purchased from the van which comes round every Saturday – breast or loin of mutton, or brisket of beef – and is mostly foreign, though some country labourers will not touch the 'furren tackle,' and abhor all tinned goods. A short while ago a dealer was selling sausages in the village at threepence a pound, best fourpence. The carter's wife did not like the former kind: 'they burned their mouths so, and made the children cry awful.' At Christmas all the labourers receive a large piece of prime beef, from eight to twelve pounds, and very many a ton of coal at Michaelmas, besides a sum of money. Their drink consists chiefly of tea, very weak – this they have three and very often four times a day – and many keep a small barrel of ale in the house, too, or else fetch it from the inn.

As to the farmers themselves, they live much better, and have the best of everything – beef, mutton, pork, lamb and veal, game and fish, whatever is in season, though here and there you find one that is 'skinny' and 'near', intent on making a pile at the expense of his stomach and appetite. Farmer B—'s choice came out at a gathering over which the vicar presided. Happening to discuss the price of foodstuffs, and of bacon in particular, he amused everyone by declaring his preference for 'that long thin, straked stuff – well, you knows, sir, the be-elly piece!' It is a point to be noticed that those farmers who are strong and hearty in health, fond of a bite and a sup, and whose cellars are well stocked with cider and ale, are always the best natured. Teetotal farmers are usually parsimonious and near, ready to extract the last ounce of labour from the individual; anyone will tell you that in the villages. 'They teetotal vawk bent no good to nobody,' they say.

The village parson usually comes in for a great amount of criticism, though chiefly from outsiders; the villagers themselves are not so unkindly disposed toward him, or the squire either, though they are particularly careful not to place themselves in subjection to them. If there is anything the matter – sickness, accident, or any other misfortune – he is very useful, then; he is always willing to do, give, or lend, to each and everyone alike. In bygone years the local doctor used to accept payment in kind from the farmers and villagers – corn from the first, and bacon from the others. This practice is common in some parts to-day, I am told.

Some of the names of people in the village are interesting, and form a suggestive catalogue. For instance, there is a Shakespeare, a Church, a Bell, a Parsons, a Clark, a Sexton, a Squire, a Cross, a Large, a Head, Legg, Little, Grubb, Stone, Wall, Sharp, Thorne, a King, a Peapell, a Taylor, a Turtle, a Pike, Brooks, Bridges, Balls, Bowles, a Tubb, a Garret, a Lee, an Alder, and a Wildern.

There are a great many old sayings and rhymes, chiefly concerning the weather, used locally, which may be common enough in other quarters, but are none the less interesting. Speaking of a person who indulged in anything unnecessary, it is said: 'He got no more use for't than a cat wi' a side-pocket.' 'If you goes a borrowin', you goes a sorrowin'.' 'As black as Old Harry's nutting-bag.' 'As black as Newgate knocker.' 'As easy as pet.' 'As slick as ninepence.' 'Put your love in the kettle, and love them all a little.' 'A wet Friday, a wet Sunday; and a wet Sunday, a wet week.' 'Sunshine Christmas Day, a good apple year.' 'Rain and hail brings frost at its tail.' 'February ull fill the ditch, black or white, no matter which.' 'Sunshine and shower, rain for half an hour.' ' Mackerel sky, not much wet and not much dry.' 'If a cock crows gwain to bed, he'll get up wi' a wet head.' 'Rain afore seven, dry afore eleven.' 'Just enough blue in the sky to make a man a pair of trousers'; and so on. This last saying might have had its origin over the Channel, since the Dutch wear blue trousers.

Other sayings common in our time are as old as humanity itself almost. Such are, 'Like father, like son,' and 'Every man to his fancy, as the man said when he kissed the cow.'

When a farm fire occurs, all the villagers turn out to assist in mastering the flames, and to lend a hand at the pumps. There was a great fire in the village when I was a boy, involving the loss of twenty-two ricks of hay, corn, and mustard, an engine and thresher, a steam grist mill, and a whole pile of buildings. The most amazing thing to me, at the time, was that no one seemed to make very great efforts to put it out; it was more like a festival than anything else. The farmer himself walked about smoking a cigar; others were engaged serving out bread, cheese, and beer to the men: there was no sign of sorrow or regret visible. We farm boys stayed up all night enjoying the fun, and crept sleepy to work late next morning, and were well scolded by the cowman; we ought to have been there milking long before. The poultry pen was burned with its occupants; more than one boy helped himself to roast fowl and turkey.

There are very few living now who can call to mind the old agricultural riots, though Robert Brooks, who is eighty-six, can just remember them. He says the rioters used to march in a gang, blowing horns as they neared the village, and calling on the farm men to help them break up the machinery. The gangs were composed of the roughest of the farm labourers, who came strangers to the place, and demanded the surrender of the new-fashioned implements. Farmer Brooks, of Stanford-in-the-Vale, smashed his up himself, to prevent their falling into the rioters' hands; and when they came to Bury Town, the farmer there had all his machinery hauled out in a field, and shouted out, 'Ther 'em be, look! Smash 'em up, mi bwoys!' but the rioters, with a touch of good-nature, passed by his and left them intact. Such of the rioters as were apprehended were transported to the Cape of Good Hope, or Van Dieman's Land, or Gibraltar. Many innocent persons suffered. One old fellow of Highworth declared he was in bed at the time, but the authorities suspected him, and he had to go. Looking back at this date we acknoweldge the mistake of the revolution, but it was not so clear to the labourers of that generation who were faced with the loss of their immediate work and livelihood.

Perched upon a slope of the hill and surrounded with magnificent elms, spruces and cedars, is Basset Down House, the home of the old squire.

The gardener's cottage is situated in the corner of the orchard at the foot of the slope, the way down to which, through the shrubs and rockeries, is called 'the crooked walk.' Here he dwells with his two sons, who help him with the work, and his aged mother, Granny Ferris; his wife has been some time dead. At the bottom of the orchard, in white-painted hives, are twenty lots of bees, which discover the gardener's hobby and recreation.

It was five o'clock – the gardener's teatime at the cottage; he came up the path wearing his green apron, the badge of his profession, and almost dragged me inside. Here I was immediately presented to Granny and the boys. She was busy filling the teapot, and wiped her hand in her print apron before offering it to me for the salutation. The kitchen was bright and cheerful; everything was tastefully arranged, and the table was set.

'Come an' 'ev e a cup o' tea,' Granny exclaimed.

'Thanks, Granny, but I've had one tea.'

'Don' matter. Breng the cheer up an' 'ev another. I don' know who you be though.'

'I've just called to see you, Granny, and have a chat, you know.'

'To see I? Ther's some 'oney, look. Jes' try that. You'll like that.'

'Is this your own honey?'

'Why, yes, to be sure 'tis, out of our bees.'

Granny is tall and stoutish, with a chubby, cheery face, grey eyes, strong features, a little masculine, hardy and healthy looking, wearing a white sun-bonnet on her head, and as active and nimble as many a young woman of forty. Her son, the gardener, inherits the chief of her physical characteristics. He, too, is tall and sturdily built, with a squarish face, arched eyebrows, thickish nose, bronzed cheeks, and a square bit of grey beard of the Brother Jonathan type.

'The fust swarm o' bees I can remember was when I was a little gel,' Granny went on. 'My dad bought 'em off a farmer at Broad Town, an' I went along wi'n. A gied aaf a suverin far 'em. I was too little to know what money was then, an' I said: "Oh, dad! you oni gied 'e a farden for thaay." Then I 'ad to stop at 'ome an' look aater 'em.'

It was amusing to listen to Granny's account of her girlhood days. She would not go to school, but always wanted to be with her dad, who was woodman, gamekeeper, and village constable combined. So she wore breeches and a little coat like a boy, and helped her dad cutting the underwood at tuppence a pole or faggoting at five shillings the hundred, or worked the heavy cross-saw, to which her dad had affixed a small rope for her tiny hands, and climbed the trees and drew up the rope with twine to attach to the top, with which to pull the tree over when it was sawn through. Later on, at the age of fifteen, she had a set of ferrets and terrier, and went about dressed in a white smock like the farm boys, and was the official local ratcatcher. The price for a rat – paid on production of the tail – was tuppence. She presented her bill on St. Thomas's Day, as the children went 'gooding' at the farms. At one time she had a whole sovereign to draw in a lump.

The conversation concerning bees brought to light several curious customs and superstitions which survive in the locality, and in which Granny believes, though the gardener several times intervened and declared we had 'done wi' they old times now, an' was goin' in for something more modern and up to date.' One of the old customs was that of telling the bees of the death of the owner, or of a near relation of the same. As soon as the death occurred it was imperative to 'tell the bees' forthwith, otherwise it was confidently believed they would all die in the hives. Again, on the death of the squire, it was the custom to 'tell the bees' immediately, and to affix a little black crape to the hives just above the entrance. When the King died it was usual to tell the bees of the fact. This time it was thought they would scatter the news broadcast as they flew about, and make all Nature acquainted with it.

If a swarm of bees settled on dry wood, that was a certain sign of death in the owner's family. A short while ago, at Basset Down, a labourer's daughter was lying ill, and a swarm of bees happening to alight on some dry wood, nothing could dissuade the mother from believing it was a sign of the girl's death. When a visitor called to inquire after the patient, the mother declared she would die, adding: 'An' 'er knows it as well as I do, for the bees bin an' settled on dry 'ood.' Strange to say, the young girl died the day following. Another curious custom is that of visiting the hive on Christmas Eve to hear the bees talking. Questioned as to this, the gardener was sceptical; but Granny believes they talk that night, and she is certain the two queen bees hold a conversation just before the swarming. Then, she says, if you listen at the hive, you may hear the old queen saying, 'Out, out, out, out,' and the new one responding, 'M-m-m-m.'

The old habit of ringing the bees, so as to call them home, still continues. The gardener keeps a small tin for the purpose; but Granny, anxious to give a practical demonstration, seized up the shovel and poker from over the fender, and beat them noisily together, saying: 'This is my bell, look!'

If a swarm of bees had settled on another person's premises, you could not claim them under the old law, unless you had first 'rung' them.

Presently Granny rose from her arm-chair to refill the teapot, and I discovered a dark object spread over the back of the seat.

'Why, Granny, you've got a badger's skin!' I cried.

'Yes. Yen 'e a beauty! I bin offered ten shillings for 'e,' Granny answered.

Then the gardener chimed in: 'Who was it as killed the dead badger? You tell 'e 'ow you killed the dead badger.'

'No e didn't kill the dead badger, neether.'

'Yes you did.'

'No e didn't.'

'Yes you did, now.'

'Knows e didn't. A wasn' dead no more than I be. You brought un 'ome in a sack one Sunday marnin'.'

'You was main frightened an in, wasn' e?'

'Well! a was gwain to bite ma, wasn' a.'

'Bite, no. A was oni gaspin' for breath.'

'But did you really kill the poor badger, Granny?' I inquired.

'Ha-a. 'E put a coord round 'is neck, an' then slipped un droo the chink o' the door, an' draad un right up, an' I 'it un wi' a girt stick. When I was along o' my dad I killed 'em many a time.'

Badgers used to be eaten for food by labourers and gamekeepers, and were thought highly of, and especially badger's hams, which were counted a delicacy. Granny had oft-times cooked them. The fat of badgers is still considered of great value by reason of its softening qualities; there is nothing so penetrating as that, according to the rustics. It is even claimed that if you place it in the palm of the hand it will go right through, and come out at the back. It was especially in demand for anointing the ears of deaf people, and for use in cases of acute bronchitis, swellings, and inflammation. Granny's last pot of badger's fat is just exhausted; people come from far off to beg a little of it.

The badger, if taken when young, may be tamed and taught to fraternize with the domestic pets; it is amusing to see it playing with the young puppies. The badger is the largest of our carnivora, and has been known to turn the scale at twenty-nine pounds. Besides young rabbits and wasp-grubs, it is fond of eggs, fruits, beetles, frogs, and mice. Like the otter, it is being continually hunted down; but if our legislators did their duty, both these would be protected, seeing they do not upset the balance of Nature, nor live to the prejudice of mankind.

The ballad-singers came regularly to the village, every Christmas, when Granny was a girl. There was a band of minstrels, and one preceded the others, carrying a great wooden bowl for the ale upon his head. As they walked they sang an ancient piece beginning:

> 'Wassail, wassail, all over the town,
> Our toast is white, and our ale is brown;
> Our bowl it is made of a sycamore-tree
> And a wassailing bowl I will drink unto thee.'

The bowl was replenished at every farmhouse; all the company quaffed from it, and wished good health to the farmer and his wife.

At this time Granny picked up her sewing from the small table and began to stitch away.

'What are you making, Granny?' said I.

'A shirt for 'e, look,' pointing to the gardener.

'But can you see to do it?' I continued.

'See? Of course I can see. Jest you zamin that.'

Then the gardener interposed again: 'Bless tha, 'er's as mischifful now as ever a was. A sawed a tree down t'other day, an' a's agwain to 'elp fetch thaay elms down in the spring.'

'Aa, if I be alive, awhever, I be gwain to 'ev a cut at 'em. E med as well wer out as rust out,' she declared.

The woodman's cottage stands in a little hollow place immediately under the hill. It is overshaded with dense beech-trees that shut out the sun till the evening part. He was filling his pipe and preparing to go for a walk, but put it back in his pocket, and sat down in the arm-chair. I made some remark about country-people.

'Well, the country-people, thaay *is* the people, byen 'em,' the woodman replied.

I readily assented to this, and the more heartily perceiving the splendid specimen before me. He is of middle height, bronzed, and well-seasoned with out-of-doors work, with iron-grey hair, strong, kindly eyes, firm and erect, as hard as the oak to look at, and possessed of a manly spirit, agreeing with the freedom of his occupation. The room was large and spacious, and everything was spotlessly clean; the faint sweet scent of the leaves was borne in from outside. A big log burned in the fireplace; it was a typically rustic interior. On the table was a pile of books.

'Even you find time to read, then,' I observed.

'Yes, thenk God. I can read, an' I can see, an' I can thenk. Ah! ther's a lot as yent right bi a long way it. Ther yent the right spirit in people. Tha be all for downin' a man as dwunt come up to thaay, or as'eve done a bit o' wrong Let a man be as bad as 'e ull, ther as bin some time in 'is life when 'e 'ev done good.'

'Are you always engaged with the trees?' I asked.

'Well, chafely, you know,' he replied, 'eether cuttin' or trimmin'. Besides that, I mows the outer lawns, feeds the swans, mends the roofs wi' thatch er tiles, an' does anything tha's wanted an ma.'

'Did you ever eat a badger?' I ventured.

'No, but I knowed thaay as did, an' squirrels, too,' he answered. 'Plenty o' people 'ev ate thaay. An' why not? Tha lives on the best an't, an' be as clane as a noo pin.'

The woodman's early days were hard and stern. 'My father was eighty-eight when a died, an' a worked seventy years out on't. I've bin for a year an' not tasted nothin' wi' mi bread, an' very often not much o' that, wi' flour £5 5s. a bag; yet I'll lay we was stronger an' hardier than the young uns to-day.'

'That was the barley-bangers,' I said.

'Aa, barley-scawters, barley-dampers, and pot-cyeks, we called 'em,' he continued. 'My owl' mother made some 'underds o' thaay. Most thengs was terrabul dea, but bacon an' cheese was chep, an' we could get dree pounds o' whey butter for a shillin'. I minds the owl' carter very well at Broad Town. A was comin' 'ome from church one marnin', an' maaster stopped un an' said: "I thenks t'ood be chepper for you to bake yer own bread, John." "Aa, zo do I, maaster," John said. "E got it aal but the flour an' the 'ood." ' Here the woodman's eyes sparkled; he was touched with the finger of fun and gaiety.

'Did 'e yer about Gargey Narton? Gargey was carter, too, an' 'ad bin out somewher, an' got lost one night down Broad Town way, an' yerd the owld owl a hollain' up in the trees aboove 'is 'ed "Whoo-oo-oo!" so a shouted out: "Garge Narton, sir, the honestest man as ever lived." '

'Then there was Mark Drew the cowman. Maaster sent 'e to the next farm wi' a sow, an' when a went to fetch un back a brought the wrong un.

"Why, Mark, you brought back the wrong un," master said.

"No I hent," said Mark.

"Yes you hev. This yent the right peg."

"Eec 'tis, maaster."

"But I tells tha chent."

"Aw tis, bless e, maaster."

"But this yent my peg."

"Eece 'tis, bless e."

"Well, I *knows* chent, then."

"Daal if I didn' thenk, comin' along the road, a was a bit too 'eavy in the yer, maaster," Mark answered.'

'Then there was Jimmy Mower, the owld carpenter, as cut the corner off. Jimmy was gwain to Devizes, an' went terrin' acraas a carner ground o' young woats. When a got aaf waay awver a was skeered a bit, an' a said to 'isself: "Well, I can back-zoord, an' I can kick legs, but daal if I can run a mossel if anybody comes." Then a yerd a gallopin' behind, an' up come the farmer on 'is owld nag.

"Hey!" he shouted, "ther's no road yer, mun."

"I knows chent, maaster, an' I byent agwain to stop to make narn, neether," Jimmy answered un.'

Wootton Basset, from which Basset Down derives its name, has been famous for its perfervid election enthusiasm and riots, though there are none living at this time who took part in them; but Jesse Giles, a big burly labourer, with strong features, little goatee beard, and pronounced nasal twang, can tell of the Cricklade riots, in which he took part, over half a century ago. All voting was in the open then; the voter merely shouted out the name of his favourite candidate before a pigeon-hole in the wall of a house. there was a small, narrow way, fenced off with a low rail, along which the voters passed. The crowd was tightly packed all along the rail, and close to the voters, the most of whom wore the old-fashioned top-hat. As the voter called out the name of his candidate the crowd cheered or yelled; the tall hats were seized off the voters' heads, and tossed into the air, or knocked off, or bashed down over their eyes, amid convulsive shrieks and laughter, and the wild din of the onlookers. The next day – the day of the declaraion of the poll – huge crowds were sent down from Swindon in barges, armed with sticks and cudgels, hammer-shafts, stones, and bottles, intent on a disturbance, while all the countryside, chiefly democratic, had flocked in, too. Each party had its band of musicians, who paraded the streets, followed by a long train of supporters, fully armed, cheering and shouting. The poll was declared about noon, and then the fighting began, to the discomfiture of the invaders, who were driven off pell-mell, through mud and water, in all directions, and often ducked in the Thames. The old women of the town ransacked the faggot-piles for cudgels; there they stood, with their arms full of great sticks, and sold them at a penny each to the rioters. Blood was freely shed; there was no quarter given, and none expected, and the few constables present were powerless to quell the uproar, which was continued till midnight and the early hours of the next morning, though the wardens of the law managed to arrest a few of the ringleaders, several of whom were transported, and worked in the mines, and came back with their pockets full of golden sovereigns, to the envy of the local farm-labourers and folks.

10

WROUGHTON, HODSON AND CHISELDON

At Wroughton, 'Dicky' Austin, the old church clerk, nearly ninety years of age, lives in a small cottage halfway down the hill, together with a middle-aged daughter, who tends him in his infirmity. He is tall and upright, silver haired, with large kind eyes, prominent nose, and thin side-beard, but his old hand trembles, and his head shakes visibly; he cannot converse much since he had the seizure last fall. The little room is packed full of furniture, and the walls are hung with pictures: works of art some of them, including a painting of Richard himself, done by the vicar's wife, and given to the clerk sixty years ago, or more. Upon a chest of drawers stands a stuffed brown owl, and a pile of books containing records of weddings and funerals, dating back nearly two centuries. Old Dicky has been clerk, gravedigger, and undertaker combined all his life, as were his people before him for the last 300 years, and the records certify that during Richard's tenure of the office he buried no less than 3,000 dead in that moderate-sized churchyard. How he found room for so many graves is a mystery; he must have dug out the old bones time after time; it is no wonder the tombstones are all packed and piled up together in heaps confusedly.

The old clerk has many quaint stories to tell, of the coal merchant, who, coming to be married, frequently interrupted the clergyman with unlooked for questions and remarks, and tried to sell him 'aaf a ton' in the midst of the ceremony; of the wayward villager who came home late from the inn, and fell into the open grave, and had to be rescued the next morning; of the sporting parson, who, time after time, went a-hunting, and forgot the weddings and funerals, and how they used to leave the corpse in the church porch all night till the next day, while the mourners went back home again, and how he used to disappoint the bride and bridegroom, and cause the wedding to be postponed for a week or a fortnight, until the Bishop was apprised of the facts, and severely admonished the defaulting vicar. Such are the tales old Dicky has to tell, with many smiles, and a few tears coursing down his poor old cheeks, but it all seems so very long ago, and no one comes to talk with him about it, and refresh his memory, especially since he has not been able to get out to see his old neighbour, Granny Hunt, who lives a stone's throw adown the hill.

Granny is aged ninety-six; she would shame many a one at sixty. Her cottage door was wide open in the afternoon; she was busy scouring her candlesticks. 'I doos this every day o' mi life,' she declares. 'The candles as e gets nowadays tha do guttur so. 'Tis nothin so good as it used to be.' She is tallish and stoutish, stooping a little, though not much, with fine features, face deeply wrinkled, but with fresh, ruddy cheeks, robust and healthy looking; if outward indications are at all trustworthy, she should easily complete her centenary. Her cottage is small, consisting of one tiny room and a pantry downstairs, and two small bedrooms above. The walls are pasted over with illustrated papers of sixty and seventy years ago, which give an antiquated air to the interior. Here and there are photographs of soldier and sailor sons, taken when the art was in its infancy, and one or two fine old coloured engravings. In her young days Granny did spinning and weaving, and also straw-plaiting, which were regular industries in the village; every cottage had a loom or a wheel in those days, which enabled the poor folks to obtain a livelihood.

'Have you lived in the cottage long, Granny?' I asked.

'Lived yer, yes. Never lived nowhere else, as e knows on,' she answered. Then she went on to talk about her father who was carter, her husband who was carter, and her son who was carter, of feasting and revelling, back-swording and leg-kicking, working for a penny a day in the fields, whipping-stocks, windmills, watermills, and other old-fashioned paraphernalia, until I felt to be whirled back a whole century, and to be lost to the present time altogether. By-and-by I found time to question her again.

'Do you enjoy good health, Granny?'

'Good 'ealth? Lar bless tha, no. E caant' walk no distance wi'out a stick, that e caant.'

'But have you never had any severe illness?' I ventured.

'Ye-es, severe illness, ye-es; but nothin' saarious, awhever,' she answered. 'My 'usband, look, 'e drapped down dead at the table yer, one Sunday a dinner-time. I was just gone into the panterny, an' the vittals was on the table, an' I yerd a naise, an I sed: "Lar, Willum, whatever be at? You bin an' knocked the leaff o' the table down;" but a niver answered ma, an' there a was, crooched up dead, jest wher you be now, look.'

Hereupon Granny, aged 96, began to apologize for the small fire, and then she piled on the lumps of coal, picking them up with her fingers, while I blew the fire with the bellows, and brought it to a flame. Presently I fished out a small coin and a package for Granny, which raised her up to the seventh heaven. 'Lark a massy! Why, 'tis a sixpunce, yun it? Is 'e fer I now? Lar now, dwun e distrust yerself. You be the best friend I sid for many a day.'

'I've got something else besides,' I said, rummaging forth a second package from underneath my coat, and undoing it. 'Do you know what this is, Granny?'

'Why, 'tis holly! No, chunt. 'Tis mistletoe, to be sure 'tis. Jes' thenk o' that now. 'Tis Christmas to-morrow, yun it?' she exclaimed.

So I held the mistletoe over Granny's head and kissed her cheek once or twice, and she kissed mine, and insisted on getting me a cup of hot milk, after drinking which I went outside and ran straight into the old shepherd, who had just come from his sheep upon the downs, and was going home to tea.

Abraham Ashton is a witty old fellow of seventy-five years, whose whole life has been spent with the sheep about the downs between Wroughton and Andover. He is of moderate height, with merry, sparkling eyes, a prominent nose, ruddy, healthy cheeks, clean-shaven face, a fringe of beard under the chin, and billycock hat on the head. He wore a thick sack, fastened with a buttonhook in front, around his shoulders, another tied round his waist, and carried a third, containing a heavy load, at his back. On seeing me he plumped this down by the roadside, and put on a broad smile.

'I got summat yer to show e, look; summat as you never seed afore,' he began, as he fumbled at the sack on the ground, and presently brought to view a monster turnip, certainly the biggest I had seen, and which he handled with great pride. Then he went on:

'Yelleky, look! Did e ever zee arn like that afore? No, that you never did. What d'e think a 'e, then? An' as sound as a bell right droo, look!' Here he flicked it with his thumb to prove its solidity. 'Tha hallus ses as ya caant grow turmuts in a garden, tha do, but this un was growed in one. The howl' carter jest gin in to I. This is one o' the 'Amshur turmuts, ya know, one o' thaay as the owl' yeow nibbles out an' then draps a lamb aside on it, an the lamb crapes into 'n fer shelter. Tha never wants no shelters up ther aside the turmut uds. Tha gets ship as beg as donkeys, yelleky. I got some an 'em up a top ther, now, look.'

'And how do you manage that, shepherd?' I inquired.

'Feeds 'em, mun; feeds 'em. Gies 'em some grub for ther bellies, tha's the oni way to do't. But tha wants a lot o' lookin' aater, else ya'd soon lose one haaf an 'em. Tha sucides therselves, ya know.'

'Sheep commit suicide? But how?' I asked.

'Why, tha gorges therselves to death, an' lays an' rowls over an to their backs, an' does all sarts o' comical thengs,' he continued. 'Tha be jest like ladies an' gennulmen gwain to a beg dinner, or like little childern at a taa-party; tha yets an' yets, an' stuffs therselves up till tha caan' do nothin', an' ther tha be, blowed out like barrels. Tha dwun' know when tha've 'ed enuf, de zee.'

Here I offered the shepherd a smoke, but he refused it. 'No thenkee. God bless tha, never smawked in mi life. 'Tis oni a 'abit, the same as drenkin' an' swerin'.'

Then he proceeded to talk of the fold again:

'Sometimes us haes 1,000 yeos, an thaay'll gie us 1,200 lambs, 200 per an moore, but chent all plaain saailin' wi' um. Back in '79 purty nigh every ship an thase downs died, aa, an' hers an' rabbuts, too. Tha 'ed the flooks, tha's summat in the liver, 'an ther was no stoppin' on't. I wur down Amesbury way, then. Tha's wher tha feels fur daylight. Tha never haes nar a clock upstairs, yelleky, but tha jest puts ther 'and out a winder, and feels for daylight, then tha knows 'tis time to get up in the marnin'. But yer's owl' Saayer John a-comin, thees better go along o' 'e, an see what tha cast make on in, for 'e's too dry fer we chaps. Dost yer what I be a-tellin' on in, John?'

'Aw, aa. I can yer, mun; but I knowed what thy oondermentin' was afoore to-day,' he replies.

Sawyer John is a slight-made man, pleasant and witty, full of cheerful gossip, and of varied experience. He is dressed in a corduroy suit, with billy-cock hat, and wears a white kerchief, tied in a bow, and with the ends artfully arranged, around the neck, which gives him a swagger appearance. His old head is frosty white; his eyes are nearly closed with continual smiling; the cares of life sit lightly on his shoulders.

'I looked for you at the Fox and Hounds, but your corner was empty,' I said.

'Aw did e, now! Was any o' the bwoys up ther?' he replied.

'About half a dozen, all telling yarns of foxes, one against the other,' I answered.

'Aa, thaay owl' foxes! Us used to hae some games wi' thaay, ketchin' 'em in the pits, and sendin' em into Wales for the huntin'. 'Eve seed the owl' gamester?'

'Why, you are all old gamesters. Which do you mean?' I replied.

'Aw, Fightin' Jack, o' Broad 'Inton.'

'That's Theobald, isn't it?' I said.

'Tha's 'im,' he continued. 'Mi lard was ridin' acrass 'is bit o' land one daay, an' up comes the owl' chap an shouts: "Wher b'e gwain to yer, then?" So mi lard pops us 'is dooks, an ses: "Dost thee want a bit o' this?" "Aa, get off that 'oss, an thee cast hae as much ant as thees wants, an' a bit moore, too," t'other said, but mi lard chocked un down aaf a suverin' an telled un to come round tomarra, a was too busy to stop then.'

The business of hand-sawyering, like every other trade of the countryside, has almost ceased to be now. The steam saw has crept into favour everywhere. All those with big estates, and very many of the farmers, too, keep a set of the tackle. The old pits have fallen in, or have been filled in, and are seldom met with. The occupation of a sawyer is distinct from that of a woodman. The woodman merely fells the timber, and trims it; the other cuts it up ready for use. The sawyers are very clever at their work, and are capable of many creditable feats. All kinds of uses, and even door-panels, were cut with perfect accuracy, over the pit, though no one would pretend that the process was cheaper or better than the modern method. Years ago the sawyer and his wife used to leave home, during the summer and harvest, and roam all over the downs, at mowing and reaping, and return again in the fall, but that has long since come to an end, there is no work to be had now, outside the ordinary everyday duties on the farms.

King's Mill, the fifth on the stream, is about five minutes' walk from Sawyer John's cottage. The old building is of three stories, and is much dilapidated. The huge water-wheel is within, enclosed in a kind of closet, like a dungeon.

The old mill carter is still living, in a cottage on the hill-side, tended by his son and daughter, and surrounded by a merry troop of grand-children. He is of moderate stature, stiffly built, with shortish nose, clean-shaven face, and robust complexion.

'Ah! I've hed some thousands o' sacks o' flour an my owl' back, all an 'em two 'underd an' a quarter,' he tells you. 'Us used to carr' 'em up the steps as ef tha was bags o' wool; us was as 'ardy as ground twuds in them times. The men grows taller an' begger, nowadays, but they byent so strong by a purty deal, an' us didn't hae none too much to eat, neether. I've bin from one Christmas to another wiout tastin' a bit o' bif. Us used to cut off a slish o' bacon an aat it raw, wi' a bit o' bread, as sweet as a nut. We carried flour into Wales when 'twas five pounds a bag, an' hed the owl' mill 'ouse stocked wi' whate from top to bottom, an' piled up in the yard covered wi' tarpaulins, an' dree or vower teamms a-waitin' to come in, an' no room to turn round. Ther was 'leven on us implied, besides millwrights, carpenters, blacksmiths, an' odd men an' wimmen for sortin' the bones for grindin' into manure. These went through a special cylinder, an' come out a'most like flour. We ground they sixty years ago an' moore.'

The carter had had many experiences on the road, when the countryside was infested with thieves, who waylaid the waggons, and stole what they could from the vehicles. At one spot, going for Salisbury, where trees overhung the road, the thieves used to fasten hooks to the branches, and when the waggons passed underneath, these caught in the bags and took them off the load. Corn was also conveyed loose in barges along the canal, and the boatmen, by a crafty device, used regularly to steal it. The plan was to stand small sticks amongst the corn and trickle water down them, which caused the grain to swell. When they came to their destination the corn was measured out; all that remained belonged to the boatmen.

At Wroughton, the majority of the cottages, underneath the hill, are very old, made of chalk or stone, with thatched roofs, and whitewashed on the outside. Here dwell the farm labourers, the agricultural part of the population; nearly all those who are engaged at the neighbouring town live lower down, in houses of brick and tile. These are really not villagers at all, since they merely come home to sleep, and spend the week-end; there is a great difference between them and the agricultural folk proper. One would imagine that work in the town, and at the factory, with a crowd, would make the men more keen, intelligent, and interesting, but that is far from being the actual case; as a matter of fact, though occupying a slightly higher level as regards work and wages, they do not posses as many individual features and outstanding characteristics as do the true rustic labourers; they have lost all charm and picturesqueness of habit and language.

It is pleasing to meet with the oxen at plough and harrow about the farm, or attached to the cart and waggon, gathering up the hay in the meadow, or the sheaves in the cornfield. The sight of the ox-teams, yoked in pairs, trudging slowly and peacefully along in the furrows, is always a delight, bringing back to mind days of long ago, and old-world customs, centuries before the steam-engine, and when horses were of greater value, comparatively, and were required for more exalted, though not more honourable toils, than that of ploughing the land. Oxen are cheaper than horses for work on the land; they eat rougher food, and are hardier into the bargain, and when they have worked for a few years they may be fatted and sold in the market at a good figure.

Richard Ashton, the ox-carter, dwells in a lonely cottage by the roadside over the downs towards Hakpen; the stables and yards for the oxen are situated in a field a short distance away. The carter is medium in height, stooping a little, with head thrown forward, fair-sized belly, jovial face, laughing eyes, and ruddy cheeks, a picture of health, a very good type of the rural labourer, his slight physical deformity notwithstanding. As a young man he served with the colours, and he is still included in the list of the National Reserve, and caused great amusement at a recent assembling and review of its members locally, when, in the presence of a huge crowd, he marched past with the rest, carrying in his hand a stock of rations, with which he had provisioned himself for the day, ingenuously tied up in a big red dinner-kerchief.

It was evening when I came to the cottage. I found the carter, with his wife and three sturdy children, busily engaged partaking of a hearty and substantial hot meal: meat and soup, with suety dumplings, cabbage, potatoes, and

Ploughing with oxen at Bromsgrove Farm, Wootton Rivers

tender, juicy turnips. A monster blue enamelled teapot was set on the hob, and the kettle was steaming away over the fire. The carter's head was leaned well over the table, and his elbows were sprawled out. He was busy with a second helping of the food, and could not tarry yet awhile; the young people quickly finished their meal and prepared to play a game of rings on a board in one corner of the room.

The carter is very proud of his oxen, and views the animals with real affection, and tends them with jealous care. He is acquainted with their needs and ailments, is able to discriminate between good, bad, and indifferent beasts, to train them to the toil, and make them useful and docile, understands the proper period of their usefulness, and when they should be superseded, and will not have them ill-used on any account. Their horns are tipped with small brass caps, like balls, to prevent them from goring each other, and no prodding or 'fooling' with the beasts, by the lads or undercarters, is ever allowed.

The oxen perform all the various duties to which the ordinary farm horse is liable; such as plough, harrow, drill, hay and corn-cart, turnip-hauling, conveying the manure from the yards, and machine-hoeing. Little Betsy Horton, the quaint old woman who dwelled in the village below in the valley, used to lead the old farm bull in the cart, and attached to the implements, and amused the neighbours with the oddness of her remarks. 'What 'ev e bin at to-day, Betsy?' this one inquired, with a smile.

'Aw bin up yander in the lower ground, a 'oss 'owin' wi' tha bool,' she replied.

The ox-carter's day is not a very exacting one. In the summer the teams go out at 7 a.m., and finish at 3.30 p.m., and in the winter the hours are from 7.30 till 3, with an hour for dinner. In the winter, when the oxen lie in, they have to be foddered, which makes extra work, but oxen feed much more quickly than do horses: they are not long in filling their bellies with sweet hay, or nourishing oat straw. When the sowing is in progress the carter helps with that, and receives extra money, and all overtime is paid for. His ordinary wages are 14s. a week, with a large new cottage, and a quarter of an acre of land. 'If I was in the townd I should ef to pay six shillin' for mi 'ouse, an no garden, an' work a good many more hours, too; so I be a main bit better off yer wher I be,' he says.

Near the little village of Hodson, in a small opening of the fir plantation, and almost shut out of view, is the gamekeeper's cottage, immortalized in Richard Jefferies' 'The Gamekeeper at Home.'

Benny Haylock, the old gamekeeper, and the subject of Jefferies' pages, was a most eccentric person. He would not allow people in the woods under

Chiseldon Church

The Gamekeeper's Cottage, Hodson
Both illustrations are from drawings by H.E. Tidmarsh

any pretext whatever, but ordered them all unceremoniously away, frightening the timid with his gruff voice and threatening language and behaviour. It would not have done for him to have whole troops of young people coming to gather primrose and violet, anemone and hyacinth, and wandering about the woods at their pleasure, as they do at this time; he would have stormed and raged like a lion. He would not allow even the lady of the House to walk in the woods when the young birds were hatched, but would roughly order her outside, as though she had been an utter stranger, and a suspicious character. One day, when the woodman and his mates were removing some timber from a plantation, the squire came on the scene followed by a small house-dog. 'Now, you fellows,' said he, 'make haste and get out of here before Haylock comes, or you'll be in the wrong.'

'Aa, an' so ull you, too, sir, if 'e do ketch ee wi' that ther dog,' the woodman replied.

Immediately afterwards Haylock came up. Standing stock-still, and looking at the squire's dog with great displeasure, he addressed the master: 'What have you got there along with you? Take the thing out o' the 'ood this minute. I ull not have it in yer, an' you knows it. I ull not have the birds worritted with the damn thing. If you can't come into the 'ood without 'im, stop out altogether yourself.' After this he turned and hurried off, crashing noisily amid the dried steams of the bracken, and muttering loudly to himself

The old fellow wore the top hat everywhere about the woods, and, notwithstanding his rudeness and bluntness, was a sterling example of his profession: 'a faithful protection to all kinds of property,' as Jefferies styled him. The villagers still remember how he slew all their cats and made a carriage rug from their pelts; they never forgave him for that, though it was done in the interests of the game in the woods. He never partook of but two meals a day – breakfast and supper – and seldom came home, after leaving the cottage, till the evening, weekdays and Sundays the same. As he walked about the woods he ate Indian corn, a quantity of which he always carried in his pocket. When the young gentlemen visitors were out shooting, they had to abide by his instructions, and if they failed to bring down the game, he made scathing comments on their marksmanship, and ground his teeth at them, and told them they could not hit a hayrick, nor a barn-door.

The old keeper was not destitute of wit, and amused them all, sometimes, with quaint tales and exaggerations. One day he came into the gardens, with face aglow, eager to tell them a precious bit of information.

'I've seen this mornin' what I never seen before,' he began. 'I allus know'd hedgehogs was fond of eggs, but I never know'd 'em to cart 'em off a dozen at a time afore. What do you think I've jest bin an' seen? I warn you wunt believe it, but I stood an' seen it wi' my own eyesight. I seen the hedgehog come along to the pheasant's nest, as ad 'leven eggs in 'im, an' I thought I'd jest see what a *'ood* do; so I stood up, quiet like, an' never made a sound. When the hedgehog come to the nest a smelled all round 'im, as if a was countin' the eggs, then presently a took one in 'is mouth, then rolled over on 'is back into the nest, picked up all the eggs on 'is bristles, an' off a went as 'ard as a was able, and left I thunderstruck. I never seen sich a thing afore, no, that I never did.'

Tommy Weston, aged eighty-five, who was ploughboy, sheepboy, carter, and bailiff by turns, dwells in a small cottage in the middle of the village of Hodson, with his wife and maiden daughter, who is a keeper of pigs, and haulier for the village, going regularly to the railway-station for coal, and delivering parcels on the way. Tommy is tall and erect in stature, finely built, square and boney, with a pleasant face, smiling mischievous eyes, and high, arched eyebrows, a fresh ruddy complexion, well-seasoned with the down air, and stiff, bristly grey hair, standing straight up from the forehead, which gives him a quaint appearance, and which is yet perfectly in keeping with his general features. His clothes, scrupulously clean, are of corduroy, and he wears a small thin kerchief wound twice about the neck, and tied in a cunning little knot, a fashion dear to the old type of labourer, but which is passing away now. Both husband and wife are hard of hearing.

''Tis a great denial to have 'em both deaf. It do wear I out so to make 'em understand,' the daughter exclaimed. Then she addressed her father, in a shrill voice, shouting in his ear: 'Faather, 'e wants you to tell 'e about the owld times.'

'What owld times?' he inquired, with a merry twinkle in his eye.

'Why, the *howwld* times, as used to be, when you turned the windmeel, an' done the grinndin'.'

'I don' know nothin' about no owld times; I furgets it,' he replied.

'Thelleky! tha's what 'e allus ses,' the daughter exclaimed disappointedly.

'Never mind, let me try,' I answered. Then, tugging hard at the collar of his coat, and pulling his ear towards my mouth, I began: 'You're the finest man in Hodson.'

'Whuh?' replied he.

'You're the finest man in Hodson,' I repeated. 'If you don't take care the recruiting sergeant will have you, yet.'

'Ha! ha! ha! He's too late bi seventy year. He ought to a come afore. Them owld times wasn't much good to nob'dy. All as thaay troubled about was manhood, an' scawtin' about.'

'Manhood?' said I, puzzled, for the moment as to his meaning.

'Tha's it,' he repeated; 'manhood an' strength. Tha didn't trouble about much else. All tha could think on was 'ittin' one another about; an' the rougher tha got trated the better thaay liked it. I've sin 'em grip one another, an' the blood runnin' out in strames atween ther fengers, all down ther bodies, an' thaay was jest landed then. Jimmy Whorl, the carter, had a hand as beg agyen as mine. He was out in the ground one day wi' 'is teamm o' fower 'osses, an' a wanted 'em to 'come hither,' an' cause tha hoodn't do what he telled 'em, he went up to 'em, an' hit 'em ahind the yer wi' his fist, an' knocked 'em down, all fower on 'em, one aater t'other, flat on the gorund; an' that's as true as I sets in this cheer. An' he was killed 'isself in the end, fightin' wi' another fella.'

'Good heavens! Then what was *he* like?' I exclaimed.

'A fine strappin' chap as ever you seed, he was, I warn,' he went on. 'That was on Burderop racecourse. When tha brought owld Jimmy whum, his brother went to look at un, an' aater a seed the marks, a said:

' "Tha be good marks, tha be, all fair an' squer, an' honourable gied; an' ef the chap as done't were afront an ma now, be daal'd ef I oodn't ev a packet at un miself too." A wanted to 'ev a dab at un, simly.'

It is furthermore said of Jimmy Whorl, the carter, that one day, when a harrow was wanted for use away over the downs, there being no horse and cart available to convey it up, he went into the farmyard, clapped it on his back, and carried it up to the field, two miles away. The harrow was an iron one, in three sections, and weighed something over two hundredweight.

Hereupon the daughter interposed with: 'Will you 'ev some elderberry wine, or be you a tee-tot'ler?'

'I should like some, if you please,' I said. So she fetched out a small jug of the wine, and warmed it over the fire, as is usual with this kind of drink, and reached down a tin of biscuits from between a set of ancient brass candlesticks standing on the mantelpiece, and granny gently and shyly pushed a big orange into my hand, while Tommy sat smiling, and thrumming on the table with his fingers.

The Elm-Tree Inn stands in the centre of Chiseldon village, near the railway, and close to a clump of elms, from which the house derived its name. Before the railway was made there was a broad space, called the Square, before the inn; when a way had to be made for the panting iron horse, with hoofs of thunder, and sinews of steel, the old village meeting-place had to be cut into; the swarm of brawny toilers with pick and shovel attacked it below, and cleaved a passage through the deep chalk up to the open downs above.

Here it was that the feasts and revels were held, with the inevitable back-swording, wrestling, and other games so dear to the older generations of people. Challenges had been issued all round the neighbourhood for wrestlers and single-stick players, stages were erected in the square; there stood the challengers crying out: 'Will any young gamester come upon the platform?' The inn had been decorated, without and within, for the occasion; and a mighty bundle of top-hats – fifteen or twenty, trimmed with coloured ribands, and all bound together – was hung out from the signboard.

Formerly the Elm-Tree Inn was a picturesque thatched house, but now it has been rebuilt and modernized; stone, wood, and straw have given place to brick, tile, and concrete, and the interior has been made to match with the outside. The old style of seat and furniture has gone with the walls; pewter pots have given place to glass mugs; landlord and all have been metamorphosed. The nearness of the railway has been responsible for the transformation of things at the inn; where there is continual contact and intercourse with towns-people the atmosphere of the village inn is bound to be changed. Here, now, in the winter evenings, instead of the village gossip of ploughing, threshing, reaping, revelling, and the rest, the talk is chiefly of the town: not half as manly and interesting as the hearty speech and ready wit of the independent crowd shouting to the landlord for better beer, and singing snatches of song, some of them well worth remembering, such as this of the old carter's, rarely tender, and suggestive of a beautiful story:

'We never speak as we pass by,
Although a tear bedims her eye;
I know she thinks of our past life,
When we were loving man and wife . . .'

On the opposite side of the road from the inn stands a small foundry, with yards packed full of all kinds of agricultural machinery and implements, of various degrees of usefulness, some falling all to pieces and entirely dilapidated, some stable in parts, and some only slightly defective, awaiting repairs, then to return to the field or farmyard. Here are sets of steam-ploughing tackle, with the huge engines and cultivators, horse-ploughs, reapers and binders, threshing-machines, drills, harrows, horse-rakes, elevators, farm-waggons, and other paraphernalia of the countryside.

Little by little, the old machinery – that which cannot be repaired – is broken up, and the parts utilized for something or other – everything comes in once in seven years, the foundry foreman says – the castings go back into the furnace and are re-melted, the wrought-iron is returned to the smith, who works it up into other shapes, and fits it for new uses, and all that is unfit for local purposes is sold away for ship's ballast, to keep the keel steady against the heaving, rolling waters and buffeting tempest.

The village foundry has existed for nearly two centuries, and, though it is only a small place, it has sufficed for the immediate needs of the neighbourhood. It is chiefly repairs that are executed, and not new machinery made, though there are a few new implements constructed, and especially heavy farm waggons and carriages. Nearly every village of any importance had its foundry till a few years ago, and though the number has diminished, there are still many to be met with here and there: there are no less than seven or eight within a radius of twelve miles of the village.

The foundry staff proper includes the working manager – a fine type of the village engineer, tall and square, with ruddy cheeks, bluff and hearty, and clever at his trade, having a practical knowledge of everything connected with his work, in strong contradistinction to the ordinary railway works official, who is crammed full of theory, and lamentably weak in practice, relying on the draughtsmen and mechanics for everything – two smiths, a boilermaker, three fitters and turners, a moulder, and three or four carpenters and waggon-builders. These occupy a small group of buildings connected together, and are able to see each other at work, to communicate with, and consult one another on various points, and to work co-operatively, which is impossible in the big factories of the towns. Here the moulder steps in to see his casting being bored in the lathe, viewing it with real pride, or the turner goes out into the casting-shed, and takes the part in his hand, while the moulder views it fondly, and feels it over and over, bright and smooth with the tools, with an eager inquiry: 'How is a? Is a aw right? How do a cut? Nice an' soft, yen a? A wasn't burned. You can kip the metal gentle and mild, or you can burn't up an' make it as brittle as glass. Tha's the caster's lookout.'

Here also the smiths and turners work side by side, or the fitter and turner goes to the forge, lights it up himself, makes his own tools and uses, and is clever in many ways; there is no jealousy, for that is a natural condition of things at the village works.

The casting shed is a small stone-built place, long and narrow and ancient-looking; its walls are cracked with the great heat, and appear half ready to topple down. The floor is of sand, black with continual use in the frames, and there is a heap of it just inside the door, waiting to be made up again; it is used many times over for the moulds. The moulder is highly intelligent and very talkative. He lays particular stress on the value to be got from an experience of village foundries, where the workman is required to have a knowledge of many things. 'I worked in them big works five year, an' I can tell you, mister, you learns more outside at these small places in one twelvemonth than you would ther in a lifetime. An' why? Cos they wunt let e learn nothin'! Ther's sheens for this, an' sheens for that; everything's cut an' dried, an' ther you be, slavin' like a nigger all yer time, at the same owl' job, an' a girt fool at the end on't; an' if you got to move out anywher' else, you be no good at all; you don' know nothin'.'

It is a well-known fact that the choicest smiths are usually those who have had their forge in the villages. It was said of honest Mark Fell, at the railway works, that 'he could make anything you like, from a shut-link to a steam-engine,' and he was only a village blacksmith in the beginning.

The old schoolmaster dwells a short way from the foundry, in a modern cottage, surrounded with piles of books and fusty-looking papers and documents, belonging to an age long past, before the present manner of teaching came in vogue. He is tall and grey, cautious in manner, and not disposed to talk much of his school career. 'I am going to have a big bonfire very soon,' said he, pointing to the books on the shelves.

I suggested he should give them away to someone or other.

'Give them! You coldn't give them to anyone,' he replied. 'Who wants books nowadays? I've offered to give them away, time after time, but nobody would have them. They're no good now. Everything is changed in the educational line. They don't do any plodding now. It's all education made easy. They go the short way at it. There was no near cut across the fields in my time, and you were only paid on your successes; so that if you did not do your work thoroughly you lost your allowance; but now they get their salary whether they do good work or not.'

The schoolmaster remembers when the ballad-singers went from village to village, singing their rhymes; he had helped to train them when he was a young man. These strolling minstrels frequented all the feasts, fairs, and revels along the downside, and gave an exhibition of their skill. They carried bundles of ballad-sheets with them, and sold them to the rustics at one penny each. The old carter of Woolstone, a few miles into Berkshire, declares that hundreds of these sheets were disposed of at a single fair time. The number of singers varied; there might be four, or no more than two. Very often it was a man and his wife and they sang alternately, in response to each other. The ballads were some grave, some sentimental, and others comic or satirical. The old carter could only remember two lines of a satirical piece, dealing with the eternal question of authority in the home. After a proposition, relating to home rule, had been set forth by the female singer, the man responded:

'I do decline, and you shall find *I* will the breeches wear,'

the answer to which was:

'Oh, no, not I! for I will die, but I will have my share.'

Though the subject-matter of this fragment is crude enough, there can be no doubt but that there was some good material circulated in this manner. One can readily understand, from this, how it was that the countryside was vocal in the old days, since every cottage contained sheets of the ballads, the airs of which had been taught the people by the singers at the feasts; they could not fail to make a deep impression on the villagers.

11

BADBURY, LIDDINGTON AND WANBOROUGH

Badbury Plough Inn stands some little distance from Badbury village, high upon the roadside, where the main way comes up from the valley to pass over the tops of the downs. The sign-board, hanging over the doorway, is characteristic of the place. Here is depicted a team at plough, and underneath is a rude rhyme, which runs as follows:

'In hope we plough, in hope we sow,
In hopes we all are led,
& I am here to sell good beer
In hopes to get my bread.'

As to the games and sports, and 'goings on' at the old inn, it is impossible to know all that. 'Nobody knows what *hev* bin carred on ther, afore now; summat o' everything, you med depend upon't,' the old carter declares, with a sage wag of the head, and in a voice little above a whisper. Back-swording, wrestling, and prize-fighting were of the most ordinary occurrence, and bull-fighting too, according to one account. This last sport took place in a small field at the end of the hollow; it is a further proof of the hardihood of the old-time rustics, and their love of fierce plays and games.

The ancient Britons revelled in cock-fighting, so it is no wonder it was indulged in throughout all the villages here so enthusiastically till half a century ago. The old road-mender has told me of the cock-fighting as he sat grinning in the chair, gripping his ground-ash stick tightly with both hands and leaning hard upon it, looking at me with his grey head a little on one side and his eyes brimful of mischief.

'S'pose thees yerd tell o'tha cock-fightin'?'

'I've heard you old folks speak of it, before now.'

'Thees't a laaf't if thees't a bin ther, I can tell tha.'

'What do you know about it?'

'Bin at it miself, mun, many a time.'

'You been a cock-fighting!'

'Ha-a!'

'Tell me about it.'

'Ust to brade 'em a purpose, dost know. Ther was two or dree sarts an 'em. Ust to gie 'em port wine; veed 'em wi port-wine sops. My hi! that made 'em upstrapalous. Couldn' owld 'em, you. Never let 'em zeed one another, thas know'st. Ust to cut ther spers off when tha was little, and clip ther wings. Didn' thaay croww! Ther ust to be reg'ler clubs fer cock-fightin' all round, mun — Stratton, an' Wanborough, an' Bushipstone. Ust to challenge one another, an' put tha money down – vive pown' a side, an' sometimes moore. Someb'dy watched fer tha cunstable, an' at it we ust to go, mi lads.'

'Used to have a ring, I suppose.'

'Aw aa, a cooass; us ed a reng. Then ther was tha two 'owlders. Tha ust to stan' in tha reng, one aache side, an' 'owlde tha cocks. Didn' thaay struggle! Tha 'ed tha piccid steel spers strapped an ther vit, dost know. Bymby tha lets loose an 'em. Off thaay goes, mi lads, straight at one another, an' the feathers did flee. Sometimes tha killed one another the fust go; tha 'ed to kip an till one an 'em was done for. I calls to mind one day, when tha was at it, one cock fled at t'other an' bowled un awver flat on 'is back, an' ther a led, kickin' 'is death-kick. As soon as a fell down, mun, up jumped tothern a top an in, an' begun a shoutin' "Er-er-er-er-err-r" as proud as a paacock. But 'e was a bit afoore 'is time. While a was a-crowin' ther, bagger if tother didn't kick 'is sper right droo ees 'ed, an' 'ee died fust aater all. An' it didn' allus end wi cock-fightin' neither, you. Us often 'ed to pick em up an' run awaay wi tothers aater us. Tha ust to saay: 'We byet e a cock-fightin', an' now ya got to 'ev summat else;' an' at it tha went, else tha cut off as hard as tha was able. There was some gwains on at that time, thee medst depend upon't.'

The hollow in which the mill formerly stood is called Badbury Bottom. Jonas Goddard, the eighty-year-old carter, lives with his son and daughter-in-law in a small cottage facing the houses in the Bottom. Passing round the corner of the house I discovered the old carter busy with pick and shovel digging a mighty pit. He was short in stature, sturdily built, and a little corpulent. His features were strong and square, hair grey, short grey beard, pleasant mouth, and merry sparkling eyes. His trousers, much too small around the waist, were drawn together and held with a bootlace; he wore a corduroy jacket, and a waistcoat of the same material, with big brass buttons, each stamped with the head of an animal: a dog, a fox, a horse, a bull, a camel, and a dromedary; a small billycock hat was perched upon his head. He was born at Winterbourne Basset, and came of the old stock. His grandparents had a family of eighteen, he was one of twelve, and his own children numbered half a score.

'You had ten children!' I exclaimed.

'My wife 'ed,' he answered quickly.

'And brought them all up?' I continued.

'Hoo, aa,' replied he, 'an' oni 'ed seven shillin' a wik to do't wi'. I bin pitchin' whate for a whole wik, an 'ed nothin to ate but bread an' a i-nen, an' never 'ed a day's illness in mi life. But I couldn't get on wi' the barley dampers. What we liked was whum-made loaves wi' the clungy vains,' (veins of glutinous matter). 'The chuldern oodn't ate it nowadays, tha be pimpered up so, but put 'em an tha land, an' tha'd ate anytheng then. Tha gets this schoolin' an' tha wunt work; you caan't get a civul answer vram 'em.'

The carter is possessed of an indomitable spirit, and was a member of the Agricultural Union as long as that existed in these parts. He went to a farmer one day, and asked him for a job.

'Be you a Union man?' the farmer inquired.

'Yes, I be, gaffer, an' a stiff un, too.'

'Don' want you, then,' the farmer retorted,

'Then you can do wi'out ma; but I shan't channge fer nobody. You can get another fella.'

'Yer, wait a bit, I'll gie tha a trial,' the farmer said, and engaged him straightaway, and proved a good master.

Nearly all the farmers on the downs settled up with the men once a year at that time. Whatever the men required for present use they let them have, and paid the balance in a lump after harvest; the men liked this method very well, because they were sure of a good sum in the autumn. If the man had overdrawn, the farmer allowed him to do some piece-work in the summer and harvest, and squared up in that way; very often it was only a matter of form, to give the man an opportunity of getting clear. The farmers gave the workpeople much food, and often killed fat sheep and sold the mutton to them at 4d. a pound. They also let the men have a sack of wheat at a cheap rate, when they wanted it, and allowed them to pay at their leisure, settling up annually. For fuel, the farmers gave the men the bean stubbles in the fields. The corn was cut off so as to leave a long stubble; this the women pulled up, and the farmers drew it home for the men, and stacked it in ricks. Now the bean stubble is ploughed in so as to keep the ground hollow. All the villagers turned out to help at wheat harvest. Sometimes the reapers had £1 an acre for cutting, and the average savings of a family during harvest was £9, according to the account of old Jonas.

'Dabber' Cox, the chief cowman, corroborated the carter's statements about earnings, but, pressed for a considered opinion, he thought that a man who would stick well to work is a little better off, though not much, now. He sat at the table and devoured a monster tea of bread and meat, looking exceedingly well satisfied. The cowman resembles a Grand Vizier in appearance. He is yellowish in complexion, with long nose, bushy eyebrows, broadish mouth, and thick black hair and beard, which was full of chaff and hay, where he had been carrying the trusses.

'I wonder the dog 'adn't a vlod out at e. 'E's main shanky, 'e is,' he exclaimed.

The cowman is descended from a distinguished local family. His grandfather, who was head carter, went to work regularly till he was eighty-four, and then was kicked in the head and killed by a young colt which he was 'breaking in' in the field. His father was carter, too, and a famous backsworder. He turned professional, and traversed the whole southern part of the island from Devon to London, and beat all the champions, including the famed men of Somersetshire.

'Nobody couldn't vetch blood out o' 'e. 'E was byet 'ard, 'e was; 'is owl 'ed was as 'ard as iron,' the cowman says. This sturdy Wiltshireman, after conquering everyone at home, afterwards went out to Greece and played there, but was killed there in the end.

The head cowman's position is one of responsibility, and the wages are higher than usual for the post; he received £1 a week and his cottage, and, in addition to this, '1s. for every caaf as drapped alive an the land.' The fogger retains a few of the old superstitious beliefs. He declares a farm cannot carry one-hundred cows, it must be either ninety-nine, or one-hundred-and-one; 'if you tries to kip jest a 'underd you'll be sure to lose one an em, bi vallin' in the ditch, er caavin' down, er zummat,' he says. He furthermore believes that a black calf is a sign of ill luck to the herd; until recently it was the custom to kill it, if one should be born.

Henry Brunsden, of Coate, the broken-down farmer, nearly ninety years of age, who nursed the infant Richard Jefferies, and gave him the freedom of his occupation, to shoot, fish, and otherwise amuse himself in his boyhood days, was ruined by a big milk swindle. A London firm contracted with him for 260 barn gallons of milk a day, and when he had become deeply indebted to all the farmers round about, whose supplies he took, he was suddenly made aware that the firm was a bogus one, and that he was a ruined man. His long hair and thin beard are snow white; his face seems to be all smiles, his head shakes slightly as the result of his great age, yet he is a veritable chatterbox. His sons laughingly tell him to 'stop it,' and 'shut up,' and tease him with this and that; he yields to their commands with an affectionate smile, and a gentle inclination of the head, but soon commences again in great glee, and faster than before. His memory is remarkable; he can quote poems and recite rhymes innumerable, and compose them himself, too; he commemorated his eighty-seventh birthday in one of these, while sitting in his arm-chair by the fireside.

'O'er Life's road, rough and uneven,
I have dragged to eighty-seven.
What have these years left for me?
Nothing but infirmity.
Sitting in my chair content,
Thinking of the years I've spent,
Of the future, and the past,
Wondering how long life will last,
Thanks I give for old and new,
And that's the most that I can do.'

The village of Liddington is situated about half a mile from the top of the hill, grouped upon a terrace adown the slope, and round about the head of a coomb. The cottages are very old, and nearly all chalk-made, and they seem to have been built, some here and some there, facing this way and that, in rows or pairs, or isolated, wthout regard to plan or design. Wherever a building was wanted, there it was made.

A good many villages have characteristics peculiar to themselves. Thus, the inhabitants of one place are noted for hard-headedness, of another for wittiness, bluntness, sturdy independence, soberness, noise, quiet, or political fervour, and the fighting spirit. By some means Liddington has obtained the reputation of being a 'newsy place,' so that the quality of inquisitiveness would seem to apply to the inhabitants there. It was said you could not pass through the village on foot without being accosted by someone or other requiring to know where you were bound for, and what your business might be. A friend of mine, recently, on being acquainted with the matter, refused to believe it, and made a wager that he would pass through the village unchallenged; but he lost the bet, for he had scarcely entered the street before someone – a total stranger – smilingly addressed him with a cheery: 'Hello! where be you off to this way, then?'

The inhabitants are spoken of collectively as 'The Liddington Pig-diggers.' This came about, in the beginning, through a remark let fall by a rustic about digging for a pig upon the hill-top, which was wrongly received by the hearer, and clownishly construed into meaning that he had actually been digging for a pig, in the same manner as the folks of another village were accredited with having raked after the moon. The true interpretation of the remark is something far different. It was an ancient privilege of the parishioners to go upon the downs flint-digging. This they did in spare time, and when other work was slack. The flints, when unearthed, were sold for road-making and repairing, and the money was very often used to buy a pig for the cottager's sty. Accordingly, it became the fashion, when one was about to go flint-digging, to say that he was going to dig for another pig; and so the story became current that pigs were dug out of the flint-beds upon the hill, and the villagers were branded with the title of 'Pig-diggers.'

It is well known that dialect survives longest in the villages, though it still remains in most of the provincial towns, too, where the population is consistent, and where there are not many factories. But besides dialect, with its many quaintnesses and local variations, such, for instance, as: 'Yella,' 'Yellacks,' 'Yellocks,' 'Yelleky,' 'Yilliky,' 'Thelliky,' and simple 'Lacks,' and 'Locks,' ('Here, look,' and 'There, look,') you often hear Elizabethan expressions made, too, such as, 'Gad,' 'Begad,' 'God's truth,' of 'This is God's truth,' or 'Code struth.'

The population of Liddington, in common with their neighbours, regularly indulged in the old sports, games and autumnal revels. The great event of the year was the feast, held at the inn, which continued for a week, and the opening of which was always marked by the cutting of an acorn pie, in continuation of an ancient custom, the signification of which is not known now. During the week the street was lined with stalls and booths for dancing and mirth; here Fiddler Jack played, for a penny a tune, and the children played at 'snuff-boxes,' and 'spandabs.'

Besides acorn pie, the villagers used occasionally to make a dish of 'pibble sup,' (pebble soup). At first thought it would seem to be a difficult matter to do this, but the cottagers say it is 'yezzi anuf, when you knows the waay.' First of all you obtain water, and boil it in the pot, adding a bit of bacon, several potatoes, a little salt, some celery, a cabbage, turnips, and ketchup, and afterwards drop in a small pebble, and well boil the whole, and you have the soup complete.

The poor people of the down-side still eat many herbs which would not appear palatable to dwellers in the town, but which, as a matter of fact, are both agreeable to the taste, and highly wholesome too. In this list are stinging-nettles – used also for tea – hop-tops, charlock, boiled rhubarb leaves, boiled lettuce, dandelion leaves and roots, sorrel, wild landcress, and succory. Potatoes were very cheap during the first half of the nineteenth century, when wages were low about the downs; they could easily be obtained at 2s. 6d. a sack. There was a special kind of potatoes common to North Wiltshire, called locally 'Yarth evvers' (earth heavers) by reason of their great productiveness.

North Wiltshire was always famed for its bacon; it was a chief part of the staple food, of farmers and labourers, too. The farmers, however, only ate the hams, gammons and chine, and the best of the pig-meat; they gave the inferior parts away to the labourers, together with the imperfect cheeses, and occasional presents of mutton. Both masters and men ate a good deal of the bacon raw, and especially when in the fields; but so great was the power of their digestive organs they seldom felt any inconvenience arising from it.

On the hills, and in the valley, too, down to recent times, the farmers, instead of paying Sunday wages for milking, used to give the men their breakfast and supper, of bread, meat and ale, and the amount of fat bacon consumed at such times is almost incredible. One morning, at a small farm where there were only three to sit down to breakfast, the farmer's wife had brought out a whole belly-piece, of six pounds, boiled, and set it on a large dish, and when the meal was finished there were about two pounds left. Hereupon the carter addressed his two mates:

''Eve you chaps finished?'

'Aa,' they replied.

'Don' e want no moore?'

'No,' they answered.

'Byen agwain to lave that mossel,' the other proceeded, and took it from the dish and ate the whole piece, without bread.

Immediately afterwards the farmer's wife looked in and roundly scolded them for not calling out for more meat.

'But we 'ed anuf, thenk e, missis,' one said.

'I never thinks you 'ed anuf when you cleared the dish,' replied she.

The road that passes through the village of Liddington up over the hills being a chief highway to London, it was frequented with much traffic, and especially in the early days, before the railways were made. Then the huge, heavy waggons, laden with burdens of produce for the far-off Metropolis – ordinarily drawn by eight horses, but requiring no less than thirteen to fetch them up the long steep hill – plied regularly up and down; the jingle of bells and crack of the carter's whip, with the rumble of the waggon wheels, were heard every day along the rough flint roads. The chief produce carried this way was flour, with other food-stuffs, such as beef, mutton, veal, bacon, butter, eggs, and cheese. Halfway up the hill, in an even space, stood large stables; here the horses were changed, and the carters rested, sometimes sleeping in their vehicles, and sometimes at the inn. After leaving the village they proceeded by way of Hungerford, Newbury, and Reading; it usually took them two days to reach London from Liddington, a distance of seventy-three miles. Considerable quantities of food were stolen from the waggon *en route*, by thieves and idlers, who regularly subsisted on what they could purloin from the vehicles, and the waggoners themselves used often to feed on the contents of the load, skilfully cutting off pieces of beef and bacon soon after the start; it is a common saying, about the countryside, that 'a slysh (slice) is not missed off a cut loaf.'

Young New, the aged carpenter and wheelwright, at one time also village constable and mail contractor, had often lent assistance to the waggoners to haul their loads to the top of the steep hill. He made his own mail-van, and selected his horses for the journey with the post, which lay between Swindon and Hungerford. The roads were very rough at that time, and were often blocked with snow in the winter; then the mail-man always carried a shovel, with which to dig his way through the drifts. Before the railway was made coal was conveyed by barges, along the canal. One year the canal was frozen over for fifteen weeks, and there was a coal famine along the down-side. The ordinary price of coal – locally – in the year 1830, was 50s. a ton.

Local letters cost 4d. to deliver, and the postman traversed the down-side daily, for twelve or fifteen miles, mounted on a donkey; for this he received 10s. weekly. Newspapers cost 6d. each. The farmers co-operated in the purchase of these; one newspaper had to suffice for half a dozen farmhouses.

The old carpenter held the post of village constable for twenty years, before the institution of the County Police. This office was one of responsibility in those times, and was not unattended with danger; the old man bears many scars as the result of encounters with roughs in the execution of his duty. The chief offenders against the law were gipsies, tramps, and travelling navvies; there was seldom any trouble with the villagers. There was no regular salary attached to the post of constable; the only sum he received was 5s. every year when he went to the court to be sworn in.

His personal equipment comprised a loaded baton, and hand-cuffs for the prisoners. Several times, on making arrests, when the prisoners would not walk to the town, four miles away, he had clapped the hand-cuffs on him securely, tied his feet and legs together, and hauled him along on his back to the cells. At a neighbouring village the constable was often required to lodge prisoners for the night, on their way to prison. To hold them secure he had two mighty staples driven into the strong woodwork, one each side of the wide fire-place, and the culprits were chained up to these all night, while the constable took his rest. If there were three prisoners, the great, heavy pig-killing bench was brought into requisition, and the third was unceremoniously chained down to that; there was small fear of escaping from such a custody.

A short distance from the ex-constable dwells the old thatcher, of over ninety years, who enjoys as good general health, well-built, with aristocratic features, strong, clear, brown eyes, dark hair and beard, only just tinged with grey; he is very erect, and he walks firmly. 'I ates an' drenks as well as ever I did,' he says. He was sitting by the fireside, lamenting a wet afternoon, and wearing a thick pair of nailed boots, leather gaiters, and an old frayed, blue felt hat on his head. If it had been fine he would have been at work, for he cannot be idle; all that morning he had been busy wheeling manure from the cow-yard to his allotment.

Mr William Pope, Postmaster at Alton Barnes
(previously in the Honeystreet sawmills)

The village policeman, Constable Coles

As a boy he played 'trippant' from school to go with his father; then he began to thatch by himself. Altogether, he had thatched over 3,000 ricks, besides innumerable cottages and farm-buildings. The average number of ricks he thatched per annum was 50, though sometimes they came to not far short of 100. For thatching a rick he received 2s. and his food for the time; with good luck he could cover an ordinary sized rick in from four to five hours. For cottages and farm-buildings the price was 3s. 6d. a square, a square being of 10 feet – 100 feet in all – and his services were required in no less than ten parishes. When there was no thatching to be done he turned his hand to the making of sheep-cages, and built cottages of wattle and daub, or rubble (chalk-stone), and sold them to poor labourers, or let them at 1s. a week. By doing this, and by following his work as a thatcher, he became fairly well-to-do, and is now the possessor of many 'housen,' and other property in the place. A larger number of the cottages, and farms, too, along the hill-side, were built on the 'life-hold' system. The builder agreed to pay a sum of money down, securing the ground for his lifetime, and when he died the house reverted to the landlord, or his next of kin might pay down another sum, and secure it for its own lifetime, and so on.

The old thatcher's interest in life is as keen as ever it was, and his memory is unimpaired; all the scenes and events of his past career roll before his eyes in an unbroken panorama. He remembers the 'mobbin'' and 'sheen breakin'' – the agricultural riots of 1830 – and how his father lifted him up on the garden gate to see the 'cavaltry' go by, to quell the disturbances. His mother used to take her children to leasing in the cornfields. She wore a very large red cloak, 'as ood kip out no end o' wet'; when it rained she gathered her little ones together under the cloak, as the hen gathers her chicks; there they stayed till the storm was over.

He had often seen the revelling and back-swording, but had only been upon the stage once himself, then he got a broken nose with his opponent's stick, and that quenched his ardour for the game. The youths of Liddington went footballing on Sundays, and the young thatcher accompanied them, much against the will of his father, who was a local preacher. One Sunday, on the way back from a distant village, where he had been playing, he called at the little chapel, where his father was preaching, and the parent respectfully asked the congregation to 'make room for the bwoy,' adding, 'dursay e's tired, for a bin a futballin' aal day.'

There is another nonagenarian living a short way from the thatcher. This is Maslin, the old carter, who has spent all his life on the downs around Liddington and Marlborough. 'This owld 'and o' mine 'ave sowed twelve acres o' whate in a day many a time, an' sometimes as much as sixteen acres. P'raps you oodn't thenk that,' he says, with a proud smile. He also remembers the riots of 1830, and saw them 'smaishin' up the sheens' in the farmyard, when he was a boy. The rioters' chief hatred was of the threshing-machines; these they attacked with especial violence, and afterwards assailed the farmhouse, and demanded money and food from the farmer. When the horse-threshing machines first came out the corn was not thrown into a drum, as at present, but was fed between rollers, which conveyed it into the thresher, as in the case of the chaff-cutter. Four horses, attached to as many levers, supplied the power for this threshing-machine. In the centre of the ring, round which they walked, was a kind of cage, in which a boy stood, to drive the animals. At first only the biggest farmers had one of these; then, after a time, they found their way into most farmyards where there was much cornland. So, also, when the drill was invented, farmers used to hire one from the foundry or warehouse, until such time as they could afford to buy one for themselves.

The old carter, with long, grey hair and beard, fine features, and kind, smiling eyes, is delighted to talk of the hard but happy times of yore, when the bright cornfields, full of reapers, stretched for many miles, and the crowds of women and children afterwards came to lease in the stubble, while the stroke of the flail sounded 'thwack, thwack, thwack' in the barn all the winter, and the teams came forth to plough in the matches held yearly upon the broad downs; he had many times carried off the prize for this as a young man – *e.g.*, £4 for the head-carter and £2 for the under-carter. There were two styles of ploughing in vogue – the 'flat work' and 'brick work'; the former kind being when the earth is turned over flat, and the latter when it is turned up edgeways. The allotting of the prizes depended upon the taste of the judges for this or that kind of furrow; but brick ploughing is usually considered the best for harrowing and cleaning. The carter thinks the old wooden ploughs were much better than the new iron ones; they left the ground rougher, but you could clean out the couch better; the new style is better to the eye but worse for the crop.

Whenever the teams went out on the road the carter received what is called 'road-money,' and some times 'straw-money,' too. 'Straw-money' is the money derived from the sale of straw used to cover the corn and other produce in the waggon. This the carters usually sold to innkeepers; each waggon carried about a shilling's worth, and sometimes more.

It is a singular fact that a great many of the down labourers, and especially carters, have a shrill, piping tone of voice quite peculiar to them, and which is not to be met with anywhere in the valley. This can only be accounted for by the climate of the downs, and the continual breezes there; such conditions must of necessity tend to affect the voice in time.

A favourite dainty of the carter's, years ago, was a large kidney potato,

Mares and foals at Fyfield Manor Farm

enclosed in a jacket of barley-meal paste, and baked that way. This 'made anybody a good breakfast,' the old man declares; and though it was frugal fare indeed, the healthy, hearty, sturdy folks seem to have derived wonderful strength and muscle from it.

The little cottage at the foot of the hill is typical of the carter. The great, long-handled whip, adorned with numerous brass ferrules, hangs on the wall behind the door, while here and there, about the room, are numerous decorative brasses, well polished, with a set of bells, buckles, and straps for the horses, a hempen halter, and the broad flag dinner-basket, lying on the floor underneath the wall.

> 'Crack, crack, goes the whip, I whistle and I sing,
> I sit upon the waggon, I'm as happy as a king;
> My horse is always willing, and for me I'm never sad,
> There's none can lead a jollier life than Jim the carter's lad.'

There are those to-day, and especially the town bred, who turn up their noses at the sentiments expressed in the words of the old rustic songs, and pretend the breezy cheerfulness and jollity of carters is a myth, but they are mistaken. The fact is, the towns do not understand the country, and the countryman's simple feelings and natural joy in the freedom of the life out of doors; it is as natural for carter boys to whistle and sing as it is for them to eat their breakfast or dinner; what is more, when you are mounted in the waggon, off on the road, or down the fields, you cannot resist a feeling of elation and optimism; there is a real inspiration to joy in the time and place, the company of the horses, and the motion of the farm waggon.

The manufacture of soap and candles in the villages is a further proof that the countryside was entirely self-supporting, and independent of the towns. In Wanborough alone, the people grew their corn, ground their own flour, made their own farm implements and waggons, and harness for the teams – with leather from their own tan yards – made their own footwear, spun their own flax, wove their own woollens, made their own clothes, and manufactured their own soaps, candles, and rush-lights.

There was no gas, or electricity, or even lucifer matches then; only the old tinder-box, with flint and steel. The tinder-box was replenished with linen rags, which had first been held to the fire, and scorched brown. Then there were the sulphur matches, which the rustics made themselves, at dinner-time, or in the evening, cutting up, and shaving the wood with their pocket-knives and dipping the ends into the brimstone, and allowing them to dry. When a fire was required, the cottager took the flint and steel, and struck a spark, which fell upon the tinder and ignited it, not to a flame, but causing it to smoulder – or 'swilter,' as the rustics say – then a sulphur match was applied and kindled, which was the instrument for communicating the fire from the tinder-box. When linen rags were scarce the cottagers were driven to many expedients, and, if everything else failed, there was the goodman's shirt – all rustics wore white linen shirts in those times – the tail of which was unceremoniously ripped off, and baked, to provide fuel for the flint and steel.

There were several kinds of soap in use among the villagers formerly, the chief of which was the grey Bristol soap at 1d. a pound, and black soap at ½d. a pound, that is, before the imposition of the duties. White soap was imported from the Continent, chiefly from Spain, and bore a duty of 2d. a pound. In time the home production was taxed, too, to the extend of 1½d. a pound, and the most rigid precautions were taken to prevent the soap-makers from escaping the duties, while severe penalities were inflicted on those who broke the law. The villagers' soap was made with the lees drawn from ashes of potash and lime, boiled up with tallow and oil. There were two processes – the half-boil and the final boil. The first of these half prepared the soap, the second finally purified it, and made it ready for cutting up for use. The rustics often used soap as an aperient medicine, swallowing it in the shape of pills, or dissolving it in syrup, or warm milk, thereby putting home manufacturers to yet another use, and so escaping the payment of doctors' and apothecaries' fees.

Almost every village of any size had its malthouse and brewery, and produced the old-fashioned brown farmhouse ale, and supplied the local inns, or those farms and cottages, the occupants of which, through lack of knowledge, equipment, or convenience, did not brew their own. There were three qualities of the liquor: strong beer, fresh beer, and ale; and whatever modern temperance advocates may allege, the old folks of the down-side are unconquerable in the belief that it was drinking plenty of wholesome ale that made them strong and hardy.

Some of the farmers made cider, and gave that to the men, instead of ale. At one farm alone they made 3,000 gallons a year, and consumed the greater part of it in the summer and harvest. During the cider-making, the men lived in, and had everything found, beside extra wages. At such times it was usual for the farmer's wife to make monster puddings of cruttons, currants and sliced apples. This was an especial favourite with the men, who ate huge quantities of it. 'Lar, maaster,' the old rustic exclaimed one day, 'I do like yoor mince puddin'. I awps yool 'eve some moor when we comes agyen.'

There were many quaint sports and games held in the village and neighbourhood of Wanborough in by-gone times, but they are all at an end now. The oldest of these festivals was one called the Lot Mead. This took place at mowing-time, and was the occasion for much merriment and feast-making. There the leader of the games appeared wearing garlands of flowers, and the mowers were entertained with one pound of beef, and a head of garlic apiece.

Another annual event was the Cow Fair. This was a great gathering and sale of beasts, at which all the farmers of the locality attended to inspect the show, and to make purchases. There was much cattle from Hereford and Wales, which filled the villagers with astonishment; they were especially struck with those 'with the whitey faces.' After the sale, the remainder passed up Callis Hill and away over the downs to London. When the herds of cattle passed through, they were sheltered in pens or yards, at the inns. A guide preceded each herd by one day, and arranged for food and water along the road; there was no telegraph then with which to despatch messages beforehand. Oftentimes the number of cattle passing through exceeded 800 in a week.

When the heavy waggons, conveying food and fodder, went through, as at Liddington, the farmers around the village killed their fat sheep, calves, and pigs, and despatched them off with the rest. Dealers travelled with some of the waggons, buying and collecting food-stuffs along the journey.

There were great flocks of sheep kept upon the downs above the village formerly, and many depredations were made on the folds by the hungry poor. The old rustics still point to a spot where stood a great hollow pollard ash-tree, in which the carcases of the stolen sheep were concealed. The menfolk of several families used to visit the field, kill and carry off a sheep, dress it, and hang it up in the hollow tree; the mothers went at night and cut off a portion as required. The first thing to be done when a sheep was missed was to search the cottages of suspected persons; by carefully following this plan, a sheep was never found at one of them.

In addition to the Cow Fair was the Autumn Fair and Market, held under an ancient Charter granted by King Stephen in 1252, when the booths for contests and amusements extended for a mile along the roadsides; and afterwards came the Feast, or 'Revels,' at which the inevitable back-swording and wrestling took first place. Then the old village band turned out, with their quaint instruments, the chief of which was one called 'the serpent,' being in fact, a brazen serpent in a coil, into whose mouth the player blew; and, besides this, the 'horse's leg,' so-called from its resemblance to the limb of that animal. The rest of the band was made up of fiddles, piccolos, and clarionets – 'clarnets,' as the rustics call them. On Sundays the serpent went to church, and was played from the old gallery, to the great admiration of the smock-frocked farm labourers.

'Dobbin Sunday' is the name given to the day for the distribution of charity bread to the poor of the village. The bread was made into small rolls and loaves, and the distribution took place at church, on the Sabbath. After the folks from the neighbouring town took to attending the ceremony and obtaining the bread in order to waste it, the day of the week was changed, but 'Dobbin Sunday' is still remembered by the villagers.

Jonathan Keen, the old farm hand, nearly ninety years of age, remembers the old sports and games, and regularly frequented them when they were held on the village green. He is big made, tall and boney, a fine physical type of the rustic, but he is trembling and feeble now. 'I feels mi age terrabul. 'Tis a hard job to get about much,' he tells you. When he was nearly eighty the mare in the stable kicked him severely, and broke two of his ribs; but even then he walked home unaided, the distance of a mile. As a boy, before he was fourteen, he could carry a sack of wheat with the men, while his wages were no more than 2s. 6d. weekly. His school chum, the ninety-one years old thatcher, of Liddington, pays him a visit occasionally, and Jonathan never omits to remind him of the fact that he stole his marbles in the lane over eighty years ago, when they were minding the cows. 'We was oni bits o' urchins then,' he adds.

The old man was a distinguished gamester in his younger days; there is nothing like the old times and amusements, according to his view. 'The owld games ought to a bin kipt on wi,' he says. 'Us could hae a bit o' fun then, an' 'twasn't allus rough; 'twas oni now an' agyen as us 'ad a bit of a row, an' then 'twas nothin'. We bwoys ood run fer miles to see a bit o' back-zoordin' an' wrustlin'.' His old head is covered with scars – several of five inches in length – which he received at play with the single-sticks, but these are his marks of honour; he feels no disgrace in the possession of them. His legs, too, are covered with marks of the wrestlers' boots; but he is not ashamed of them, either. The wrestlers were forbidden to have iron tips on their boots, so a great many used to soak them for a month in horse urine; this made the leather very hard, and they were enabled to kick their opponents black and blue.

One of Jonathan's old mates had both his thumbs bent right back in the wrestling, which happened somewhat curiously, from our point of view. There was a trick in wrestling called 'reining up.' This was to get your two thumbs into your opponent's mouth – one each side – and force him backwards with it. How difficult that must have been may be surmised from the dislocation of the thumbs; but the other's mouth must have been very hard to occasion it.

The Wanborough back-sworders were very clever with the sticks. It was a common exercise to practice with a lighted candle on the table, and, so skilful were the players, that they could time after time extinguish the flame without bending the wick. A favourite trick of the players was to strike each other on the funnybone, and then take immediate advantage of the blow to break a head. After the sword-play at the 'Revels' the company was entertained by the prize-winners, who paid for a repast of bread, cheese, and ale at the inn.

But the darling sport of old Jonathan was cock-fighting, which was far more frequently indulged in than the sword-play. The champion cock of the whole neighbourhood was one 'Boney,' who had slain dozens of competitors, and, though minus an eye, was still unconquerable in the field of game-fighters. One day a game-breeder brought Jonathan a small rough cock.

'Ull e buy a good little tom?'

'I don' mind! 'Ow much?'

'Aaf a crownd to you. An' 'e's a game un,' the dealer replied.

'I'll 'ev un,' said Jonathan, and he took the bird home.

Immediately a challenge was issued by 'Boney's' owner, and accepted. When the time came round the birds were brought out, the small cock crowing lustily under Jonathan's arm.

'E's a good un, I back. A crows like billiool,' the umpire remarked.

Soon after the start the small rough cock gave a mighty bound, and struck poor Boney's other eye out, blinding him completely, and ending his career in the ring. Boney understood and felt his defeat very much, and ran about squalling with rage and pain. 'I took my little cock, aater tha, an' slenked along whum as ef I'd bin an' killed a fella, an' didn' Boney's missis let it into I!' quoth Jonathan.

'Ya ant a zeed thaay little kines it, 'ev e?' remarked he, rising from his arm-chair, and reaching down a small box from the mantlepiece. The 'little kines' proved to be a collection of Roman money, coins impressed with the figures of Constantinus and other of the Emperors, which the old labourer had found from time to time about the fields, and digging in his cottage garden.

At the boxing and fighting matches which took place in out-of-the-way spots, the mothers of the young men frequently attended with whips and whipped their sons up to the line, calling them cowards if they gave way at all. Old Betty Seymour, who dwelled in a small cottage by the canal-side, regularly attended the matches, and often gave active support to the combatants. The London, Somerset, and local teams of back-sworders met annually at Coate, in a contest for the championship, and thousands of people attended to see the games.

How vexed the old bootmaker was to think he had wasted precious time watching the sword-play, when a young fellow. 'What, I to stand here and watch this ungodly work! To see men knockin' one another about an' the blood a runnin' down in strames,' said he to himself one day at the Revels. He would do so no more. After leaving the games he got over in a field, and, kneeling down on the grass, asked God to keep him from the back-swording, and never attended another contest afterwards.

A short while ago the vicar invited him to church to hear a sermon, and was afterwards indiscreet enough to call on the old man to beg a compliment.

'What did you think of the sermon?' said he.

'What did I thenk o' the sarmint? Why, I didn't thenk nothin' ant. Ya dun't understand the Gospel!'

'Yes I do,' the vicar replied.

'Why don' e praach it, then,' the bootmaker answered. 'I never yerd sic a skippin' awver in mi life. 'Tis a fine beg buildin' ya got, but 'tis some middlin' poor stuff praached inside on in.'

The old bootmaker, though past ninety, is hale and hearty, and uncommonly vigorous. He is quick and keen in conversation, has a clear, strong voice, and warms to his subject amazingly; he would put many a youthful orator to shame, and overwhelm him with his unanswerable logic and wisdom. Strongly and sternly Puritanical in view, he interprets your thoughts, and sums you up in a moment; you feel his quick, penetrating gaze piercing you through and through, and are quelled in his presence.

Though at such a great age, he still works at his trade, and earns a few shillings, repairing the villagers' boots. When, many years ago, his master died – who left a fortune of £2,300, acquired at the village shop – he took on the business, and made boots for all: farmers, labourers, game-keepers, and the rest, warranted all his goods for twelve months, and gave a year's credit, which he had no cause to regret, as long as his dealings were with rustics; only the jockeys and town folk defrauded him of his money. The country labourers used to settle up every year at the end of harvest. He had been to the village of Bishopstone, three miles off, and collected £70 in three nights. There are practically no boots made in the villages now; instead, the folks go to the nearest town and purchase cheap pairs, which are all to pieces in a few months. Jonathan Keen was still wearing a pair of everyday boots made by the old shoemaker eight years before; he would have worn out half a dozen pairs bought at the town in that time.

12

ALDBOURNE, BAYDON, LITTLE HINTON AND BISHOPSTONE

All the roads about the downs are made of flints. These are obtained in two ways, with very little difficulty, and always near at hand; there is very little charge for hauling, and no railway carriage, as with most other stones and materials. A great many of the flints are picked up on the ploughed land after the harrowing has been done, and then the farmers sell them to the road authorities. This work is done by women, who are paid at the rate of 1s. a square yard, twenty bushels being counted a square yard. The down-land quickly dries after the heaviest rains, and the work, though laborious enough, is not altogether uncongenial; the women can earn 8s. or 9s. a week, when the weather is fine.

Flint-digging also is carried on by men everywhere about the downs, and is done at the piece rate: 2s. 6d. a square yard being paid for all flints duly dug out and riddled. The flint-beds usually lie immediately under the turf on the high parts; you have merely to turn back the top spit, loosen the stones with the pick, and shovel them out. Generally, each man has his own station and tools, and works singly. His apparatus consists of a pickaxe, a stout iron drag, a steel fork with eight grains, a shovel, a riddle, or "ruddle," (sieve) and a wheelbarrow. Along the winter and spring he has a moveable shelter made of a couple of close hurdles covered with a rough canvas sheet; whichever way the wind is setting he adjusts this against a stout prop, and works behind it. Like most other rustic labourers, the flint-diggers believe in the horseshoe as a sign of luck; you often see one nailed in the centre of the hurdle at the top, as they fix them over the doors of the cottages. Flints which are gathered up from the ploughed land are better for road-making and repairing than those newly dug out, being much harder and more durable, by reason of their long exposure to the sun and atmosphere.

Formerly Aldbourne was much bigger and more thickly populated than it is now. A century ago the inhabitants numbered 2,000; but they are shrunk to 1,100 to-day, and the migration still proceeds apace, though the men go not so much to the towns as to the colonies, which is a mark of courage in them, and is not to be deplored too much. But the chief cause of the village's prosperity was its cottage industries of spinning and weaving, which made the villagers peculiarly independent and self-supporting; it is said there was not a cottage in the place but had one or two looms worked by the women and girls, whose average weekly earnings were from 9s. to 10s. 6d. In early times, down to the close of the eighteenth century, silk-spinning and weaving was the chief industry; after that time fustian and linen-weaving was in vogue, and silk gimp-making – the ornamental bordering in upholstery – which finally gave place to willow-weaving and plaiting. Besides these purely cottage industries, there was a bell foundry, and a general foundry, a soap and candle factory, two wind-mills, with powerful machinery impelled with six large fans, malt-houses, rope-walks, and a chair and table manufactory, which is still active, and where everything is hand-made, with the exception of the table-tops and seats of the chairs.

The silk-weaving was the oldest industry. The last of the home employments was the willow-weaving and plaiting, which has not been discontinued above sixteen years, and which might be revived, if the cottagers would do it; but they are disinclined to undertake the work again, so this important trade has fallen to decay, though there are manufacturers ready and anxious to take the woven material when it shall be forthcoming.

Willow-weaving was done with the loom, and the process was almost identical with that of woollen and other stuffs. First of all, the young withy poles and trees – and sometimes lime-trees also – were cut, and the bark removed. Then the wood was sawn up into pieces a yard long, and the small logs split into quarters. After this it was passed on to expert cutters, who, with the use of specially contrived hand-tools, cut the wood into very thin strips, and separated the fibre, tearing it apart, into something smaller than wheat straws. These fibres were tied in bundles and afterwards passed on to the weavers, who wove them into sheets a yard square. When the squares were done, they were received into the proprietor's depot, and despatched off to London for hat-making, and some of them went abroad, too, to be utilized for the same purpose. The material was very tough and pliable, and would last a long time, in any weather.

Willow-plaiting moved on the same lines as the weaving, but this was done without looms. Here the willow was cut into thin strips with hand-planes, and the women and girls plaited them, using five strips at a time. This fabric the folks called 'tuscin,' which may be the local rendering of 'Tuscan.' About fifteen years ago willow material was displaced by compressed paper, but this would not stand the wet, and the London manufacturers came and tried to revive the industry, but to no purpose. A company was formed in the village, and the looms were got into order again, but the cottagers would not take to the work any more, so the looms were carried off to the towns, and the experiment tried there, but it was unsuccessful.

The manufacture of chairs on the easy-going, old-fashioned lines still proceeds in the village of Aldbourne. All the work is done by hand, and is of the most skilful and efficient kind; there is a great demand for Aldbourne chairs all round Wiltshire and Berkshire, and the output is often at the rate of 100 a week. Every kind of chair is made, together with a few tables, though it is chiefly chairs, large and small; polishing and all is done on the premises. The wood is obtained in the locality of Marlborough, and, except the elm-boards for the seats, it is cut up with hand-saws. The frames of the chairs are chiefly of ash, and the legs of birch and beech. Some of the chairs in olden times were made of yew; these lasted for a century, or a century and a half, in constant use, but none are made of that kind of wood to-day.

The skill of the village chairmakers, and especially of the turners, is most remarkable; though I have been for many years acquainted with all kinds of elaborate turning in metals, I have never seen anything made so simply, quickly, and beautifully, as are the ornamental legs and spokes of the chairs and tables, and everything made, too, without gauges, absolutely to the eye, with unerring precision. The lathes are very primitive and simply constructed, but remarkably effective, machines. There are merely two sharp steel centres, fixed in 'dogs,' for holding the rough wood, and a wooden rest for the tools before, with a treadle underneath. From the time of taking up a rough piece of wood for a chair-leg from the ground, and handing it back, perfectly turned, as smooth as marble, with not the slightest tool-mark about it – except for the ornamental cuts – is no more than three minutes.

The work proceeds by easy stages, the master and owner toiling with his men; there are no stringent laws framed for employees: 'If there were, they would be useless,' the master says. 'It is best to jog along comfortably together. If they want a pipe of tobacco, I tell them to slip outside and have it; and if it is wet they go into the next room where there is no danger of a fire; it would never do to attempt to proceed on the lines of the big factories here in Aldbourne.'

As well as being skilful, intelligent, individual, and independent, the folks of the ancient weaving village are noted for longevity; life is usually lived to the full in the majority of places about the down-side. Granny Bird is one of the oldest inhabitants to-day. She is over ninety years of age, and is as nimble as a top; she skips all round the village in a few moments. When the beautiful, bonny, rosy-cheeked boys and girls come out of school in the afternoon, they always run up to Granny in the street, and shake hands with her, with pretty modesty and bashfulness. 'They allus does that whenever

Preparing to burn bristles off slaughtered pigs in the Angel Yard, Marlborough

they ketches sight o' I,' Granny says. She points to the high tower, which she climbed as a young girl, and to the large square before the church, round which they ran for gown lengths nearly a century ago, and to all the cottages in view, where the busy shuttles plied to and fro, in happier days than these, and she remembers all sorts of feasting, sporting, and revelling, but this is at an end now; only the old, grey tower remains unchanged, with the evergreen downs, that lie all round like the billows of a mighty ocean; all the rest is passing away.

Living near to Granny is the aged roadmender and back-sworder, who continued his daily work till he was nearly eighty-five, and, on the other side, the old bricklayer and well-digger, who has carried out many difficult tasks, and bored no end of wells about the downs, and assisted at opening the ancient barrows on the hill-tops. In addition to this, he has had much to do with dew-pounds, and has frequently measured the dew-fall, which, according to his statement, often amounts to three inches in a night, during a thick mist. The water in the ponds attracts the mist, that may be seen rapidly drawn into the pools; the mist will fill the ponds much more quickly than would an ordinary shower of rain.

From Aldbourne the road climbs steeply up the high downs to the east and continues away, rising higher and higher, till it reaches the pretty village of Baydon, nestling amid tall elms and beeches, and surrounded with fresh green meadows.

There was one sturdy old family in Baydon, known and celebrated for miles around, by reason of their prowess in wrestling and back-swording. This was the Beckinghams, who were blacksmiths and farmers, too, skilled in the art of ironwork, and also in that of tilling the earth. The combination of blacksmithing and other trades with that of farming was very common formerly; nearly every proprietor of the forge had a few acres of land, and kept horses and cattle.

The last of the kind living at Baydon is old John Alder, who was carpenter, wheelwright, and farmer, thereby uniting yet another trade with that of husbandry, and being doubly qualified to construct carts and waggons, since he was not only a good judge of materials, but was also versed in the actual use and running of the vehicles, and could put his own handiwork to the test. He received his tuition as a boy in the village, and considered himself fortunate to get 16s. a week as a journeyman, fifty years ago.

The old wheelwright has retired from farming now, and lives at the little shop with his grown-up daughters, who carry on the business of the village Post Office, and sell all kinds of curious odds and ends, such as are in demand in country places: as marbles for the children, and whipcord for the farm-lads, needles and thread, hooks and eyes, and buttons for the good-wives, shoes for the feet, hats for the head, clothes for the body, sweetmeats, james, pickles, foodstuffs, pictures, newspapers, clothes-pegs, postage stamps, and a host of other sundries, of varying degrees of usefulness. The little room within – the window of which looks out upon the old Roman road by which the Emperors used to pass – contains many curios; bits of antique chinaware, books, stuffed animals and birds in glass cases, the most interesting of which is a 'dove-cuckoo,': a dove crossed with a cuckoo, which was shot in the high beech-trees standing by the roadside.

The openness and strategic disposition of the downs between Russley and Lambourn make them an ideal ground for military manoeuvres; many brilliant spectacles have been witnessed here in modern times, and many mimic battles fiercely along the slopes and plains, amid the wheat stubble and turnip field. Here we small boys used to come, tramping ten miles from home in the happy harvest holidays, and be inextricably mixed up and confused with 70,000 or 80,000 troops, driven this way and that, now in the firing line, exposed to the terrific fusillade of the infantrymen's rifles, now under the heels of the cavalry, nearly trodden to death, running mile after mile, thirsty and sweating in the hot sunshine; at one time scolded out of our wits by the testy corporal, at another chaffed and encouraged by the fat, jolly cavalry sergeant, loitering among the sweet-smelling turnips, and singing a snatch of song by himself:

'The girl I love, and the horse I ride.'

The thin red line of the infantrymen, stretching as far as ever the eye could see, the glint of the sun on helmets, and the flashing of sabres, with the boom, boom, of the cannon, and the continual crack, crack, crack, of the rifles, formed a scene never to be forgotten; though we somehow managed to lose our tiny stock of pence, lying down on the beautiful short turf studded with harebell and scabious, and had to perform the long journey home on empty stomachs, singing as we passed down the narrow lanes of the valley.

There are two small blacksmiths' shops in the village of Little Hinton, one of which, half tumbling down, is held by a farmer, who merely does a job now and then when he feels disposed, and repairs his own implements; and the other in daily use, by the old blacksmith, John Johnson, or 'Young John,' as the villagers playfully name him. His shed – which he built himself – is of iron, and stands immediately alongside the school playground, through which he crosses, in dirty weather, to gain the forge, stepping on wooden boxes to assist him over the low fence. At playtime the children come out to watch him at work, to hear the roaring bellows and tinkling anvil, and to see

The Mercer family at Milton Lilbourne Forge, where Forge Cottage now stands

the bright yellow sparks whizzing out, and shooting through the small doorway. The old smith is very fond of the children, and they love him in return; 'Young John' is a familiar figure, and a favourite with all the villagers. The farmer gave him the ground, free of rents, for his forge, glad to have a regular smith in the place; 'Young John' executes all the small repairs to the machinery and implements, and shoes the horses, settling up with his patrons every three months.

The little forge is a curious place, containing all kinds of rough tools, with other odds and ends, and everything is in a muddle, as is usual with the village smithy. The bellows for the forge are in a tiny box-like place behind where the smith stands; there are several iron 'boshes' for the water, and the dust-like coal is kept in a large two-handled pot, which once did service over the kitchen fire. The chimney is a very simple contrivance, being merely a milk-churn, with the bottom knocked out, hung in the iron roof, the broad bottom forming a kind of bonnet, to carry off the smoke and sulphur. This suits the old blacksmith very well, because, as he says, he 'can look up the chimmuck at night, an' see the stars a-shinin' outside.'

The smith is tall and boney, but none too robust since he had the severe attack of bronchitis last fall, which played havoc with him; he is hard on seventy now. In manner he is extremely gentle and agreeable, a lovable man, with a playful, yet serious mind, full of quaint sayings and sparks of wit, able to converse on matters of the deepest import, and to make rhymes while he beats out the fizzing metal on the anvil. His voice is soft and mellow, and he sings the tenor part in the choir at the tiny church; he has been a chorister all his life, from early childhood. He is ripe for a chat at all times, whenever you care to look in upon him, and is desirous of taking everyone up the coomb to see the ancient dwellings, to tell you the names of all the hills, and point out the spot where the old grey mare 'Merriman' slipped over the steep side of the coomb, and tumbled down one hundred feet with a load of manure behind her, shattering the cart to fragments, but escaping unhurt herself. He has no mate to help him at the forge, except when he has an extra heavy job in hand; then he gets an old neighbour to come and give him a blow, but he 'soon gets out o' bread' (breath). His hammers are all named: there are 'Slogger,' the sledge; 'Dragon,' the intermediate one; and 'Useful,' the hand hammer. When he wants either of them he cried aloud: 'Now, Useful!' 'Come yer, Dragon!' 'Stop ther, Slogger, till I wants tha agyen!' Where 'Useful' is not big enough, and 'Slogger' too mighty, he 'goes at it, an' 'its into 't wi' Dragon, an' yarns mi bit o' rooty' (bread).

He remembers when the terraces in the coombs were cultivated and grew famous crops of wheat. The ploughing of the sides of the coombs was done by oxen, which are more surefooted than horses, and the corn grown there was of an extra good quality, because of the great heat, and shelter from the wind. The old fellow has pondered on the formation of the coombs, and is convinced they were made by water action, but, being unskilled in geological lore, his opinion is that they were washed out at the time of the Flood. Besides being blacksmith and choirman, 'Young John' scares the birds from the wheat in the fields, and is empowered by the farmers to shoot rabbits and destructive birds. Many fieldfares visit the coomb in the winter months, in search of food; these the old man takes with the gun, and boils them into broth; the smithy is often full of feathers plucked from birds obtained in this way.

A short distance from the blacksmith's shop lives the old thatcher, Steven Gray – whose brother, of the same trade, after half a century of work on ricks and roofs, fell from the top of one in the autumn, and was killed outright – and also Bill Adams, the carter, whose old dad drove a team of eight horses with one of the big waggons plying between Gloucester and London, before the railway-line to the west was made, or even thought of. When the track was laid hundreds of people swarmed off the downs, and ran for miles to see the first train pass along. The engine was the 'comicallest theng' the carter 'had ever seed'; a good many of the villagers took to their heels, saying the engine had 'brawk the gyet down, an' runned away.'

A short way below Earl's Court, spanning the River Cole, is Acorn Bridge, the scene of many famous contests between prizefighters and others, before the railway was made, and brought civilization to the spot. The last great fight there, remembered by the rustics, was between two champions nicknamed 'The Mouse,' and 'The Earwig.' This time the fighting lasted for five hours, and one of the combatants fought with a broken arm for half the period.

In the centre of the village of Bishopstone is a large square pool formed by the waters of the spring, which are dammed back by the road passing along the hillside; and, higher up, beyond a series of watercress beds, surrounded with cottages and gardens, is a square troughlike place – fed by a rippling spring of crystal clearness – called William's Well, where the cottagers obtain their drinking-water, and which has never yet been known to fail. Two hatches regulate the water in the pool.

The mill stands on the opposite side of the highway, and is built up from the hollow beneath. The great iron wheel is situated outside the building, with its top slightly below the level of the pond; the third floor and entrance are even with the road. Here, in times past, the corn was brought from off the hills, and converted into flour, to supply the village and the countryside round about. The machinery is still used for gristing, but not for fine flour;

almost every day the huge wheel revolves under the weight of the foaming water, and rumbles beneath the high wall. The school, the blacksmith's shop, and the mill are all close together; the children are happy in their situation, and in the opportunities they have for viewing the several industries; they throng around the smithy door, and peer over at the mighty wheel each time they pass along, delighted to see the gleaming waters leaping down, and to view the merry fizzing sparks shooting out underneath the stroke of the blacksmith's hammer.

The village church stands about a stone's-throw from the mill. This is a fine large building in the Norman style of architecture, with a high massive tower, which has been girded about with several stout iron bands, made by the village smith in the churchyard itself. The big bell of the tower is rung every night during the winter from eight till nine, as a guide for any who may be lost on the downs. This the villagers call the 'kyfew' (curfew). The custom was instituted by one who was himself lost on the downs, who heard the bell ringing in the darkness, and was guided by it; accordingly he left a sum of money to pay the ringer for all time.

A century ago, when the villages of the down-side were infested with robbers, the thieves used to bring their plunder to Bishopstone, and conceal it in the tombs, with the bones and dust of the dead. Here, too, in times past, the poor folks used to assemble in the porches to receive their alms, wearing a red badge on the arm, containing the letters B.P. – Bishopstone Paupers – while the villagers' sheep were brought regularly to graze in the churchyard on the Sabbath, the tinkling of the bells agreeing well with the music of the anthem inside.

The old-fashioned farmers around Bishopstone and Idstone, down to a few years ago, used to give their workpeople three meals a day – dinner, tea, and supper – regularly throughout the hay and corn-harvest. The dinner was a hot meal, consisting of boiled legs of mutton, and pieces of beef, several kinds of vegetables, and a huge roly-poly suety pudding. This was cooked each day over the faggot fire in the brew-house, then it was carefully stowed in the clean bright milk-pails and carried out into the fields with the yokes. 'This used to put some life into us, an' mek us strong an' 'earty; we didn't mind buckin' in an' doin' a bit extra aater that,' the old carter declared.

A short distance from the Ridgeway are the remains of a Roman station, and, high upon the downs towards Russley, are two aged hawthorn trees, known respectively as the 'one o'clock bush,' and the 'two o'clock bush.' These are so called because the ploughmen and harvesters tell the time with them: when the sun is exactly above the first it is one o'clock. The labourers on the downs still make for themselves sundials for use in the fields. To do this they merely thrust a wand into the ground and note the shadows at the different hours, cutting out marks in the short turf with their pocket-knives.

The village could formerly boast of many industries. At one time nearly all the cottages had spinning wheels and looms, and wove woollen stuffs and willow fibre. Large quantities of hemp were grown in the neighbourhood, and the fibre prepared at Bishopstone, and afterwards sent away for manufacture into ropes and sacking. There were also premises for making whiting from the down chalk, a bone mill, a soap and candle works, and glove- and gaiter-making. Besides this there is the watercress industry, and the village has its smithy, its tailor, and basket-maker. One of the curios exhibited in the village is an old fire-engine that did service for 300 years, and has only recently been superseded. Formerly fires were very much more common about the downs than they are now; ricks and farm buildings were often ablaze: there was more incendiarism prevalent sixty years ago than there is in our day. During the time of the agricultural riots the old engine was in constant demand to put out farm fires; it is a wonder the rioters did not single out that, too, and smash it up with the new-fangled threshers and other plant.

The watercress beds lie along the bottom of the coomb, from where the spring bubbles out of the hillside, down to the mill-pond, and all about the hollows in the centre of the village, sheltered with the high, warm hedges, and overhung with the elmtree boughs. The beds are divided with banks of turf or stone, set across; a small opening is left for the water to run through, passing from bed to bed, or, if the current is too swift, that is conducted along a channel at one side, and only allowed to filter through the loose stones and so keep the cress supplied. The beds are renovated each year, in the early autumn, when all the cress has been cut.

The watercress industry, if conducted thoroughly, is a profitable one; a certain income is assured to those who are willing to pay sufficient attention to the beds. It is difficult to obtain labour in planting out the beds and cutting the cress, on account of having to stand in the water; a great many men who do this are afflicted with rheumatism. The men wear top-boots at the work, and are paid at the rate of 3s. a day. The value of the cress is not as high as it was formerly; twenty years ago it fetched 15s. a flat (hamper), whereas to-day it is sold at 8s. for the same quantity. The Bishopstone product is far-famed, and was in great request in the markets of London, Birmingham, and Manchester; but many of the beds are dilapidated now, there is not nearly as much cress grown as there used to be.

The old tailor and breeches-maker, whose father and grandfather were masters of the craft, still carries on his trade and does good business with farmers and others for many miles around, in spite of the competition of big concerns, which tend to crush out the small village workshops. But the old fellow has methods of his own, together with a rare skill in the use of scissors and needle; his customers are numbered all over the world: in Africa, Germany, India, America, and elsewhere. His father and grandfather were makers of the old leather breeches, but the old leather kinds have passed away now, and have given place to cheap corduroys and shoddy, for the labouring classes, at least.

The tailor's shop stands near the True Heart Inn, and but a few paces from Hocker Bench. The house is ancient and rambling in structure, with a roof of thick, warm thatch. Here three journeymen are constantly employed, usually seated on the floor, cutting out, stitching together, and finishing the suits. The tailor's 'goose,' 'gander,' and 'goslings,' are cooking in the oven near by, as they jestingly say: these are the three flat irons, used for pressing the seams of the cloth.

The old tailor, though drawing near to eighty, is as quick-witted and energetic as ever he was. He is tall in stature, with fresh complexion, sharp keen eyes, and a bit of grey beard underneath the chin. His speech is short and quick, with a kind of Scotch accent, and he is very deaf. Every year he issues a special almanac, prefaced with a quotation from his old Breeches Bible: 'And they sewed figge-tree leaves together, and made themselves breeches,' adding that 'improvements have been made since the first pairs.' His grandfather was the village constable at the time of the Chartist Riots; the ancient sword and staff used during the disturbances are still preserved behind the counter at the shop, with many other curios: tinder-boxes, flails, venerable books, handcuffs, Roman horseshoes, and a cow-bell, six pounds in weight, which used to hang around the necks of the cows grazing on the common lands, before they were enclosed. In the lot is a huge old leather-bound Prayer-Book, such as the rustics used to carry under their arms to church every Sabbath morning. This particular one belonged to a labourer, and has a tale attached to it. One day the parson came into the labourer's house; there was only the boy at home.

'Ha!' said the cleric, looking round the room; 'I'm glad to see you've got the good Book in the house, my boy.'

'Ya-as, zur,' the youth answered.

'And when does your father use it?' continued the parson.

'Every Zunday marnin', zur,' was the reply.

'And how does he use it? Does he stand up and read it to you like this?' inquired the vicar, taking the book in his hands.

'No-o-o! A oni sharpens 'is razzur on 'in,' replied the youth, with a contemptuous toss of the head.

The basket-maker, who is almost blind, dwells alone in a large old cottage standing by the roadside as you come up the hill. His small yard and garden are packed with bundles of withy, fresh from the beds; other bundles, some of a bright amber colour, and some stripped of the bark, ready for weaving into white wicker-work, are brought indoors, and placed under the window, or stacked in the large pantry. He has his seat on the floor in the large room, and works away unmolested, for he is his own master, and pleases himself as to the number of hours he toils, and the quantity of baskets he makes. He makes baskets of many kinds, great and small, good serviceable stuff, warranted to wear well, and, though very short-sighted, he is quick and clever at his trade. By working hard he would make three round bushel baskets a day, which would earn him about 5s. 6d., but flat cress-baskets are those most usually required. The beams of the old house are as large as trees, and the chalk walls are much worn with the wet, and almost ready to tumble down in places.

A great many of the down-side cottages and farmhouses are full of curious odds and ends, and contain numerous quaint bits of furniture, beautiful old-fashioned chinaware, coloured prints, ancient guns and implements, cups, utensils, and every description of ornament. Some of the cottagers set great store on the dainty little china services, which have been handed down from mother to daughter for generations, and love them both for their parents' sake, and for art's sake too, and are not at all deficient in the quality called taste; while others, if they do not value them as highly, still guard them jealously, and soon indicate to you that they are not for disposal. 'Aa, you be ogglin' round, you be. You'd like to get yer fingers on that, I warn, but you can set yer mind at rest now at once, you wunt 'ev it. That warmin'-pan belonged to my grandmother's grandmother, an' I don' know 'ow many 'ad un afore her, an' this yer skimmer's older than he. I 'oodn't sell none an't for a 'underd pound, no, that I 'oodn't.' Occasionally, though not often, you meet with old paintings, quaint woodcuts, and prints of parliamentary riots; books also are rare, except for the great old leather-bound Bible and Prayer-Book.

Figures and ornaments are plentiful, ranging from the old common chalk images of cocks, dogs, cats, and other animals, introduced from abroad, and sold by Italian hawkers a century and a half ago, to highly artistic groups in coloured stone ware – things of beauty that will not fade – purchased by our grandmothers. Even the stone jars containing potted meats and pickled herring were artistically made and coloured in the early half of the nineteenth century; you occasionally see some of these on the cottage mantelpiece, dearly prized by their owners.

Freaks of Nature, such as a white blackbird, or a white stoat, stuffed, and in glass cases, are sometimes found, together with owls and foxes; and here and there, though not commonly, the one and only cottage hen is discovered perched upon the back of the couch, or between the chair legs, while the happy family gathers around the fireside, gaily laughing and chatting the hours away before bedtime.

INDEX

GLOSSARY OF SOME UNFAMILIAR WORDS

A BUSH-HARROW: a light harrow, made of a hurdle or gate interlaced with brush-wood and thorns

TO CHAVE: to mix or strew with chaff, or to separate chaff from corn

CRUTTONS: bits of pork, left over from lard-making, put into a roly-poly pudding

A DROCK: a drain under a road; a *at stone laid as a bridge across a dirch; a water-course

TO FAG to cut corn with a sickle and a hooked stick

A FOGGER: a cowman

GENTILS: Maggots

LEASING: gleaning

NUGGIN: searching (as if for nuggets)

A STOWL: a tree-root left in the ground after felling; the stump of a bush or tree

WAKES: lines of hay, ready to be put in cocks

WILDERNS: apple trees run wild in a hedge, not true crab-apples